SEEKING THE SUMMIT

SEEKING THE SUMMIT
SAM SWITZER'S STORY
OF BUILDING AND GIVING

By Sydney Sharpe

Frontenac House

Book and cover design: Epix Design
Editor: Naomi K. Lewis
Front cover images: Switzer family collection
Back cover image: Ron Switzer Photography
Author photo: Ron Switzer Photography

Library and Archives Canada Cataloguing in Publication

Sharpe, Sydney
        Seeking the summit / Sydney Sharpe.

Includes index.
ISBN 978-1-897181-81-2 (bound).--ISBN 978-1-897181-82-9 (pbk.)

        1. Switzer, Sam. 2. Businesspeople--Alberta--Calgary--
Biography. 3. Philanthropists--Alberta--Calgary--Biography.
4. Jews--Alberta--Social conditions--20th century. 5. Calgary
(Alta.)--Economic conditions--20th century. 6. Calgary (Alta.)--
Biography. I. Title.

HC112.5.S94S53 2012   338.092   C2012-904913-1

Printed and bound in Canada

Published by Frontenac House Ltd.
1138 Frontenac Avenue S.W.
Calgary, Alberta, T2T 1B6, Canada
Tel: 403-245-8588
www.frontenachouse.com

To those who heal the world through giving
As Betty Switzer did
May her memory be a blessing

Acknowledgements

WHEN SAM SWITZER FIRST STARTING TELLING ME HIS STORIES, I collapsed in tears – of laughter. In the course of more than a hundred hours of interviews and meetings, my recordings were often punctuated with loud laughs. Those stories are the heart of this book where sometimes the tears are of sorrow too.

I am grateful to Sam for bringing one man's story of patience and persistence to a writer always looking for what makes our province and our country so great. Sam Switzer is a pioneer who proves that working and giving are the secrets to life. Our interviews became conversations on community and spirituality, and I treasure those many hours of insight.

I am thankful to Sam's children, especially Darlene, Lorne, Ronald, John and Mark who shared their memories and who confirmed that their father was correct in the details of his own recollections.

I am especially indebted to Darlene for her dedication to this book and to Ronald, a professional photographer, who spent many hours offering an abundance of images that he has taken over the years.

Many thanks to Laurie, the daughter of Sam's beloved late wife, Betty Switzer.

Sam has so many friends that it would have taken ten books to interview each of them and I thank all those who told a few of their best tales.

Sam's office overflows with professionalism – thanks to Carolyn Reu and Anne Christopoulos, who were incredibly cooperative.

Thanks to the *Calgary Herald,* for providing three essential photos.

I'm deeply thankful to Naomi Lewis, who edited with perfection, and to Lyn Cadence for her marketing and promotion assistance.

I am, of course, completely responsible for any errors or omissions.

Thanks, too, for all their friendship and support: Phoebe and Richard Heyman; Margo Helper and Greg Forrest; Don Hobsbawn and Wendy Langford; Rob Edwards, Jeanine Arseneault and Jamie Edwards.

My family makes my life and I thank Don Braid, daughter Rielle and son Gabriel for their love and encouragement. And thank you Mom – Norma Sharpe.

CONTENTS

PREFACE

THIS IS THE STORY OF SAM SWITZER, A MAN WHO ROSE FROM poverty in East Calgary to command the respect of the prime minister of Canada, the premier of Alberta, the mayor of Calgary and hundreds of other friends and associates who have come to know him over his long life of achievement and philanthropy.

On June 7, 2012, the Jewish National Fund of Calgary honoured Sam Switzer for his contributions to developing recyclable water in Israel's Negev desert – just one of his many philanthropic causes. Letters of congratulation were sent by the Rt. Hon. Stephen Harper, Prime Minister of Canada, Alison Redford, QC, Premier of Alberta and Naheed Nenshi, Mayor of Calgary.

"I would like to join with you in congratulating tonight's honoured guest, Mr. Sam Switzer, for his commitment and dedication to the well-being of his fellow citizens in Calgary and for his steadfast support for the State of Israel," wrote the prime minister.

Premier Redford wrote: "Sam is a leader in the truest sense of the word – not only in the business sector, where he has excelled, but in the broader community of Calgary and indeed the global community. He has demonstrated leadership through his many philanthropic efforts, contributing to the well-being of those at home and those abroad."

Mayor Nenshi wrote: "Tonight's event honours a man who exemplifies what it means to be a good citizen. For more than sixty years, Sam Switzer has been an active volunteer, supporting numerous organizations and individuals in our city. Through the Sam and Betty Switzer Foundation, his family has provided funding in the areas of medical research and treatment, education, culture and the arts. There can be no doubt that Calgary and its people are much better off for the contribution and efforts of Mr. Switzer.

"It is not surprising that his generous spirit extends beyond your borders; indeed, his is of the kind that can hardly be contained to one place. Mr. Switzer has helped build Calgary into the great city you see today, and he serves as an excellent role model to those who will lead it into the future."

The child of a poor but loving family, Sam very quickly showed a knack for building and sharing. Even then his compassion for others was obvious. His drive and generosity would grow over the decades into a remarkable network of philanthropic activities.

This is how, and why, he did it.

INTRODUCTION

SAM SWITZER LOOKED INTO THE AUDIENCE OF FELLOW MOUNT Royal University graduates and slowly grinned. What was he doing on this stage with such a distinguished crowd? It was June 3, 2011. His last graduation was 70 years earlier, when he completed Grade Nine. Now he was to receive an honorary bachelor's degree and give a speech. Had this respected 100-year-old academic institution gone mad?

Hardly. Sam's 80 years of entrepreneurial experience and success had produced the most important lessons in his life. Now he was about to impart the best of this knowledge: giving and sharing. But first he needed his legs to hold as steady as they had at his last graduation.

His daughter Darlene sat to his left, ready to assist with a comfortable chair, and his family was all around to lend their hands, but he had no intention of allowing an annoying arthritic pain to meddle with his walk to the podium. Dreams seldom come true without persistence, and Sam was not about to sit this one out. He rose, stepped slowly to the podium and grabbed both sides firmly. As he stared at the sea of youths facing him, their energy flowed through the room. At once he was a young man again, ready for life's adventures, full of confidence for the next step. Sam smiled, took a slow deep breath and began:

"Thank you, ladies and gentlemen, honoured guests, fellow graduates: I am thrilled to be here at Mount Royal University, sitting with the 2011 grads as one of you. I know I haven't put in the four years of classroom learning, but I am honoured to also know that you have recognized my nearly 80 years of entrepreneurial learning. And thank you, Mount Royal University, for measuring entrepreneurial success through commitment to community and helping others help themselves.

"My last graduation was 70 years ago when I completed Grade Nine. I had a passion for fun – who doesn't at age 15, or any age? But I also had, and still have, a passion for learning. I looked eagerly towards high school and beyond. But my beloved mother became blind, my dear father was frail and my family needed me in the small grocery store they owned in East Calgary. My formal education stopped cold.

"From the age of five, I was wired to work. Nearly everyone was, in our impoverished community where dreams died fast. The Depression ate away the dignity of working people, depriving them of work, food and home. My parents, Myer and Chaiya Switzer, four older sisters and I lived in the main floor of a house on 6th Ave and 4th St SE. It was just three blocks from the police station but right next door to the hub of the red-light district.

"Remarkably, at the age of five, I became that district's ice supplier. I'd go down to the train tracks on 10th Ave and 1st St SE and wait for the train to pull up to empty ice. I'd gather the pieces that dropped between the rails and put them in the little wagon my parents gave me for my birthday. Then I'd race home to the ladies next door who'd give me five cents a load. Those women carried a heavy load themselves. They helped me understand early on that compassion and kindness can take the sting out of the most biting of circumstances.

"My ice-wagon business taught me another early lesson: control your costs. Because my stock cost nothing, this was a very good business.

"I was 13 when I started delivering drugs – prescription drugs. For my bar mitzvah, my parents gave me a bicycle that I soon put to work. Farrow's Drug Store was right across from the Palliser Hotel. In the winter, I got five cents for delivering the medications, often riding my bicycle up North Hill.

"Again, the costs were minimal, except for my frozen face, fingers and assorted appendages. Another early lesson: always be hands-on, especially when they're frozen to the handlebars.

"My first car was a 1917 Model T Ford that my cousin Benny and I bought for $15. It took us six months to fix the wreck. A year later, Benny bought me out for $25, which I immediately swapped for a 1926 Chevy four-door convertible. Now, this wasn't a convertible by design, but by luck – all bad. There was no roof and the four doors were nailed shut, but what do you expect for $25?

"At least I had wheels to get me to a stucco job in south Calgary. The contract paid $1500, with $500 down. I worked hard and the client worked fast. So fast, in fact, that I never saw the $1000 I was owed for the finished job. From that I learned another lesson: know the integrity of partners and clients.

"My flair for sales took me into the used car business. I found a location right next to the Budget car rental on Macleod Trail. In those days, a neon sign cost as much as a building. So we simply put an office on stilts, up where people could see us clearly.

"A woman came in crying, saying she was so overworked and overwrought that she needed a vacation. Would I buy her car?

"Of course," I said and gave her a good price. She took her money and I never saw her again – probably because the transmission was full of sawdust.

"A fellow came in wanting a Buick. I found a two-year-old model with 25,000 miles. A week later, he stormed in with a wrecked transmission. Turns out the car actually had 125,000 miles! I learned another lesson: Do not go into the used car business.

"Then I found my calling in construction and real estate. From apartment building and rental to hotel and motel ownership, I learned the lesson you all know: location, location, location.

"Throughout these adventures and so many more, I've learned that you don't make mistakes. Rather, they are missteps – I prefer to call them the best learning experiences – that ultimately point you to where you want to go.

"Along the entrepreneurial road, it is not how, but with whom you grow. I have been blessed with close friends and family, especially my six wonderful children, my three loving stepchildren, and all their great kids. I have had the immense good fortune to live and work with the love of my life, my late wife Betty. I cherish her memory.

"Important to me, too, is my faith. I spend an hour each morning in prayer and ask God for guidance.

"Success is not measured by how much you have or how much you earn, but how much you share and how much you give. It is the simplest act, yet it reaps the highest reward. Entrepreneurship and philanthropy are the two sides of the same coin. Toss it high, and you will always win.

"I will treasure my honorary Bachelor of Business Administration degree – entrepreneurship, just as I treasure the honour and privilege of being here today with this distinguished class of 2011.

"Thank you, and the best of entrepreneurial luck to my fellow graduates. May your opportunities grow into successes and may your community reap the benefits."

Chapter One:
The Ice Boy

"I know the Great War was hard on my father and he saw many horrors, but there's just one that he told me," Sam recalls quietly.

Sam's parents, Myer Switzer and Chaiya Geldman, married just a few years before the First World War in their home of Radom, Poland, and welcomed their first child, Rebecca, in 1912. The coming of the war forever imploded their conventional Orthodox life. The Russian army quickly conscripted Myer and his two brothers, Max and Gershon. There was no choice, as every Jewish man knew. The front went right through Radom, just 95 km south of Warsaw and 70 km north of Kielce.

Sam heard the story many times.

"He was with the rest of his unit, taking a break and waiting for further orders when the call of nature came. He wandered into the woods, and then slowly headed towards camp, just enjoying a rare moment of quiet."

A massive blast shook the earth. Myer fell to the ground in shock. After a time he slowly crept back into an eerie silence. And then – nothing. The enemy shell had obliterated the entire group. Everyone was dead, except him.

The carnage he saw that day would never fully leave his psyche, but Myer resolved to leave Radom, even though he and his family had survived this war. He knew the antipathy towards Jews would simmer until the cauldron of bile boiled over. He was right, of course. Another pogrom erupted and swiftly shattered shtetl life. This hate-fueled fire enflamed Poland and so many other parts of Europe. Within a generation, it would engulf the entire planet in the Second World War and immolate tens of millions of innocent victims including more than six million Jews in the Holocaust.

Myer's sister Bella Singer, who was already in Canada, had the foresight to realize her family would never be safe in Radom. As she sponsored her loved ones, each savoured his or her ticket to freedom. The main objective was Canada, a country so immense, with fields so full of promise, that a bounty of plenty was there for any with the health, strength and resolve to come and work. At least, that's what the Canadian government ads implied.

"Immigrants were bombarded in their homelands with Canadian government propaganda showing a rich, bountiful and completely mythical life on the frontier," Don Braid and Sydney Sharpe wrote in *Breakup: Why the West Feels Left out of Canada.*

"Even the artistic techniques were extremely devious; posters ignored the emptiness and vast skies of the prairies, focusing instead on busy, plentiful fields and foregrounds. Ducks looked as fat and juicy as turkeys, cattle as big as boxcars. One poster showed a beautiful woman in angel-like robes sailing over farmsteads, scattering wheat from a basket to the fields below. Some of the scenes look suspiciously like the European countries the propaganda was aimed at. Many immigrants attracted by this misleading advertising jumped at free homesteads, but had no idea they were heading into a primitive, remote and difficult land where they would have no political or economic clout."

Each person Bella brought to Canada grabbed any kind of work to pay her back so the next family member could be sponsored. Often they worked on the Jewish homesteading colonies near Calgary. The new arrivals felt responsible for those left behind, so they in turn also raised cash to sponsor their own immediate relatives. Bella first bought tickets and "guaranteed" two nephews, Charlie Switzer and Saul Bleviss, who left Radom for Calgary in 1912. A few years after the First World War ended, Bella began bringing six of her brothers and sisters from Poland to Canada: Gershon Switzer in 1920; Sam's father Myer Switzer, in 1921; Mendel Switzer in 1923; Mindell Bleviss in 1927; Rifka Belzberg in 1928 and Jacob Switzer in 1929. Together with a flow of nieces and nephews, Bella also sponsored her sister, Jessie Fishman. Tragically, her other sisters, Sarah Aizenman, Faiga Cyngiser and Noma Farber would die in the Holocaust, along with most of their family members that hadn't emigrated.

Even as the First World War raged, Myer and Chaiya had been blessed with the birth of daughter Lily, in 1916. Just two years after the war ended, in 1920, another daughter, Jessie, entered the world. Myer wanted a life of promise for his growing family, not the pandemonium of daily dread. Escape to Canada and a new life had drifted about in his dreams ever since his sister Bella had moved to Calgary with her husband Abraham Singer in 1910.

It became Bella Singer's mission to make Canada home for as many of her extended family as could escape Poland's virulent anti-Semitism and establish a new life. She was directly responsible for more than 300 relatives taking that treacherous route from Radom to Calgary, Canada and points beyond. Had Bella Singer not rescued these near and distant relatives from poverty, disease, intolerance and deceit, thousands of their descendents would not exist today.

"When you look at what one tiny woman did, it was massive," Sam Switzer reflects. "We called her 'Auntie Meema,' and she was an amazing human being with a huge heart and indomitable will."

Sam's father, Myer, was one of the earliest to follow his sister to Calgary. Throughout their lives, the two siblings remained close and confiding friends. Bella had been the youngest of Wolf Baer Scwajcer and Chaya Leeba's children until Myer, their ninth, was born. (The children were Mendel, Mindell, Faiga, Rifka,

Sarah, Jacob, Jessie, Bella and Myer.) After their mother became ill and died in 1884, Wolf Baer married Miriam Rzeczynski, who bore two more (Noma, and then Gershon). Thanks to Bella, many of those children, grandchildren and great grandchildren made it to a new life in Canada. The Scwajcers changed their name to Switzer at the immigration dock. By 1924, the persistent pogroms were taking their toll, and finally the 77-year-old patriarch was convinced that he must set off, too. Bella paid his passage and Wolf Baer prepared to leave Radom. The extended family waited in Calgary to hear he had safely boarded the ship.

"I was in the basement," Bella's son Jack Singer told writer Tyler Trafford. "Sam's father came over to see my mother. He was crying, weeping. He said that he had heard Wolf Baer had passed away in Poland."

Even before Myer received the upsetting news, it was hard to picture Wolf Baer making the perilous trip, given his frail health.

Getting to Canada and then Calgary from southern Poland was a journey fraught with danger and betrayal. Those lucky relatives with a $62 Canadian-Pacific ticket to Canada from Germany (the price would later double), courtesy of Bella Singer, were embarking into the unknown. Armed with passage, cash and suitcase, each young émigré needed to make his or her way to Antwerp and board the ship to Halifax.

For a Jew, applying for an exit permit from Poland was akin to asking a jailer for a cell. Leaving Radom for Germany required secrecy and secure routes. Broad daylight worked only if the bribed guards lived up to their end of the bargain. Night crossings could make the heart stop, but at least didn't rely so much on the vagaries of human trust.

Once on German soil, the hopeful emigrant headed for Antwerp and Canadian immigration officials who tested his or her medical and financial health. Good eyesight and a minimum of $25 were crucial, as well as the paid-in-full passage to Calgary. The relatively calm Antwerp docks betrayed little of the two-week journey to come, an intimidating voyage across the North Atlantic, always a war of wills between the ocean and the vessels that sailed her.

When the ship docked in Halifax, Canadian immigration officials greeted the newcomers with more questions and exams on health, wealth, where-to and why. Once free of the incessant prying and prodding, they boarded the Canadian Pacific Railway to Calgary, to gaze from an uncomfortable bench as the train snaked across a wilderness filled with rocks, grasses, bald prairie and loneliness.

The exhausted Myer arrived at Bella and Abraham's rooming house in 1921, eager to repay his sister and earn the fare for Chaiya and his young daughters to leave Radom. He was told there was work in the Jewish farming settlement of Rumsey-Trochu, about 160 km northeast of Calgary.

In 1906, a romantic had described an area "where grass was up to a horse's belly, lakes and sloughs were fresh and productive with wildlife and game, and wildflowers were everywhere."

The settlement was 10 km west of Rumsey, on the east bank of the Red Deer River, and soon 75 Jewish homesteaders had established their colony. The following year, just 18 km away, another adventurous group of Jewish settlers formed a colony just east of Trochu in the valley on the west bank of the same river. The settlement was kickstarted by the Jewish Colonization Association, an international aid group formed by the French Jewish philanthropist Baron Maurice de Hirsch and others, including Moses Montefiore, in 1891. (The Jewish colony in Sibbald, just west of the Alberta-Saskatchewan border was named after Montefiore.) The JCA provided seed funding for colonies across the prairies, allowing an opportunity for Jewish farmers and pioneers to seek a new life.

Settlers were attracted to the prairies for the quarter-section homesteads (160 acres or 65 hectares) available to any willing to prove them up and pay the $10 administrative charge. The farmer needed to clear, plant and harvest 40 acres (16 hectares) as well as build a home, within three years. The successful homesteader not only received the final land deed but was eligible for a contiguous quarter section at a fee of $10. The lure of free land was popular with prospective farmers and politicians alike; although what seemed heaven-sent to the poverty-stricken settlers too often proved to be from a lower region of the firmament.

Sir Alexander Tilloch Galt, Canada's High Commissioner to London, urged Canadian Prime Minister John A. Macdonald to accept Eastern European Jews fleeing from pogroms after Alexander III was crowned czar.

"From what I learn these Russian Jews are a superior class of people, partly farmers, but generally trade people," said Galt. "I found American Jews were actively promoting emigration to the United States, and I thought what was good for them could not be bad for us."

Through inaction, Macdonald thwarted Galt for over a year before finally agreeing. Author Max Rubin notes it was "another eight years before Jews decided to settle permanently in Alberta."

The debate on easier Jewish entry into the Canadian frontier made clear Canadian politicians' image of the perfect settler. Clifford Sifton, the minister of the interior from 1896 to 1905, knew exactly what he wanted: "A stalwart peasant in a sheepskin coat, born on the soil, whose forefathers have been farmers for 10 generations, with a stout wife and a half-dozen children."

Sifton's dream was the bedrock of a judgmental immigration policy that opened its doors wide for "peasant stock," but just as quickly closed them when that stock's ethnicity, or religion, displeased the bigoted bureaucrats and politicians who guarded the gates.

For a few brief years until the mid-1920s, the immigration gates unlocked, especially for family members and farm workers. To an immigration official, Myer would seem suitable since to unite with family in Canada, he was eager to work on the West's farming frontier.

The Rumsey-Trochu colony was the most successful Jewish farming settlement in the country. When European borders opened after the First World War, numerous immigrants from Poland headed to the homesteading settlement.

"The Rumsey and Trochu colonies were established on fertile

soil, and enjoyed much higher annual precipitation than the Jewish colonies in the dry belt of Saskatchewan," writes Albert Stein. "So, if they were lucky enough not to get wiped out by hailstorms or grasshoppers or early frost, the early years were bountiful. By 1920, the Jewish population in the district was 238, and over 10,000 acres were under cultivation … Land values soared and wheat, under the open market system, reached a speculative high of $2.21 per bushel. But when the Canadian government abandoned the wartime Wheat Board in 1920, and returned grain marketing to the Winnipeg Grain Exchange, growers were left at the mercy of the grain cartel."

The settlement struggled with the droughts of 1921 and 1923 that had felled the hopes of farmers across the West. Myer and the other new arrivals were accustomed to hard work but hardly prepared for the harsh prairie farming conditions coupled with the lack of rain. The drought led to crop failures that disillusioned even the heartiest of farmers. Many had mortgaged all they owned for machinery, seed and more land. When months with little rain coincided with depressed grain and cattle prices, too many faced farms of dust and vanishing returns.

"Prices of grain and cattle were manipulated down, and by 1923 had brought ruin to thousands of farmers, especially those who had obtained large mortgages to [buy] expensive land," explains Stein. "The Rumsey and Trochu colonies were not spared; many farms were abandoned.

Between 1921 and 1923, nearly all the settlement's newcomers headed back to Calgary and neighbouring towns. Myer, too, returned to the city and an uncertain future, but he was sure of one thing; he was not going to face life any longer without Chaiya and the girls.

In Calgary, there were still odd jobs for a man willing to put his sweat into his vision of family reunited. Myer earned and borrowed the funds for his family's passage. Then he waited. Until Chaiya and the girls stepped down from the rail car in 1923, Myer couldn't believe they had really managed to complete the risky journey of no return from Radom. At last, life would be free from the constant threats of death. Poverty was almost a trivial problem by comparison. Ultimately, Myer's extended family, as Max Rubin notes, would wield considerable influence within and beyond their East Village roots.

"The coming of the Switzer and Shumiachter families to Calgary changed the Jewish community's social makeup," writes Rubin. "While the Shumiachter family had been in Canada since before the First World War, their extended family was still in Russia. The Switzer family had already begun the process of emigrating from Poland before 1918. The large size of both families, coupled with the fact that most of the family that came to Canada went to Calgary, made these two families dominant in the social and economic life of the Jewish community."

As Chaiya Switzer went into labour at the Calgary General Hospital, she prayed her child be born healthy. It was February 25TH, 1926, nearly three years after her fourth child – another beautiful daughter, Dinah – had graced their lives in this same place. Myer was 41, but Chaiya was already 46 and unlikely to ever again be admitted to the maternity ward.

With the startling cry of the newborn, their baby slipped into this world. His parents were ready to cry, too, for the infant was both healthy and male. Ousher Zalic Switzer became his name, but Sam Switzer was the name he would come to be known by, a name given to him when he registered for grade school.

From the moment his mother carried him home, Sam was adored by his older sisters. He delighted in running amok in a household full of girls. The joy and play within the home masked the poverty and misery waiting outside. The family lived in Calgary's desultory East Village, where dreams were delivered on the flip of a coin and too many ended in the gutter. It was an impoverished community awash in spent souls crossing swords with the law.

Yet it was also a neighbourhood of hope, as recent immigrants imagined a new land free from the pogroms and brutalities of countries they had fled. The East Village was the crossroads for eagerness and despair as every new resident envisioned days of prosperity. For many, the poverty would be but a way station on the road to rewards for perseverance and hard work. Or so they prayed.

The early Calgary Jewish community set up their mini-shtetl just south of the Bow River and east of Centre St and 12ᵀᴴ Ave. There were Jewish grocers, bakeries and kosher butcher shops, as well as second-hand stores.

They even established their own loan societies. In 1931, the Switzer family and their extended relatives formed the Polish Jewish Family Loan Association, whose stated object was "solely to aid members who are temporarily embarrassed financially, by loaning small sums to members of the society."

No interest was charged, everything was done on a handshake and all the loans were repaid, says Sam, whose father was one of the many founders. A generation later, the sons of the founders continued the loan society, meeting at the Summit Hotel, which Sam had built and owned. The Polish Jewish Family Loan Association still operates today.

Historian Jack Switzer explained that similar "Free Loan Societies" took root across Canada and were "based partially in the Talmudic principle of 'gemilut Chasidim' – acts of loving kindness." He quoted fellow historian Harry Gutnik: "A loan was not to be considered charity and therefore damaging to the recipient's self respect, but simply a temporary support, perhaps even an obligation upon the group as a whole."

Once a person in the Switzer extended family was gathered in Calgary, he or she had an immediate network for what was needed, whether spiritual, social or financial. This shtetl contained it all: shul, food, clothing, and shelter. Advice was free.

Baby Sam came home to a rental on 7ᵀᴴ Ave SE; but within the year, Myer and Chaiya had put their meager earnings into a home they actually owned. Just two blocks away, at 511 6ᵀᴴ Ave SE, the two-storey plaster-clapboard boasted a main floor with dining room, living room and one bedroom for the family, as well as another five rooms upstairs.

As soon as Myer and Chaiya saw the house for sale, they

wanted to buy, but they wondered how it was even possible and whether the $500 asking price was too steep. Family and friends suggested a man who understood the vagaries of the real estate market. So much so, in fact, that after their meeting, the man himself bought the coveted dwelling, then quickly tripled the cost, and offered the house for $1500.

"He was an expert at buying," says Sam dryly. "Also selling."

The stunned couple, concerned the next house would be far beyond their reach, paid the price.

"All six of us lived on the main floor while my mother rented out the five upstairs rooms," recalls Sam. "My sisters slept on tables in the dining room, where I found a spot to sleep, too. My parents slept in the only bedroom downstairs."

The family quickly took to the new home's important advantages. The House of Jacob Synagogue (at 325 5TH Ave SE) was only two blocks away. Closer still were Shuler's Grocery (on 4TH St and 6TH Ave SE) as well as two kosher butcher shops. Martin's Bakery (at 415 4TH Ave SE) was the most popular shop on Sundays.

"They were famous for bagels and pumpernickel bread. On Sunday, everyone in the Jewish community came to buy – it was a ritual, and we'd get together to chat and chew!" remembers Sam.

But the disadvantages were too obvious to ignore. Their home also boasted one of the best places to observe the endless comings and goings of the neighbours. Prostitution and bootlegging defined the area, but the local police were often rebuffed in their attempts to shut down houses of ill repute. The station may have been only three blocks away, but that did little to hamper the area's star attractions. Raiding Calgary's red-light district proved as futile as permanently shutting the world's oldest profession.

Notoriety didn't begin in the East Village, but it certainly grabbed hold of what was once an integrated thriving community. The red-lights grew up slowly, as the East Village's own website explains.

"By the start of Calgary's pre-First World War boom, around 1906, East Village was a bustling community with a mix of residential, commercial, service, institutional and industrial activity.

"Over the years, blacksmith shops gave way to iron foundries, livery stables to service stations, single-family homes to apartments or 'flophouses.' But business gradually moved west and residences sprawled out from the centre, and, by 1941, the city medical officer of health declared EV part of 'Skid Row,' the site of what is now politely called 'undesirable activity' but was then referred to in police blotters as bootlegging, prostitution and the like."

The East Village transition from respectability to "Skid Row" was in full swing, but this hardly deterred the former residents of pogrom-plagued Radom. Myer and Chaiya brought the values of toil and tenacity, imprinted in their Polish Jewish upbringing, to their life together in Canada.

"My father worked with a horse and wagon, buying and selling rags, bottles and used clothing," sister Dinah told writer Tyler Trafford. "He would holler, 'Any rags? Any bottles? Any used clothes?' I couldn't believe how loud he hollered. I would go on the wagon with him."

One day, as Myer jumped from the wagon to sell his wares, he tripped and fell to the ground. His leg snapped, and just as suddenly, Myer's days in the rag trade were over. He sold the horse and wagon for a temperamental truck and even more tentative career: buying and selling cattle.

"Father would wake me early in the morning to help him start the truck," adds Dinah, who was just six at the time. "I would sit on the floor and hold the pedals down with my hands while he cranked the motor by hand."

Some mornings, when her father drove her to school, Dinah would ask for a penny for candy.

"It still bothers me. He had a long leather purse and would press it open, and inside would be maybe a couple of dimes, a quarter and a few pennies. I know now that he needed that penny more than I needed candy."

Myer's move from rags to cows met with patched roads and even patchier returns. Every rancher had a poignant tale to tell. Ever the kindly buyer, Myer paid too dear a price to see a profit.

"If all it took were hard work and long hours, my father would have been a millionaire. Sadly, he just didn't have that aggressive quality that you need to be a businessman," says Sam wistfully.

Myer rose before dawn, driving his truck more on resolve than results, always accompanied by a faith in what the day could bring and a will to make it happen.

What kept the family solvent was the persistence and ingenuity of Chaiya and her two older girls, Becky and Lily. They also rose early while the three youngsters, Jessie, Dinah and Sam, were allowed to sleep later (but only until they were old enough to earn.) "How lucky I was," adds Dinah. "We had nothing, but I didn't know."

Her two older sisters did. Becky and Lily rushed from the home at dawn to buy crates of eggs from the Sheinin family wholesalers. They walked door-to-door, selling the eggs for two cents a dozen. Their regular route through the red-light district caused Chaiya some serious concern.

"It was a challenge for my sisters," says Sam. "My mother would try to talk them out of going to certain houses. Occasionally, she might have been successful."

The family survived because everyone worked as soon as they were able. Relying on the money the girls earned meant Becky and Lily would never attend high school. Education, so highly valued, fell flat in the face of poverty.

Yet the joy of childhood never did, even though Sam's working life began at the age of five.

"My parents bought me a wagon for my birthday," recalls Sam. "It was red and shiny and I couldn't wait to play with it."

Sam's wagon wasn't filled with children's dreams, but with life's demands. The little boy with the wagon was now earning a living. The ladies who bought his train-dropped ice for five cents a load were well known to the police blotters as living off the avails of a house of ill repute. To Sam, they were customers of a far different sort. He became their supplier – of ice. It was his first job.

"They were very thankful for the ice and I almost never left without a sweet or a few pennies more. Those ladies were always kind to me."

His sister Dinah described Sam's early slogging. "Jessie and I had it easy. We went to school and played. Sam worked like a dog. He earned every cent. I didn't realize what a hard, hard life it was for them. I thought it was fun. My life was very sheltered. Sam was a very hard worker all his young years."

Yet Sam never felt oppressed or overworked at such an early age. "Work was life," he says. "It was what you did for the family. Besides, I was spoiled rotten."

Dinah insists he was not spoiled, although the family was crazy about him. "My mother called him 'my precious little one.' He was a clever boy and the best brother you would ever want. He is a wonderful brother and a fantastic son."

Sam echoes his sister's words as he recalls a home rich in love. "We had nothing, but we had everything."

Especially his mother's cooking, which Sam rhapsodizes about.

"I loved her chicken, and goodness knows we had it so often, I had to love it," he laughs. "But it was her sourdough bread that everyone praised. Her crust was to die for. I've never tasted bread that was better. And then there was my sister Lily who made the best chocolate cake around. Of course you couldn't get enough. Even if it hadn't been the Depression but a time of plenty, you could never get enough of Lily's cake and Mother's sourdough."

Twenty-first century foodies pursuing their slow food movement would do well to look to the past and the meals of mothers like Chaiya Switzer.

"If those very plates of food were served today, they would be considered completely organic and homemade, a true treat," explains Sam.

As the Depression raged in Canada, this was all Chaiya could afford to feed her family. It was called the Dirty Thirties, and canned food – much touted at the time – cost far beyond the family's means.

"We bought chickens from Maclean Auction (on 10TH Ave and 10TH St SE) and brought them to Rabbi Smolensky, who killed them in a barn behind his house. We used every part of the bird. The ladies would pluck the chickens and save the feathers for pillows and bed spreads. The rest, you name it and we ate it."

As a growing youngster working his wagon, Sam lived for food. "Model Dairies were famous for their ice cream and Bridgeman's chocolate was *the* bargain chocolate. For five cents you could buy a bag of broken chocolate pieces. I can still taste them. Of course Olivier's Chocolate was considered Calgary's finest – and I'm sure it was if I could have afforded it then!"

Sam also remembers Union Milk, but not for the calibre of the spilt cream. Instead, he was intrigued by the surreal sight of horses that seemed to suspend themselves high above the ground. At least that's what it looked like to a youngster perched in the synagogue, looking through the window for a horse to take flight. Perhaps the steed would swoop down for Oush and off they'd go into the sky.

"They were so grand and beautiful, and I just allowed my imagination to soar. Union Milk was right across the street from the synagogue. They kept the horses on the second level. It was quite the sight seeing these horses clip-clop down the big ramp. I got lost in this strange scene sometimes hoping they'd just take wing and fly. But no horse ever lost its step as it made its way down to the milk wagons. At the bottom, a man would hook the horse to the milk wagon and then pull a blanket over the wagon so the milk containers wouldn't freeze in the winter or sour in the summer."

Sam certainly had ample opportunity to study the horses as they walked down the ramp. That's because his father prayed in synagogue twice a day, often taking Sam by the hand as they walked the few blocks together.

"My father was a very religious man, and he went to synagogue every morning and evening. He brought me whenever he could because he wanted me to have a sound understanding of our religion, to be respectful and observant."

Myer had the strongest of reasons to believe in his God and pass those lessons to his son.

"God had spared his life from that blast in the Great War," says Sam. "There was no part of my father that didn't feel that forever."

Myer was especially grateful to Bella, knowing he was one of the first in the Switzer chain of migration that removed most – but not all – of his relatives from the growing clouds that piled up over Europe, raining hatred and death. Chaiya had longed to return to Radom one more time to see her family. In 1934, she embarked on the long voyage to her past, a place where anti-Semitism was in full force with pogroms erupting at the whim of wickedness, and where a Jew who could readily return to Canada was grateful for her very life.

"I don't remember my mother talking to me about her trip – after all, I was only eight. But I do know how very glad she was to get home and be living in Calgary. She missed her family that remained in Radom. Of course, she would never see them again," says Sam solemnly.

In the Radom area alone, over 380,000 Jews died in the Holocaust. Sid (Sucher) Cyngiser was one of the few to survive the slaughter of the ghettoes, concentration camps and death marches. The grandson of Wolf Baer's third child, Faiga, Cyngiser saw his grandmother, mother, sisters and then father perish under the brute evil of Nazism. His turn was near, but on April 7, 1945, the allies freed the shattered survivors.

Everything had been torn from Cyngiser but his spirit. He ended up in a German hospital for Holocaust survivors, where he saw a woman crying after an orphan called her 'Mother.' The woman, Bronia, broke down at the tragedy of the motherless child.

"She was crying, so upset about it," Cyngiser told the Mount Royal University 2012 Holocaust Symposium. "That's when I knew she would be my wife."

Bronia and her sister had lost their mother to the Nazi genocide. When the three were starving in Auschwitz, Bronia's mother would take her meager piece of dried bread and tear it in half for the two girls.

"I feel so much guilt still, because I survived and she did not," Bronia told the symposium.

As Cyngiser slowly recovered his health in the hospital, he was asked if he had any American relatives. Miraculously, he recalled his great aunt Bella's Calgary address. Sid Cyngiser arrived in Calgary on December 28TH, 1949. For over 50 years, Sid and Bronier Cyngiser have brought the stories of courage and survival to tens of thousands of students for whom the Holocaust is an evil never to be repeated.

The Cyngiser's good friend, Aron Eichler, was rounded up in the carnage that stole his childhood, and nearly his life, in Cieszanow, Poland, near Lvov. He barely survived the concentration camps and emigrated to Montreal in 1949. Aron moved to Calgary and eventually married Sam's second cousin, Ida Zysblat, whose grandfather Jacob was the older brother of Sam's father. Sam and Aron became fast friends. Eichler rose to be principal of I.L. Peretz School, and as an educator he knew he must tell his story.

"I've transmitted stories of the Holocaust to students in high school and universities for the past 30 years," says Eichler, whose wife was always by his side. Sadly, Ida has passed on. "They need to know what happened in the Holocaust, the unspeakable sins of inhumanity. If I have forgiven the Germans for what they did, I have not forgotten. No! The next generation must know what happened. If not, then we really won't have learned anything."

For their profound suffering, the Cyngisers and Aron Eichler want only to prevent future generations from living such horror. As Eichler says: "We must work together for a world where people believe in the goodness of humanity and where harmony and mutual respect can thrive."

This is exactly what every one of Wolf Baer Scwajcer's descendents wanted when they left Radom and what they live for today. While rewards awaited many after generations of toil, the challenges are just as fickle. Historian Alan Mendelson quotes the great scholar Louis Namier: "Who is a Jew? For Gentiles, anyone whom they want to belittle or stigmatize."

Namier continues: "Harried, he is blamed for being restless; kept out or kept down he is described as pushing or assertive; hurt, he searches for compensations and is called vain, blatant or self-indulgent; insecure, he yearns for standing, power and wealth:

which sometimes protect him, but more often expose him the more to attack."

The extended family of Bella Singer and her brother Myer Switzer were grateful to have made it to Canada before the tidal wave of anti-Semitism swept through the government of William Lyon Mackenzie King. While Canada had opened its gates to the great immigration thrust of the late 19TH and early 20TH centuries, it bolted them shut during and after the Second World War, the time of European Jewry's greatest need.

Irena Karshenbaum writes that: "R.B. Bennett, who had spoken at the ceremony for the laying of the cornerstone of the original House of Jacob in Calgary in 1911, was prime minister from 1930 to 1935 and Opposition leader from 1935 to 1938, but he refused to help the Jewish community."

Mackenzie King and his high commissioner to Britain, Vincent Massey, wanted no Jewish refugees in Canada and found their Director of Immigration enabler in the ardent anti-Semite, Frederick Charles Blair.

"I suggested recently to three Jewish gentlemen with whom I am well acquainted, that it would be a very good thing if they could call a conference and have a day of humiliation and prayer, which might profitably be extended for a week or more, where they would honestly try to answer the question of why they are so unpopular almost everywhere," Blair wrote in a 1938 letter to a colleague.

"I often think that instead of persecution it would be far better if we more often told them frankly why many of them are unpopular," Blair continued. "If they would divest themselves of certain of their habits I am sure they could be just as popular in Canada as our Scandinavians."

Blair finished penning his bigoted poison with this remark: "Just because Jewish people would not understand the frank kind of statements I have made in this letter to you, I have marked it confidential."

Blair was rigorous in implementing not only his but the concurrent intolerant views of Mackenzie King's wartime government. In 1945, when journalists asked one of his bureaucrats how many Jews should be allowed into Canada, this was the shocking reply: "None is too many."

It's a disgraceful period in Canadian history, one chillingly chronicled by Irving Abella and Harold Troper in their book, *None is Too Many: Canada and the Jews of Europe 1933–1948*. From 1919 to 1933, Canada admitted nearly 40,000 Jewish immigrants. Then, as Jews fled from certain graves, Canada had the disgraceful distinction of accepting the lowest number of any western nation: 5000. Compare that to the U.S., which had its own anti-Semitic strategies, but still managed 200,000. Palestine admitted 125,000, with Britain at 70,000, Argentina at 50,000, China at 25,000 and Bolivia and Chile, with 14,000 between them.

One of the shameful tales in this immoral immigration saga is the fate of the 937 Jewish passengers aboard the S.S. St. Louis. Trying to escape the evil assaulting Europe, the terrified travelers embarked on one last voyage of hope on May 27, 1939. Journeying across the Atlantic to Cuba, and then Florida, the ship was refused entry at every port.

Halifax was the last hope, and it was there that Blair played his self-scripted anti-Semitic screed to his perfection. It was his policy to personally examine – and refuse – every Jewish refugee application. None was too many.

Dubbed the voyage of the damned, the S.S. St. Louis was to become one of the most poignant pictures of anti-Semitism in the early stages of the war.

"We can only hope that some hearts will soften somewhere and some refuge be found. The cruise of the St. Louis cries to heaven of man's inhumanity to men," wrote the *New York Times* in an editorial.

The bleak mood on board the St. Louis filtered down through the melancholic games of the children:

"Are you a Jew?" asked one of the guards.

"Yes," answered the child at the barrier.

"Jews are not admitted," snapped the guard.

"Oh please let me in. I'm only a very little Jew."

No part of Canada's political landscape was immune to anti-Semitism and zealots like Blair. Alberta's Social Credit party, which ruled the province from 1935 to 1971, had too many members in thrall to a Scottish engineer named Clifford Hugh Douglas. While he had initially developed the notion of Social Credit, a good part of his doctrine relied heavily on a malicious hoax called the Protocols of the Elders of Zion. Major Douglas blamed the Depression and all economic ills on an international banking conspiracy dominated by Jews. When Douglas called Jews "parasites" in 1938, Social Credit Premier William Aberhart disowned him in a statement to the Alberta press.

Yet in 1946, with six million Jews dead in the Holocaust, Major Douglas continued to publish his poison in the British newsletter, *Social Crediter*. It was wholeheartedly repeated and endorsed in the *Canadian Social Crediter*, which was printed in Edmonton by the Alberta-based party.

"In 1947, Manning lost patience with the Douglas-inspired anti-Semites on the board of the *Canadian Social Crediter* and sent in one of his lieutenants, Drumheller MLA Gordon Taylor, to fire the whole lot," Sharpe and Braid wrote in *Storming Babylon: Preston Manning and the Rise of the Reform Party*.

In a 1982 interview for the University of Alberta archives, Ernest Manning had his own view of anti-Semitism in the Social Credit Party.

"One time in the House I made a speech repudiating this thing. I said, 'This is the viewpoint of individuals; it is *not* the position of the government, it is not the viewpoint of the Social Credit movement in Alberta. It never has been, and it never will be.' And I pointed out that in any political party you could find anti-Semites. There was nothing peculiar about the Social Credit party… there isn't a political party in existence that doesn't have somebody that's anti-Semitic, or anti-Catholic or anti-something. But it's grossly unfair to say that that is the position of the party."

Still, it was frightening for Jews who had fled the pogroms and violent anti-Semitism of Europe for a promised land of tolerance.

Jews in Alberta were often barred from jobs, clubs and certain societies precisely because of their religion.

"My sisters tried to get better jobs in the big chain stores, but they couldn't get anything because they were Jewish," recalls Sam.

Much of the prejudice remained covert rather than overt. Certainly there were doors that would remain shut for more than half a century, and it became a point of principle to seek invitations from the very club officers who had turned a thumbed nose decades before. Even today in Canada and the U.S. there are companies and clubs that prefer their roster remain quietly free from any kind of diversity.

Calgary historian Jack Switzer remembered the shadows of prejudice reflected in the places Jews chose to avoid. "The adult community was more passive about it. But the Jewish community was quite concerned by some of the followers of Aberhart in Social Credit."

Yet as youngsters, neither Jack, nor Sam earlier, felt the reins of bigotry holding them back. "I never sensed anti-Semitism as a child or teenager," said Jack Switzer, who grew up primarily in the late 1940s and 50s and, sadly, passed away in January 2012.

"I didn't experience it personally like my sisters did," says Sam, who was a child of the Great Depression. "In a sense, the district where we lived was like a ghetto. We were isolated but also insulated."

As a young boy, Sam was content, for all that he needed was contained in this small shtetl in the middle of Calgary, where he was nurtured and cherished. Sam knew who he was, and the ghetto produced in him the resolve of a racehorse rounding the turn of a rut-filled track. His strength of character would see him through a series of ventures as varied as the prairie sky. While he would travel afar, he would never leave the community that allowed him as a child to believe in the flight of horses and dreams.

CHAPTER TWO:
THE GROCER

THE BUSINESS GENE STREAMED THROUGH SAM'S VEINS, EVEN when he was a five-year-old boy selling ice. But it was so much more than that. At this tender age, Sam learned to trust his instincts. He could tell almost intuitively when to unload his precious ice cargo with a prospective client and get paid. Knowing when and where to pull his metaphorical wagon would prepare Sam for an entrepreneurial career that would surprise even him. It all started at home.

"I was so lucky to have all that support from my parents and sisters," he says. "I had to help my family. I had to succeed. My mother and sisters were working long hours and I couldn't let them do it alone. I couldn't let them down."

Yet nestled in that passionate commitment was the quest for fun and adventure. If there was a race or contest close by, and a reward of sweets, Sam was there at the starting line.

"The Palace Theatre on 8ᵀᴴ Ave held Saturday morning yo-yo contests. All you had to do was spin your yo-yo and be the best. That was the only way I was going to win the prize – a bottle of coke and a piece of chocolate plus new yo-yo string. How else was I ever going to get that kind of treat, including a cowboy movie, for nothing?

"There were these twins in my class at Haultain School – Doug and Dick Moffat – who were so good that they travelled throughout Canada and the U.S. as yo-yo champions. When they weren't in town, I won. I actually became the yo-yo champ of Alberta."

Sam practiced how to loosen and tighten the string as well as twist it into the middle of the yo-yo. The basic forward pass seemed simple – at least to him – and Sam quickly learned the loops. He mastered the around-the-world trick where the string shoots out and circles the yo-yo centre, then snaps back.

"I got to the point where I didn't think about the routine, but just did it. Actually, all I really thought about was the chocolate."

With his edible winnings in his stomach – and the yo-yo lace in his pocket – Sam would stroll by the familiar stores on the street. "I'd talk to relatives at Ralph's Furniture and then look at the suits at Jack's, just a block west. Later, they had the zoot suits, and I imagined wearing one of these fancy wide-legged styles with a waist so high that it would fit over my head."

He'd continue walking past the stalls in the market where so many Jewish merchants got their start. Today, Calgary's glass-paneled city hall covers all those memories. Luckily, the city planners also chose to renovate the glorious original sandstone municipal building. The two structures sit as separate epochs joined at the municipal hip.

"I used to go to the dentist at city hall," recalls Sam. "He had an office in the basement where he'd look at my teeth, see some he didn't like and give them fillings. You got what you could in those days with no money. It was always pretty painful. I don't think they knew anything about anesthetics. If they did, they sure didn't use them on me."

Maybe the cries of the kids still live in the walls and halls of the old building. Certainly some of city council's debates seem like pulling teeth. Many years later, when Sam was in his 40s, he thought he might run for council. He attended many of the meetings and studied the way they ran.

"I spent hours of my time watching the aldermen. They'd take two hours with someone wanting to build a garage and asking for a zoning change. And then, when something required city approval for spending a million dollars or more, council would spend five minutes on it, or less! I realized that, too often, the alderman was a voice in the wilderness. My time would be better served as a participant from the outside looking in. At least I understood the process, such as it was. The few times I appeared at council, I armed myself with all the facts and figures and made sure everyone had them beforehand. I had learned to be prepared and quick on my feet."

When Sam hit the heady age of 10, he took the wheels off his wagon and plunged headlong into racing. The thrill of the ride would never leave him. "That's when I got into the go-cart races. I put plywood on the bottom of the wagon, cardboard on the front for a windshield, and jumped in. They'd close the 4TH St North Hill and off we'd all go. My parents and sisters never missed a race. It was so much fun, but I never won – not even once."

With five years on its battered frame, Sam's four-wheel carthorse was no longer the pristine wagon it once had been. His parents solved all that on his bar mitzvah with a brand new bicycle. It was no racing cycle, but another mean working machine.

Farrow's Drug Store, owned by Noel Adair Farrow, was across the street from the Palliser Hotel on 9TH Ave SW. One day Sam rode his bike to the store, walked in empty handed and headed out with a full box of prescription drugs.

"I became a drug pedlar – and peddler – at 13. I'd get five cents a load. Just like my ice days," laughs Sam as he reminisces over his duties as a delivery boy.

The Calgary of seventy years ago is gone – except for she who must be obeyed: the weather. Whether the sun was blazing or had slipped into hiding when the clouds rolled into town, sick people needed their medications. Dodging bolts of lightning in summer and peddling through pellets of hail in fall seemed a cursed fate until Sam trudged through far worse – the bitter whiteouts in winter.

The winter wind was so raw, Sam was certain he'd be blind before he got to the top of North Hill. Closing his eyes, he slowly peddled, feeling the cold crush any spirit lingering in his iced-up resolve. When his eyelashes froze, Sam guessed his way, longing for a warm house and an invitation inside, just to thaw for a few minutes.

"I attached this piece of plastic and cardboard right behind the handlebars, hoping it would shield me from the worst blasts of the blizzards and numbing winds. It may have protected me from a slab of sleet or snow, but barely. On the good days, though, when the sun was shining and the road was clear, the job became pure bliss as I was gliding down the hill, hoping the ride would never end."

A few months earlier, when Sam was 12, he'd stepped into the lobby of the York Hotel on 7TH Ave and Centre St and then headed down the stairs. Before it moved across the street, Gibson's Bowling Alley was in the bowels of this grand hotel, an imposing rival to the prestigious Palliser a few blocks away. (Today the gallant Palliser continues as a luxury Fairmont hotel. Sadly, only the York's brick façade and concrete friezes remain, reconstructed into the bold Norman Foster-designed EnCana skyscraper project. The original ornate poured-in-place mural of plant fronds evoked an art deco style that was unique in 1930-Calgary, the date the York was completed.)

Knowing he'd be working deep in the dark basement, Sam still had his sights set on becoming a pinsetter on the 8 to 11:30 p.m. shift. The pay was two and a half cents a line – per person each game. If the night was good, he could pocket $2.50, a tidy sum for three and a half hours work. Sam got the job and kept it for six years until he was 18. Over the years, he dropped Farrow Drugs and occasionally wondered whether he'd made the right decision. He missed the wide blue skies of his drug route, even though they were too often snatched away by a rogue storm. In the end, he knew he'd rather dodge wayward pins, bowling balls and the occasional bowler drooling in his cups.

"It was five-pin bowling, and I'd set up lines with the pins placed in a V and two sets to a line. The balls weren't that heavy and could sit in your hand. Some customers got a little rowdy, and they'd throw the ball down to us. We'd jump out of the way, pick it up and throw it swiftly back. It was kind of exciting and good fun – mostly. Every now and then, there would be one who didn't know when to stop or who would be angry about a bad game. But it was a whole lot better than bracing for a blizzard outside. Besides, the Mandarin Café was nearby. They were well known for their Chinese food and the best banana cream pie."

Sam's sweet tooth never failed him, and the treats that were bartered, earned or won deadened the sting of anti-Semitism lurking on the edges of his work life.

"My sisters got it more than I ever did. I was younger, but I saw. They didn't get hired at the national stores, so that's why they became their own bosses."

In between his many jobs, Sam went to school. His first three grades were spent at Alexandra, a striking two-storey sandstone school with plenty of windows to peer at the future. It was a small trek over the CP railway line to 9TH Ave and 9TH St SE in the Inglewood district.

"We had to walk on the railway trestle. We'd sometimes hear the train coming but we never stopped. We just picked it up and ran."

"There weren't too many other Jewish students at Alexandra. Our favourite game was rock fights. Maybe that's why. One day I threw a small stone and hit a girl on the forehead. Naturally, I was sent home. Just imagine how I had to explain that story to my mother."

His family moved briefly to 1021 14TH Ave SW. Sam spent Grade 4 at the formidable four-storey sandstone Connaught School on 11TH St and 12TH Ave SW. (Marking its 100TH birthday in 2011, the school was beautifully restored by the Calgary Board of Education, thankfully making up for the demolition of too many sandstone schools in the mid-twentieth century.)

Myer and Chaiya soon made it back to more familiar territory at 1717 1ST St SW, where Sam enrolled at the Haultain School on 2ND St and 17TH Ave SW. Another illustrious sandstone building, the first school of its kind in Calgary, the Haultain also led the school district with the first electricity and running water.

Sadly, after 70 years of service, the Calgary Board of Education condemned the building in 1962, judging it "irreparable for occupancy." Another historic sandstone structure became Calgary dust.

Sam enjoyed school, even looking forward to the occasional clash that reminded him his faith wasn't the status quo. "In those days, we always started the day with the Lord's Prayer, and that was about as far as it went in talking about God. Except for Christmas. There was always the Christmas pageant, and I ended up being one of the wise men. Now that was a stretch. I don't think I invited my family to see the show," says Sam dryly. "I do know that I then wanted a Christmas tree, but of course I never got one!"

Today, Sam says he'd like to see a prayer at the beginning of the school day. "Of course it should be non-denominational in the public schools. But it would set the tone for the day – or at least for the first part of the morning."

Sam was in his class in the 12-room Haultain School annex one day, when the recess bell rang. "We boys grabbed our coats and headed outside. We were all standing around the stove and then someone started kicking it and then all of us were taking a turn, and then we're pushing away and suddenly we've knocked the stove over. That's what heated the school annex, so all our classes had to be cancelled. Of course, we had our code of silence, so nobody owned up to it. Well, the school may not have been heated, but our teacher sure was. He gave every one of us a strapping before we headed home."

Again, Sam doesn't remember what he told his mother. "Clearly, it wasn't my most scholastic moment."

But he does recall his time in hockey, especially since Sam didn't have a clue how to skate. "Skate? I could barely stand on those metal strips. I used these clip-on contraptions that someone had discarded. Who knows where they were before being clamped on to my shoes that were way too big for me anyway? Maybe they had been part of that stove sent to haunt me. Well, take a number. My shoes were so big they could fit two of me. I inherited them from Morris Mendelman, and he always had nice shoes. At least I could grow into them – but by then the soles would be holes."

Despite his equipment deficiencies, Sam was a player for the Haultain midget hockey team where he played defence. Asked if he ever scored, he said, "Are you kidding me? I was lucky to be able to stand on the ice and not fall over. The only time the puck hit my stick was when I was holding on to it to keep my balance. I may not have been the worst player on the team, but we never had to find out. That's because our centre was a ringer – Roy Kelly. He could take a puck from anywhere on the ice and score. Thanks to him, we won the city championship a couple of times, in 1937 and 38."

Roy Kelly was the player every kid in sports aspired to be. Sam was delighted just to be on the ice with the star. For Kelly, the puck acted like putty, moulding itself into a perfect position before blasting into the net. Kelly later traded his Calgary wins for a stint with the junior Trail Smoke Eaters. He was recruited in 1944 to play left wing for the Cleveland Barons, and his professional career took him throughout the U.S. and Canada.

During those brief years at Haultain, Kelly made hockey the sport of champions for Sam and his schoolmates. In his self-deprecating way, Sam finally alludes to getting an assist or two off Kelly's skill. "If I manoeuvred the puck Kelly's way, he managed to make magic – even off the kid with over-sized shoes and fake skates!"

Sam didn't see the same kind of magic in his academic work, however. "I really did enjoy Haultain, but if I got 60 percent or more, I felt I was doing well. Those were the days when there wasn't much homework, and I didn't get to read the kinds of books that I would have liked, because I worked. Writing well was everything, and I didn't excel at that – or much of anything, except perhaps arithmetic."

Numbers were imprinted in his brain, probably because Sam worked at such a young age. He needed to know how to count if he was to contribute to the family income. In his head, he had to master adding and subtracting. This skill may not have revealed itself in Sam's school grades, but it would place him ahead of his competitors in nearly every job and career he launched. As a youth,

Sam's ability to keep a running tally proved especially lucrative in the penny-poker games he played with his pals.

Sam walked to school with his friend, Hymie Aisenstadt. "Hy was always one of the most brilliant in class. I wanted to be like him. So one day I asked him the reasons for his success and he said one word: 'Reading.' He read everything he could: newspapers, magazines, dime novels, westerns. Every month I'd give him 25 cents and he gave me some novels or westerns to read. After I finished, I'd return them and he'd hand me some more.

"When he was 21, Hy started an oil company during the Leduc oil boom. Just as quickly, he went belly up. But that didn't deter Hy. Looking for opportunities, he switched gears and got the idea for Hy's Steak House. He figured that all these oilmen needed a comfortable place to eat, drink and do deals. His first restaurant was on the bottom of a building on 9TH Ave between 2ND and 3RD St SW. Hy's was very successful, but a fire burned it down. So he moved to a spot on 3RD St SW between 7TH and 8TH Aves. A good friend who had moved to Calgary from Brooklyn, New York, Arthur Fishman, designed the cozy dark, wooded interior. I remember the backs of the chairs were covered with washed potato sacks. Hy was the first one to cook steaks on a barbeque pit behind glass windows. As you watched your food on the flames, Hy would come around and talk with everyone. He was just a PR genius and opened a string of steak houses. While the steak houses remain, Hy, sadly, has passed on."

During the 1930s and 1940s a steak dinner was only a dream for many who fought simply to eat, sleep, work and survive. These were the Dirty Thirties, named for the prairie dust storms that would clean out every crop and critter, leaving a land of barren dirt. Homeless men and women crisscrossed the country, riding the rails in boxcars, living on good will, ingenuity and luck. The dire times pushed some families to the brink and beyond; for more than a few, suicide seemed the only way out.

Yet many families pulled together, sharing what they had and instilling in their children responsibility for their loved ones and their community at large. Sam's family was one of those.

Like everyone at home, Sam was pulling his load – in his case literally. But it was his mother and especially his industrious sisters who kept penury at bay. Becky and Lily looked no further than their own neighbourhood, the grounds of the Calgary Exhibition and Stampede, for their inspiration.

Billed as "the greatest outdoor show on earth," the Calgary Stampede attracted the top cowboys and cowgirls from around the world. For one golden week the city would forget the economic blues and bask in the best who rode wild bulls and broncos. While rodeo was king, the midway was queen, and everyone wanted a turn at winning their way out of toil. There was a game for every pocket, although prizes were elusive. But there was one place where cash always produced results: the food concessions. At some point, everyone got hungry and thirsty.

Always on the lookout for another opportunity, Becky and Lily noticed the Stampede needed more food and drink stalls. They also realized quickly that a drink cost less to produce than a snack. The two devised a magic formula that tasted like true orange juice, but consisted of the juice from a few oranges, water, sugar, food colouring and more water.

"Don't forget the water," laughs Sam.

The drink may not have been freshly squeezed, but the idea certainly was. In the hot summer fairground, the mere suggestion of tangy orange juice was all revelers needed to beat it to Becky and Lily's tiny little stand.

"That's how the Stampede stall started," says Sam. "What came first: the chicken or the egg?" Sam chuckles at the age-old question and then swiftly offers his answer. "The egg, of course. The egg is the idea – orange juice. The chicken – well, it's the Depression, and no one can afford chicken on the midway. So, it's the egg, all the way – at least in those times where a successful idea could mean the difference between just soup on the table or meat and potatoes too."

Soon the Switzer concession stall offered hot dogs, hamburgers and coffee alongside the juice. The stall was so successful, the Switzer girls decided to take it across the prairies with the midway shows that travelled to the town fairs. In 1929, when she reached 16, Becky married Morris Mendelman. Three years later, 16-year-old Lily stood under the chuppah with Jack Fishman. The extended family worked with the sun in the long summer days just to generate the means to make it through the bleak winter.

By the time Sam was 10 he was helping his sisters at the Stampede stall. He had a tiny stand with some juice and cigarettes, located under the old grandstand. "What a combo," he laughs. "As I got older, I had a few ideas too. The midway workers needed a decent bite to eat. Ben's kosher deli was next to the York Hotel. I went in and bought corn beef and salami. Then I rushed over to Martin's Bakery for pumpernickel bread. I put together tasty sandwiches and sold them on the midway at three for a dollar. I sold out every time. As we travelled the fair circuit throughout Alberta, Saskatchewan and Manitoba, I would head to town as soon as we got to the fair grounds. I had my model: find the best bread and meats, make the sandwiches and then walk through the midway selling my fresh fare. The customers liked it, no one else was doing it, and I had my mini-deli."

At one fair, just on the outskirts of Moose Jaw, Saskatchewan, Sam heard an airplane. As he looked up, thousands of pamphlets scattered through the sky, and Sam gave chase. He rushed around the grounds and gathered all the flyers he could. They were ads enticing people to buy plane rides.

Except the one Sam had in his hand. "The one I got was for a free ride," says Sam, as excited as he was that long-ago day. "I was 10 years old and I was going to get my first ride on an airplane, and I didn't have to pay anything! I made my way to the airfield and gave my pamphlet to the pilot. I couldn't wait to get in the plane and take off. When we left the ground and I looked down at the wheat fields and the Moose Jaw River – I hoped to stay in the air forever. I wanted to fly, and one day I would."

The magic is still in the Moose Jaw air, especially when the magnetic Canadian Forces Snowbirds practice their air acrobatics in their very home city. And Sam did indeed go on to not only own but even get behind the controls of his airplane. But he quickly adds: "I prefer to rely on pilots who fly planes for a living rather than my incredibly lucky efforts."

By 1937, the industrious Switzers had also managed to put enough money away to buy a grocery store at 112 14TH Ave SE. The newly named Switzer's Grocery boasted a cement basement for dry-food storage as well as a cold cellar. It also featured enough room for the family to spread out – but barely. The remaining kids at home, Dinah and Sam, were expected to clerk and stock the store part-time with Myer and Chaiya overseeing the operation. There was just one problem – one enormous problem.

"My parents were multilingual," recalls Sam. "Unfortunately, none of their four or five languages was English. Their English skills were rudimentary at best. So Dinah quit school to run the store."

Dinah proved as enterprising as her older sisters, designing the store with spacious shelves overflowing with stock. Only her mother knew it was a ruse. "I had the suppliers send us dummy boxes, ones that were empty, and I filled the shelves with them. Ma used to say to me, 'Dinah, I'm going to be embarrassed if I sell an empty box.' And I would say, 'Don't worry, Ma, I know exactly where the full ones are.'"

Dinah hadn't planned to leave school so soon. Her older sister Jessie was tagged to help with the store, but she was close to finishing and wanted to complete her studies. Soon she was engaged, and on December 25TH, 1938, Jessie married Abe Sanofsky. Just six months later, the joy turned to heartbreak. Doctors discovered leukemia and Jessie's life was taken. "My mother cried for the rest of her life, thinking of Jessie," says Sam sadly. "It was such a tragedy. Everybody loved her; she was just kind and sweet."

Dinah was so distraught that her mother sent her to Red Deer to visit her older sisters working at the fair. There she met Harry Shore, the Royal American Show's train master. Soon they were engaged and, in 1942, Dinah and Harry were married. When they moved away to Toronto, Sam's childhood abruptly departed, too.

Chaiya and Myer had given Sam the unconditional love that was the bedrock of his existence. In return, he had worked most of his young life and willingly handed his mother all his earnings. Despite the harsh conditions of his jobs, Sam always had his family, school and pals to thwart poverty's pernicious path. His parents had hoped that Sam would complete his schooling, first at Western Canada High School, and then, if life allowed, even college.

Life didn't allow. Chaiya's eyesight had failed and Myer was frail. There was only one person left to manage the store – Sam.

"It wasn't a choice," he says. "My sisters were married and had their own lives, even though two of them lived down the street. I was the only one left in the family who was capable of doing it: reading, writing, adding, subtracting, shelving, carrying, cleaning, managing the place. It all seemed like such a simple decision, and my parents wished there had been another way. But there wasn't. I had to quit school near the start of Grade Ten. My parents were no longer capable of making a living. I was now responsible for them as well as myself. I was 16."

Although Dinah was off to Toronto, she remained remorseful over Sam's situation even though the outcome was beyond her control.

"The principal met my parents to persuade them to leave Sam in school," she said. "He told them Sam was very clever and he could amount to something. But my mother said she needed him."

Clearly the principal saw in Sam the very potential that would propel him to achieve and prosper. But for the next decade and beyond, Sam would be tied to Switzer's Grocery just to keep it afloat.

"Oh, I still saw my pals at the end of the day or on the weekends," he says. "The store was hockey central. In the winter, we flooded the lot behind our building so everyone could continue playing hockey. All the neighbouring kids were welcome and we'd get on the ice with or against the champ, Roy Kelly. But after February 15TH, you couldn't keep ice on the rink."

Switzer's Grocery, with its inviting coal-fired stove, was one of the warmest winter places in the East Village ghetto for groceries and gossip. Alvin Libin, whose father owned the Palace Bakery, recalls the weekend orders he'd rush to refill.

"They were big supporters of our bakery," says Libin. "They'd often run out of bread on the weekend and I'd hurry over with a new supply. I'd love to have stayed and watched the scene as I was a little in awe of Sam, who was a few years older than me, but I had to get back to work myself. During the week, of course, I was still in school."

Attached to the back of the Grocery was a barren shack that Sam soon transformed into a games room. Sam's buddies came for hockey, but if the ice was melting, poker fit the bill.

"We played penny poker every weekend if we could," recalls Sam. "The limit was five cents, but sometimes the betting would get up to 25 cents. My mother would descend around three or four in the morning and try to get us to shut it down. 'We're just about ready to wind it up,' I'd say. Before you knew it, we'd begun another round of betting. Now I don't know if that was a growing experience, but years later, a good number of the fellows went on to become millionaires."

"Willy Friedman, Harry Sherman, Dave Dworkin, Willy Steinberg, Benny Switzer, Hy Aisenstadt, Jackie Marks and Sam Hashman were a few of my friends. The first watch I ever owned was the loan from Sam Hashman. He needed 25 cents to carry on, and then lost it all over the next few rounds. So, I'm feeling pretty good wearing Sam's watch. The next day the phone rings and I pick it up. All I hear is a woman screaming on the other end. 'You'd better bring that watch back *now*, if you know what's good for you,' she says. And that's one of the nicer things she had to say. Of course, it's Sam's mother and she will not be coming over to exchange pleasantries. In fact, the only thing she wants exchanged is the watch. It turns out that the watch is worth at least $10. That's a lot of money in those days. Let's just say that if guns were legal, Sam's mother would have met me at high noon. 'It was just a misunderstanding,' I tell her. 'I've just borrowed it. Why yes, I've just finished borrowing it. Why, I'll be bringing it there immediately.' And that is the saga of my first wristwatch."

When the boys weren't dealing cards and shooting the puck in the winter, they were playing poker and striking the ball in summer. Baseball was popular anywhere on the prairies. Whether it was in the farm community of Rumsey or the bustling city of Calgary, Jewish baseball teams matched the best.

"We played the city leagues and did pretty well," recalls Sam, who pitched for his team. "Let's say we gave the competition real competition. And we never put up with any anti-Semitic slurs. I can't even remember being in a fight." Then Sam adds wryly, "I don't know if that's good or bad."

When Sam was 16, he walked past the YMCA on 9ᵀᴴ Ave and 1ˢᵀ St SE, stopped and then headed up the stairs where so many of Calgary's youth learned to swim.

"I liked water, and I really wanted to be able to swim," says Sam. "I knew from the novels I read that swimming was an important skill. So I paid for the first course and jumped in the pool. I loved it. Then we came to the diving part – that is if you want to call it a dive. I stood on the side, put my hands over my head and fell in. When I graduated to the diving board, my technique didn't. I stood on the edge and my stomach touched the water before my arms did. And that is what my so-called dive remained for quite some time. But I did learn to swim pretty well and move from the belly flop to a point where I didn't embarrass myself – well, not too much!"

As Sam passed the notice board at the YMCA one day, he stopped at a poster for a Dale Carnegie course. This was the famous motivational speaker and writer whose insights and pithy quotes encouraged people of all ages to understand and improve themselves. In 1936 Carnegie had written his bestselling tome, *How to Win Friends and Influence People*. His popular courses taught people how to boost self-confidence, reduce stress, communicate and lead.

"The successful man will profit from his mistakes and try again in a different way," Carnegie wrote. Sam enrolled and found the kind of inspiring tips a teenager taking care of his parents, plus a grocery store, needed. The value of such motivational courses has never left him, and Sam enthusiastically endorses them. He especially remembers: "Happiness doesn't depend upon who you are or what you have. It depends solely upon what you think."

Yet the Carnegie quote that resonated most eloquently, as mortal fury threatened to destroy the world in 1942, was this: "Most of the important things in the world have been accomplished by people who have kept on trying when there seemed to be no help at all." In the face of defeat, that was the very determination and courage that sent Commonwealth airmen into the skies to vanquish the Nazis during the Battle of Britain. It moved British Prime Minister Winston Churchill to praise the Royal Air Force allies' valour with these eloquent words: "Never in the field of human conflict was so much owed by so many to so few."

While the Second World War raged across the globe, Sam saw friends leave to fight, knowing he might never be with them again. Yet here he remained on the home front, full of mixed emotions, with an exemption from service. "This was a war against evil, and I wanted to fight Nazis. We all did. In 1943, when I was 17, I got drafted. But I was stuck in the store supporting my mother and father. They were completely dependent on me. Mr. A.L. Barron, our family lawyer, explained the situation in a letter to the draft board. I got a two-year deferment, and the war ended in 1945. We were overjoyed it was over, but I always felt that maybe I should have been there. Yet how could I?"

What Sam vowed to do for the rest of his life was give what he earned to his family – as he had always done. The difference was that the larger community became his extended family and the recipient of his physical and philanthropic labour.

CHAPTER THREE:
THE CEMENT MIXER

SAM'S POKER PALACE IN THE SWITZER GROCERY SHED WAS hardly a place where dreams are made, but winning pennies put him in his first car. It was a 1917 Model T Ford that had nothing going for it – or in it. Sam's dilapidated derby wagon had more power than this metal nag, but that didn't stop him or his cousin Benny (Gershon's son). They paid the price, $7.50 each, plus six months of sweat and salvaged parts.

"We got it to run and we were off – sort of," says Sam, still delighted with the memory. "One time Benny and I take it to Banff, feeling pretty good about ourselves. Here we are, two kids with nothing, and we're driving to the mountains in our own car."

But not for long. On the way to Banff, one of the tires blew and the boys had to steer the car to the dusty shoulder of the Banff Coach Rd, jack up the jalopy, take off the flat, put on the spare and continue the journey on the highway's gravel roads. They made it to the mountain town, strolled down Banff Ave, stepped in for a quick bite, walked along the Bow River, then headed back behind the wheel of the Model T. The drive to Calgary was bumpy, but they were cheery, chatting all the while. Suddenly the steering wheel started to wobble violently. Another tire bit the dust. Now the day and the road were getting dark. With no spare tire – and no time to spare – Sam stopped the car, the cousins quickly removed the flat, then jumped into their seats and bounced back to Calgary on the spent tire's metal rim.

That was enough for Sam and the Model T, but Benny believed he had a winner. He bought Sam out for $25 and convinced his brother Phil to paint the car and enter it in the Calgary Stampede parade. The once-majestic Model T was transformed into a champion, taking first prize and $50.

Sam, meanwhile, moved on to his next grand sedan. While he was young, the car was not, even though they were both the same age – 21. It was a 1926 Chevy four-door former hardtop, now no-top convertible.

"Oh it was a convertible all right," he laughs. "The doors were nailed shut and the only way in was through the roof. We had to cut and pry it off permanently. It had no seats, so we sat on a wooden bench. But what a car for $25! The motor and gears were all good, and did that car run."

Whether it was off to a party in the basement of sister Becky's or a jaunt to Penley's Dance Hall, or better yet, the dance pavilion in Bowness Park, the friends squeezed into the car and Sam steered into the night. Any time of year, Bowness Park was a destination. In the summer, the lagoon enticed the swimmer to float past the pines and the canoeist to paddle into a palace of lost pools. In the winter, the lagoon became a winding rink of ice and crystal.

For sheer zaniness, no one could touch Sam and his close friends on a wintry Sunday as they headed to one of the city ski-spots. Sam would drive the packed white Chevy to the top of Shaganappi hill and park just as everyone piled out.

"We'd immediately drain the water from the car because no one could afford anti-freeze," says Sam, chuckling. "Then we'd leave her there while we skied. For those of us who didn't have skis, we shared. When it was our turn, we'd clamp our winter boots onto the skis, buckle them in and race down the hill. Then we'd herring-bone or side-step back up and do it all over again. At the end of the day, we'd knock on someone's door, ask for some boiling water, pour it into the radiator, push the car down the hill to start her, then all jump in. It was a sight to behold. We had such fun, yet none of us had any actual money."

The early nickels, quarters and lucky dollars that any of Sam's friends earned went directly into their families' survival. Poverty may have been but a few pennies away, but Sam and his band of tight pals seldom wondered whether they'd have to curb their entertainment budget. There wasn't one. There never would be during the war or the lean years after. Everyone knew how to stretch a dollar, trade a service and bank a favour. Those who didn't learned quickly. But being poor didn't stop the group from having a good time.

In 1951, Arthur Fishman found himself at Switzer's Grocery, just after moving from Brooklyn to Calgary. Although they weren't related, he met and became friends with Jack and Lily Fishman, as well as her brother, Sam. Whether skiing, skating or dancing, Arthur was happy to join Sam and the gang.

"That's because he had met the beautiful Mary Edgar. They were quite the charismatic couple – that is, until they included me," laughs Sam. "Actually, the three of us had great times, especially on the Shaganappi ski hill or at the old Crystal Ice Palace. Her father had been with the North West Mounted Police and was quite famous in Fort Macleod, where he later was elected mayor."

After he and Mary married, Arthur Fishman would become famous himself, as a renowned interior designer whose work would grace homes and buildings throughout the continent. For now, though, he was more than happy just to be with Mary and his coterie of friends while he slowly started his business. It was Arthur who designed Sam's pal Hy Eisenstadt's downtown Calgary steak house that would gradually grow into the Hy's Steak House chain.

Sam loved a fast car – and one day hoped to own one that would actually fit that description. He dreamed of a deal where he would drive the car he wanted across the continent. Then he'd put it on the market and make enough to buy another one. One day he'd own a Cadillac.

Sam's sister Dinah, now married to Harry Shore, was living in Canada's economic powerhouse. It was an ideal opportunity for Sam to buy a car in Toronto, sell it back in Calgary and pocket a small profit. He boarded the train east and met up with Jack Edelson, another close friend, who would drive back with him. There were only a few days before they were to leave Toronto, yet Sam still hadn't purchased a car. It was midnight on one of those stunning southern Ontario evenings when a crisp fall wind blows off Lake Ontario. Sam and Jack borrowed Harry's car, with Sam at the wheel.

"We're feeling no worries, and why not," says Sam. "I'm not that many years from my East Village ice wagon, and here we are cruising the scene in Toronto. We're smiling and waving at passersby. With no warning whatsoever, a car rushes towards us from nowhere. We swerve, but he still smashes us. Luckily he hit the back, not the front of the sedan, so we're okay. But the car is toast. Imagine phoning your brother-in-law after midnight, getting him out of bed and telling him that someone has just creamed his car.

"Now Harry, who's the kindest guy on the planet, is suddenly out a car and I've got to help find him one. I also need to buy something to drive back to Calgary. At the last moment, I get a two-door tan-coloured Pontiac. Jack and I decide to travel through the northern U.S. as it's shorter and gas is cheaper there. It still is. We're driving in North Dakota and this beat-up tractor hauling some sort of combine pulls onto the road. The guy completely ignores the fact I'm traveling towards him from the east and another car is coming straight at him from the west. That car veers to avoid the tractor-combine and heads directly for us. I break and bolt for the ditch. Too late. We get creamed. Again. The Pontiac isn't a write-off, barely, and, luckily, neither are we. So we get the car towed to this little town where there's a mechanic who claims he can fix it up so we'll never know it was hit. I wish he could do that to me. But he was true to his word and we finally made it out of North Dakota. Every bone in my back throbbed as we drove back to Calgary, but maybe that was just my pride."

Over the years, Sam did manage to take the train to Toronto

and drive a car back to Calgary and sell it, without such mayhem. Besides, he loved visiting Harry Shore and Dinah, who changed her name to Diane to avoid being confused with the famous American songstress. And Sam did indeed own a succession of nearly-new Cadillacs that he conveniently sold for a steady profit.

Saturday evening parties thrown by Sam and his crew were popular in the Jewish community as events where young friends and visitors could get together for games, dances and even some kosher food. If you wanted a few hands of poker, or a little soft shoe on the basement floor, there was always a welcome from Sam and the boys, with their sisters providing freshly made sandwiches in the wee morning hours.

That's how Edward Bronfman met Sam Switzer. Edward's father, Allan, sent his son to Calgary to learn about the oil and gas business. The extended family, whose fortune was made in spirits and distilleries, would buy a controlling interest in Royalite Oil in 1950.

Edward's grandfather, Ekiel, had been born in Russia but escaped the anti-Semitic pogroms of his homeland by emigrating to Canada in 1889, homesteading near Wapella, in southeast Saskatchewan. The harsh prairie proved no place for the former tobacco farmer, and the family moved over the border into Brandon, Manitoba, where Allan was born in 1896. Ekiel and his older sons delivered wood for fuel, and after a few years were able to buy a small hotel in Emerson, Manitoba. Their venture slowly expanded into three hotels in Winnipeg. The source of the family's great wealth, however, began as the prohibition era was ending in Canada but enduring in the U.S. Spirits would make their fortune, but would also tear the extended family apart.

Allan studied and became a lawyer in Winnipeg, partnering with his brother Samuel in a mail-order liquor venture. When Samuel Bronfman started Distiller's Corporation in 1924, Allan moved to Montreal to work with the older brother. Samuel secured the assets of Joseph E. Seagram and Sons, merging the two into Seagram's in 1928.

"When prohibition ended in 1933," writes Christopher G. Curtis, "Seagram's was ready with huge amounts of well aged and carefully blended spirits, which were sold bottled to the consumer through a network of distributors, a marketing approach developed by Sam [Bronfman]."

Samuel eventually managed the Seagram decision-making. Later the liquor fortune passed to his sons, Charles and Edgar. The latter's son, Edgar Jr., would steer the enterprise into the entertainment business – a move that ultimately saw the great Seagram's assets dissipate as swiftly as a cold beer on a hot summer night.

Although Allan's sons, Edward and Peter, were excluded from the Seagram fortune, they moved to Toronto to master their own business empire, the Edper Group and its successor, Brascan Corp. That would be many years after Sam Switzer first met Edward; but Edward's stint in Calgary would serve him well on his path to prosperity and philanthropy.

On February 13, 1947, light sweet oil began flowing at Imperial Oil's Leduc No. 1, immediately south of Edmonton, ensuring Alberta's ascent as Canada's energy giant. Royalite Oil had already discovered wet gas and oil at Turner Valley in 1924. As the Bronfmans branched out in 1950, they expected Edward to immerse himself in the energy business. That he did, but he also managed to enjoy the activities and festivities of Sam Switzer and the gang.

"He was young and Jewish, just like us," remembers Sam. "So, we were all introduced and he happily joined in. Edward drove this Buick – and it was a real beauty – that he brought around to the parties. Finally, someone in our group had a brand-new car. Every so often, we'd drive to Banff in Edward's Buick. But to go, each of us had to chip in and pay for gas. In the end, it was worth it – the Buick never broke down or blew a tire, unlike a certain car I still can't forget."

Edward hoped to repay Sam's hospitality so he invited his friend to stay with his family in Montreal. The two families may have had similar origins on prairie homesteads, but that's where the parallel ended.

"We're living in close quarters above the grocery store," says Sam. "The only extra room I've got is my poker shed. Edward's home was a little different."

That's for sure. Edward's house was an exquisite Montreal mansion in tony Westmount, complete with liveried staff and chauffeured limousine.

"A stately butler in full uniform receives my dilapidated luggage," laughs Sam. "Given the state of my beat-up suitcase, maybe he needed those gloves. I'm taken to my room, which could house the entire Switzer Grocery, and told to get ready for dinner. What am I supposed to do – get a top hat and tails? Should I have a word with the butler? Should I switch clothes with the butler? I manage to make my way to the dining room, a space so massive that we could have staged derby races.

"There were maids and serving staff in starched uniforms assigned to look after the guests – including, incredibly, me. I suddenly imagine myself as one of those elegant diners at the exclusive Banff Springs Hotel in that restaurant on the second floor. Yet today I'm no longer sneaking a peak at an outside world. I'm right in the middle of it wearing a suit that looks like it wants to leave without me. Except no one's leaving, because there's food to be eaten, and it is fantastic. As I finish my soup and dutifully wait for my meat, I'm asked if I want some more. There's more? I've never lived in a place where there's more. I'm lucky if I get enough. But, of course, I accept.

"I've decided to relax and enjoy myself. I'm in a make-believe world where the food is endless and people wait on you, and not the other way around. It is so alien that I simply sit back and enjoy. I shall see what happens when I go to sleep. If I awaken in a palace, I shall enjoy the hospitality of my fantasy world until someone realizes that I have invaded their dream-world, not mine.

"It's morning and it's not a hallucination. I'm still here and there are two uniformed people waiting on me, or, for me. No, they're not carrying a straightjacket. I pass by the ballroom on the second floor.

"Now Edward and I are off to see the Montreal Canadiens take another rival down. We're being driven to the Forum in one of the family limousines, with a chauffeur. The East Village grocer boy is being driven by a chauffeur. The world truly has gone mad. Maybe they heard about that little accident with Harry's car in Toronto. Or perhaps someone dished on that North Dakota smash-up. Whatever. I've never been in such comfortable seats. They're so soft, I could fall asleep. But what if I wake up and it's all a game – at my expense. I think I'd rather see the real thing at the Forum.

"The seats at the rink are sensational. I'm right in the middle of the ice. There's Maurice Richard, that crazy right-winger. Maybe I'll just step on down into defence and let a few pucks deflect off my skate to the Rocket's handy stick. I wonder if Roy Kelly ever told the Rocket about me."

Richard shoots. He scores. The roar of the stadium pulls Sam out of his reverie and back into the best spot in the house. The Rocket and the Habs have gained another victory. And Sam is fully immersed in the fantasy that has become his sudden reality. For now.

Sam would never forget the dazzling dichotomy between his 1948 world and that of Edward. What would stay with him forever was that it mattered not that Sam was "the little grocer boy." What obviously stuck with Edward, and all who would meet Sam, was that Sam was a man of diligence, faith and trust. Besides, beyond the material world, the two young men were not all that far apart. As young Canadians, they were both children of families that had successfully escaped the anti-Semitism and pogroms of Europe.

While Edward Bronfman visited his Calgary friends, he talked about the opportunities he saw in certain stocks and bonds. Sam was a whiz at selling stock on the grocery shelves, but an absolute neophyte at buying financial stocks on the market. Eager to learn, he listened intently as Edward explained market simplicities and intricacies to the novice.

"I sure could have used one of those *Stock Investing for Dummies* books, because I certainly qualified," says Sam. "I'd never bought a stock in my life. Naturally, I needed a stockbroker. I went to James Richardson and Sons and put some of my savings into a few oil stocks. Every morning I'd get up at 6 and head over to the Stock Exchange at the start of trading and check my picks. Then, I'd hurry back to open the store for the day."

It was familiar territory, physically, anyway. The Stock Exchange was across from the York Hotel, in the building that housed Gibson's Bowling Alley. Sam skipped down the basement to the Exchange, reveling in the buzz of the boom. He was certain his stocks were up significantly, and happy to buy more on margin.

"This had gone on for about a year and a half," continues Sam. "By now I had basically borrowed $25,000 which was the amount of my Richardson's margin account. Naturally I thought I had a significant profit, but figured I'd better be sure. I started adding the numbers, then subtracting all the broker's fees, including the margin and its costs. Guess what? My massive profit came in at $2500. After all this time and considerable – all right, let's be honest – constant – worrying, I was up only $2500! I just decided it wasn't worth it and cashed everything in – sold it all. Besides, I was feeling very queasy about the market. The euphoria had tanked."

The market hadn't, just yet. Stock speculating is like star gazing. All diamonds in the sky, dazzling, but distant and impossible to possess. Sam had been investing with another good friend, Vic Bussi, whose day job was delivering bottles of dairy from his horse-drawn Union Milk wagon to businesses like Switzer Grocery.

"Vic got involved in the market big time and was very good," recalls Sam. "His stocks were up over $90,000. So he kept a high margin account of $125,000 with Richardson's. When I got worried and sold all my stocks, I suggested he might want to do the same. Vic stayed in and I couldn't convince him otherwise. When the market plunged, poor Vic went with it. He was a dear,

dear friend and I was devastated for him. His market experience haunted him even after he studied real estate and became an agent."

Sam was still working at the grocery store, feeling fortunate if the till took in $40. "And that was a good day," he says.

It was 1948, and the rising energy industry attracted workers from across the country, spurring construction in Edmonton and Calgary. Housing was tight and Edward Bronfman was living in a dank basement suite in Stanley Park, the only place he could find reasonably close to Calgary's downtown. Not too long after their Montreal visit, Edward asked Sam if he had thought about doing something with the Switzer lot that served as the community hockey rink right behind the grocery store.

"Why not build an apartment building, and I'll become a major tenant?" Sam recalls Edward asking.

Sam doesn't immediately dismiss the idea, but mulls it over. "Here I am with no skills in construction, a few savings, and Edward wants a nice place to live close to the city core. Sure, I'll just whip up some plans. And then I actually started to think about it. Why the heck not!"

"Gordon Arnott had just graduated from the University of Manitoba as an architect. We had all become friends, so he said, 'Let me design the apartment for you.' He drew up plans for a three-suite building that featured a luxury apartment on the main floor, which Edward would take, plus an additional two suites below that would be rented out. We liked the design, so I bought Gordon's plans for 114 14TH Ave SE."

Arnott was on the cusp of an extraordinary career. He had already won the Royal Architectural Institute of Canada's Gold Medal upon graduation. He was born in Winnipeg, had spent some time in Calgary, and earned a post-graduate degree in regional planning at Vancouver's University of British Columbia. Yet Arnott would make his mark in Saskatchewan, designing such award-winning buildings as the Norman MacKenzie Art Gallery, the Saskatchewan Centre for the Arts, and the Saskatchewan Pavilion at the 1986 Vancouver Expo.

"Now that I had Gordon's design, I needed to pull together the financing," continues Sam. "Edward promised to rent the main floor luxury suite. The builder said if I worked with him, he'd add my work hours and credit that amount to the cost of the construction. Not only did that keep the cost down, I learned how to stucco. In the end, we put up the building for $2500 total. I was so excited to see it finished and finally move Ed into his little bit of Calgary luxury. Well, Ed was moving all right, but not behind the store. With no warning, he's called back to Montreal. I guess his parents figured he had learned enough here."

Sam, for one, relished the adrenaline running from his toes to the top of his head as he risked his savings and health to transform a memory-filled backyard into a modest but dignified apartment building. Edward's transfer was a blow, but it didn't destroy Sam's euphoria. He had built something from nothing. The construction business was just the boost Sam needed to contemplate a career beyond Switzer's Grocery.

With the housing shortage, he was able to rent the three apartments. His two oldest sisters owned successful dry cleaning businesses and purchased homes across from the grocery store. Becky and Morris Mendelman ran Laval Cleaners in the hip enclave of Hillhurst, on the north side of the Bow River. Lily and Jack Fishman, who was also a tailor, operated Economy Cleaners in Inglewood, in a building that later housed Kane's Harley-Davidson dealership. Lily and Jack eventually moved their establishment to 17TH Ave SW where they put their own name, Fishman's, to what is one of the most respected dry cleaners in the city.

Becky and Lily could sometimes help in the store, freeing Sam for more adventures in construction. With Edward Bronfman gone, Sam well understood where promises could lead. And leave. He needed to start small. Experienced with stucco, Sam placed an ad in the paper.

"I got a job stuccoing a house in south Calgary and was thrilled because it was worth $1500 with $500 down. I bought all the material, including a cement mixer that I pulled behind my

1926 Chevy. Then I went to work, mixing the cement, applying the stucco to the house wall and getting mud in my eyes. That should have been my first clue. While I was working hard and fast, the people who hired me were even faster. They took everything I did and gave me absolutely nothing else. Their word was worthless and that's where I'd be if I'd stayed in that business. I wasn't used to dealing with liars and cheats – and I play a smooth hand of poker! That was one of my worst working experiences – getting mud in my eye both physically and financially. But I sure learned a few lessons. Become your own boss and control as much of the project as possible. Know the integrity of your client. Most of all, get a larger down payment so you have something to live on after paying for your materials."

Sam didn't stay blue for long. As he assessed the situation, he realized he had one trusty friend throughout the sticky stucco saga – his car. And he was pretty sure it needed not just a rest, but an owner that didn't expect it to pull more than its woebegone weight.

"I walked into the Maclin Ford showroom at 215 11ᵀᴴ Ave SW, where this shiny crimson convertible summoned me. She was the real thing, with a top that you didn't need to crack open with a sledgehammer. When the salesman approached, I asked him how much. '$2400,' he said. I replied, 'Fine. But I also have a convertible to trade in, too.' He was delighted until he saw my 1926 Chevy. When I said, 'Isn't she a beaut?' he replied 'That's not exactly how I'd describe it.' But I was ready: 'I can sacrifice my Chevy convertible for $200, and give you $2200 for your convertible.' When the salesman stopped laughing, he shook my hand and said we had a deal. I drove out of Maclin's in my first real convertible and I didn't have to get into it through the roof."

Sam went back to spending his time at the store, serving and waiting. He was learning his lessons pretty quickly, yet they were becoming a little costly. He yearned for the calibre of client and customer that he met at his grocery.

They were people like Izzy Florence, who helped Sam with insurance for the store. In 1955, Izzy started the prestigious Calgary Jewellery that continues today, under the able stewardship of his son, Bernard.

"Izzy truly assisted me in my growth," adds Sam. "So did A.T. Marshall and R.W. Dobisky, who provided credit for many of the goods in our grocery. His son, Danny Dobisky, became a good friend. The Barron family lawyers, starting with Jacob Bell (J.B.) and his son Robert, really gave us a hand, as they did to many in the community."

J.B. Barron, who became a theatrical impresario, managed the Palace Theatre for the Allen family. When that was over, J.B. bought the Grand Theatre and continued to bring in such luminaries as Paul Robeson and Marian Anderson. Ever the trailblazer, J.B. erected an eleven-storey highrise that still bears the family name. With his son Dick at his side, J.B. built and managed the Uptown Theatre on the main floor, while the rest of the structure became Calgary's first office tower. The Barron building attracted such global energy giants as Shell, Mobil and Sun Oil. At the top of the building, J.B. created a Frank Lloyd Wright-style suite where he resided until his passing in 1965.

These Calgary business pioneers were just a few of the people whose honour and trust picked Sam up and polished his understanding of life. They were gems of knowledge who shined with integrity, lighting a path far beyond the warm cocoon of Switzer Grocery.

CHAPTER FOUR:
THE BUILDER

SAM BASKED IN THE LIGHTER LESSONS HIS COCOON NURTURED, while refusing to believe his future was on hold. He delighted in dancing sessions at Becky's basement, where he learned to rumba, mambo, cha-cha and swing. But it was the tango that took his heart away. If he could capture this mood of mystery on the dance floor, perhaps he could also entice that most elusive of dances. Would the tango dance him to the woman of his dreams?

By 1984, Sam would well understand the great Leonard Cohen's darkly beautiful ballad "Dance Me to the End of Love." But 35 years before Cohen's haunting song, the only lovelorn thought haunting Sam was whether he would ever be able to afford marriage, and more to the point, he wondered if any woman would actually look at him.

"I had a few dance partners, but as soon as I wanted to take a young lady out for the second time, her mother usually threw me out," says Sam with a slow smile. "I guess they wanted maybe doctors for their daughters."

Sam always believed in himself, whether the second dates materialized or not. But even he started to question his prospects after falling in love, at age 21, with a lovely lass from Medicine

Hat. They were going to get married, until Sam factored in the harsh reality of his East Village life.

"How can I think about marriage?" he asks. "I'm working in the grocery store and giving everything I make to my mother. I always have. What I make is what keeps our family afloat. Where would I put a wife – in the cramped room I sleep in, right beside my parents above the store? Where would we have any privacy – in my ramshackle poker shed? She had no means, either. For the pair of us it was a pipedream."

As they called the wedding off, Sam ached to escape. Working hard was all he knew and fun with friends was his just reward. Yet everything seemed a pretense. Sam wanted a life where he had some control.

"I took off to Toronto and lived with Dinah and Harry," recalls Sam. "I got a job shelving goods at Dominion Stores and stayed there for three months. My sisters and their kids helped my mother in the store. I needed time away to think about my life. But I was learning one thing. If I ever wanted to get married and have a family, I couldn't do it working in Switzer Grocery. It simply wasn't possible to make a living. My poor parents lived starkly above the store and I didn't want that kind of existence, for them or for me. If I could prosper doing something else, then I could sustain both a family and my parents, too. I was a hard worker, an easy learner and good with money. I would figure it out for all of us."

That he did, although many a misstep, and even more adventures, would go into the businesses that built Sam's future. But first he had to leave the grocery store, and not just for an evening party but for the rest of his working life.

The party was at Moe Kowall's; Moe had moved from Winnipeg to Calgary and married Minnie, one of the Switzer cousins. He went into office and apartment construction as a developer, but for now was learning the basics from the basement as a hardware salesman for Sears. As a close pal, Moe worried about Sam and wanted him to meet a friend from Edmonton. Her name was Aneta Newman, and Moe felt she was just the kind of woman who could turn Sam's life around. He was right.

"Moe arranged this blind date between the blond and beautiful Aneta, and the definitely not blond and beautiful me," remembers Sam. "She took my breath away."

When Sam came up for air, he wondered what she'd see in him. Perhaps the tango and the other dance moves were making their mark. Then she told him she liked him.

"It must be the car," laughs Sam. "I had that brand new convertible that I buffed so it glowed like glass. Maybe she fancied her reflection on the hood. Maybe she liked the wind in her hair as we drove down the road. I know I sure did."

Sam had it bad, and it didn't help that he hadn't met her parents in Edmonton.

"I was worried they'd react the same way the others had when they met the 'grocer boy' going out with their daughter. Besides, in the summer we were in the exhibition business, and there were more than a few folks who felt we were beneath them. It was pretty ridiculous when you consider just how hard everyone worked. Hard-working and honest should be at the top of the list of character traits for a prospective son-in-law. But that was the pettiness of some people."

Aneta's family had moved to Edmonton from Punnichy, Saskatchewan, where her dad, Nelson, had been the village mayor. His family had emigrated from Russia to homestead in the south-central area between Saskatoon and Regina.

Nelson Newman sold elegant watches and exquisite jewellery at his downtown Edmonton store, Jasper Jewellery, across from the Hotel Macdonald. Aneta and her sister, Tibele, were known as the 'gold dust twins' because their father was a jeweller.

"He had a heart of gold, too," adds Sam. "We got along very well and became friends. Her mother, well, she was not pleased to meet me. When I asked Aneta to marry me, she refused to give us her blessing."

"So, you want to become my son-in-law?" she asks anxiously. "No. I want to become Aneta's husband," replies Sam.

It's Sam as a stand-up, and he's off. "I don't know what I'd do without my mother-in-law. But it's nice to dream about.

"I took my wife and her mother to the mountains," he continues. "While we unpacked, her mother went for a walk down the beautiful bush-lined path. Suddenly we hear an enormous roar. We run down the path and see a grizzly on its hind legs baring his teeth at my mother-in-law.

"'Stop that beast. Do something,' cries my wife.

"'Don't worry,' I reply. 'I'm sure the grizzly can take care of himself.'

"I have to admit things got a little tense when my mother-in-law was around," adds Sam.

"'You can't stand my relatives,' my wife would say.

"'That's not true,' I'd reply. 'I love your mother-in-law.'"

Sam steps back from the one-liners that mask the pain inflicted by the in-law who consistently treated him as an outlaw. Instead, he remembers that his fear of finding love was gone. He had fallen under Aneta's spell and yearned that it never be broken. Sam fully believed the strength of their love would generate all the energy they'd need to power a future together.

They were married in August 1952, three months after their first date. Sam was 26 while Aneta was 25. Her cousin, Rabbi Abraham Postone, conducted the ceremony, and Moe Kowall was best man. Because the new synagogue for Beth Israel congregation wouldn't be completed until the High Holy Days in the fall, Sam and Aneta were married in her family's Edmonton home.

"Everyone says it's the most beautiful house wedding they were ever at," Sam wrote to his sister, Dinah, and Harry Shore. "We've been married a day and a half and I still don't believe it, but I am, and so far, yuk, yuk, I love it. But I'm sure looking forward to you... meeting the most wonderful girl in the world, my wife."

Aneta adds her thoughts in the same letter, writing: "It is wonderful being married to your brother and we're on a honeymoon to heaven."

Their actual honeymoon was to Las Vegas in Sam's convertible. They drove south through Alberta into Montana, taking Going-to-the-Sun Road through Logan's Pass in Glacier Park. The glorious vista was as close to heaven as you wanted in this lifetime. At any time, the car could have plunged down the sharp cliffs after failing to negotiate one of the stomach-churning hairpin turns.

The honeymooners returned after two weeks and moved into the apartment Sam had built, right behind the grocery store. Finally, Sam would have his own place, in the very suite Edward Bronfman was to live. Besides, Aneta was pregnant, and the two had a plan for a new start. Sam talked to his mother along with Becky and Lily. He would leave Switzer Grocery for good, with his two sisters taking over the store. Sam would finally be free to start a small business. Why not the 300 square foot coffee shop beside the Palace Theatre? The Palace was full of precious memories from his youth, the place where he became the yo-yo champion after the Moffat twins left town. Now he would be the champion of his destiny, starting with the Yavvis Coffee Shop. While the price was steep – $6000 – and the store frontage was small – 20 feet – Sam knew he could make the space across from The Bay work, and would manage the initial cost.

"It only had eight stools, but people would rush in for a breakfast snack or lunch bite," recalls Sam. "I'd advertise the specials on the window. My favourite was an orange and onion sandwich on rye for 15 cents. Believe it or not, it became pretty popular. You could eat an entire lunch for 50 cents. Coffee was five cents and then jumped to 10. I even made my own ice cream for milkshakes or pie à la mode."

Sam traded a few buckets of his ice cream for pies that he picked up from Bob Perkins, a baker and chef, who became a good friend. Perkins operated his own restaurant a few blocks away, across from the Eaton's store. (The former Eaton's space is now part of the Calgary CORE complex.) One day, Perkins would work for Sam as food and beverage manager at the Summit Hotel, but for now the two were busy with their own small businesses.

Sam knew the importance of freshly baked goods. He rose at six and rushed to the North Hill bakeries for chocolate donuts, long johns and éclairs. "They were still steaming when I opened the doors for breakfast just before 8. Soon I had lineups," says Sam. "Lunch was the same. Everyone knew that Yavvis only sold fresh. I remained open until 8 in the evening so people who were going to the Palace could stop for a quick meal.

"I was doing all the work myself except for the few hours in the afternoon when my poor old dad came in to help with the dishes. After all the time I had put in the grocery store, he wanted to do something for me. Isn't that amazing, pitching in and washing dishes and he's nearly seventy? I'll never forget that."

"Yavvis was successful and I was making enough to have a family, which was a good thing. Before we knew it, we had two kids, with more to come. But I was working from the moment I got up at 6 until I went to bed by 10."

Sam ached to spend time with his young family. Darlene had arrived on June 6TH, 1953, followed by Lorne on November 18TH, 1954, both at the hospital – the General – where their father was born. The family continued to grow with Susan's birth on June 27, 1956, and then Ronald's on September 10, 1957. Later, John welcomed the world on June 26, 1962, and finally Mark arrived on January 18, 1964.

"Aneta would put Darlene and Lorne in the carriage and wheel them from Switzer's Grocery to Yavvis Coffee Shop. Often that's the only time I'd get with them," says Sam. "It was my favourite part of the day." And then he jokes, "Her favourite part was helping herself to the cash register."

Then he gets serious again. "The reality is that we didn't have a family life." Sam's success was taking a toll.

Aneta talked with her mother, and soon her father had an idea. "He liked the location of the coffee shop as the perfect spot for a jewellery store. 'Close Yavvis,' he said. 'Sell jewellery instead. I'll lend you $4000 in stock and give all the free advice you can stand.' I took him up on his offer."

Sam knew nothing about fine jewels but too much about long hours. Finally, he would be able to spend evenings with Aneta and the kids. Yet the transformation of the coffee shop into the jewellery store couldn't leave him without income. Sam needn't have worried. "Bill Milne had moved to Calgary and became a close friend," says Sam. "He was just starting to build his architectural business and offered to design the entire store, including the cabinets and showcases."

As Sam and Bill's friendship grew, so too did their long and successful business partnership. Born in Winnipeg, Milne moved to Calgary in 1950 when he was 23, beginning a distinguished career that was to be defined by his design for the iconic Calgary Tower. He would also plan the brilliant Calgary pathways that snake in and around the city to beguile walker, runner and cyclist alike.

Milne was a keen environmentalist, and in the 1970s secured the support of MLA Clarence Copithorne and premier Peter Lougheed to create a multi-use area within the wilderness of the Kananaskis Mountains. "Milne made a significant contribution to the plan," stated the Alberta government release. In 2008, the park within the Kananaskis was renamed Peter Lougheed Provincial Park.

Bill promised Sam that he wouldn't lose a day of income. A friend, Ed Sardachuck, built the showcases in his garage and installed them in the store on Sunday morning. (Ed Sardachuck would also move on to an impressive career in construction with Sam Hashman, rising to Chief Development Officer for Trizec Corporation.) As soon as Ed finished, Sam placed the watches and jewellery in their proper cases. Bill's unique use of space and novel design seemed to double the store's size. Its former contents, meanwhile, were safe in the Switzer Grocery basement for sale or some future use.

After two-and-a-half years of non-stop labour, Sam shuttered the windows of Yavvis on Saturday evening at 8 and opened the door to Switzer's Jewellery on Monday morning at 9. "The customers were flabbergasted," recalls Sam. "They'd walk in wanting their coffee and donut and walk out wondering what happened to their little café."

Sam wondered, too. Not about his little café, but about his little knowledge of fine jewellery. His father-in-law was an expert in high-end watches, gold and diamond rings, bracelets, necklaces and earrings. While Sam was not, he quickly learned that there was more profit and less pain in costume jewellery.

"I liked a little more fun and pizzazz in the showcase. Besides, if a rhinestone brooch went missing, I wasn't going to be out the kind of cash I would be if a diamond necklace suddenly darted out the door. I could relax a little more with my merchandise, yet become a little more creative in presentation."

As he focused more on costume baubles, Sam's business boomed. He travelled to California for copper necklaces, bracelets and belt buckles. He flew to New York for rhinestone pieces and faux pearls. Sam loved large, flashy, unique costume jewellery, and so did his customers.

"I called it chunk jewellery," says Sam. "There was no junk about it. You don't need the most expensive piece for an evening out. It's all about the way you dress and carry yourself. You should wear the jewellery. It shouldn't wear you. And everyone can wear something fun."

There was, indeed, something for everyone at Switzer's Jewellery. If you couldn't afford the Rolex watch – and few could – then a fine Bulova fit the bill.

"We became super successful with our new line of jewellery and watches, because people didn't need to mortgage their life away," he recalls. "At Christmas we'd have our half-price sale on Bulova, and the store was packed beyond the doors. There's no better bruising in the business than that from a customer crushing you to get to the sales cabinet."

Sam had already repaid his father-in-law for the $4000 worth of stock he had needed to start Switzer's Jewellery. He had hired Marsha Dvorkin Stein, who was superb at sales and whom he could trust to manage the store when he was away. Everything he had yearned for, he had: a loving wife in Aneta, two delightful children – toddler Darlene and new baby, Lorne. Yet he was restless. The poker palace was gone; all the pals had families and were busy building their own businesses. Besides, Aneta had threatened to join the tight-knit crew and outplay any hand they had.

"There's no question she could have out-foxed us," smiles Sam. "She already had. Aneta was smart and was not going to put up with me coming in that late. And I sure wasn't going to put up with her coming in that late. Our poker days were done."

The pals played on – but it wasn't poker; it was life. "Many of us became life-long friends," Sam says. "We did deals and worked with each other or passed on ideas or tips. It was about mutual respect."

Sam's was a busy life, but he was missing the buzz of Yavvis, if not the hours. Vinnie Jacques suddenly owned 2750 square feet of vacant floor space when he moved his sofa shop next door. Sam took the spot at 208A 9ᵀᴴ Ave SW and called it Sammy's Coffee Bar. He still had all the fixings from his former coffee shop and decided to test a new type of café – this one with a television. It was a first for Alberta; a TV screen for all to see as they ate their light lunch or dinner. The novel idea captured Sam's imagination. He was sure that eating while watching would be a hit. The concept would revolutionize bars and restaurants across the province, where screens would dominate the walls with every sporting event imaginable – sumo wrestling anyone?

"You could forget your worries and watch your favourite show while having a bite to eat. Then get back to work. What's not to like?"

He devised a quick-lunch menu for men and women on the run. For the supper crowd, there were fixed-price specials that included soup and dessert as well as coffee or tea.

"It was the original TV-dinner," says Sam. "Television was new and exciting, and if you didn't have one at home, you could watch it all at Sammy's."

Sam would be watching, too, but he wouldn't be doing all the work. He had learned the hard way that hard work was only one of the ingredients to success. The others were hiring smart people, paying them fairly and delegating. This time, he hired a head chef, Robert Jackson, as well as a day manager, Alberta Turner, and a night manager, Irene Fulbrook.

"It paid off of course because I've got good people at both Switzer's Jewellery and Sammy's Coffee Bar," says Sam. "I've also got time to think about making the businesses the best. And then I had a windfall."

Sam knew the jewellery business boomed before the Christmas season, and watched intently when The Bay bought the building beside it. As they were right across from Switzer's Jewellery, Sam noticed that there were a number of empty stores in the recently purchased building.

"So I talked to The Bay's manager and told him I'd like to rent one of the stores from November to January. He was happy to have the rent, and I was delighted to have the space. The extra stock was easy to buy from a store that had closed, so suddenly I had three places to manage, but I had the right people in the right positions. In the Bay space alone, we made $10,000 over those three months."

What wasn't a windfall was living in Victoria Park. Aneta, especially, was feeling cramped in the building behind Switzer Grocery. She also wasn't keen that Sam's parents lived within a stone's throw, a fact she didn't actually test but could have on certain days. The suite may have been designed as a luxury apartment, but with a growing family – there would be six children within 10 years – Aneta wanted a house large enough for everyone to get lost in. The neighbourhood that had worked so well for Sam and his sisters tested Aneta. His childhood was gone and Aneta wanted to be gone, too – as far away as possible from the crumbling, yet for Sam still very comfortable, East Village.

"I understood," says Sam. "We were having babies right away. My mother and father were always around. Of course, I didn't really mind, but it wasn't such a good situation for a married couple."

Sam was also following his sisters' example. Even though Lily and Becky started running Switzer's Grocery, they still left the neighbourhood after having children. Lily and Jack Fishman moved into the comfortable community of Rosedale on the northwest side of the Bow River, while Becky and Morris Mendelman bought a home in budding Elbow Park, just southwest of the city core.

Although Aneta had her own feelings, Sam still had to contend with the mother-in-law who believed her daughter had married far beneath her and had simply settled. "She always felt that Aneta could have done so much better, and she never neglected to let me know that," recalls Sam. "So that, plus the fact I wanted the family to feel comfortable, pushed me to find the perfect location to build our new home."

Just above the Elbow River, with a breathtaking view of the Rocky Mountains, a brand-new subdivision was opening in southwest Calgary. It was called Britannia, but all the view lots were gone. Priced at $4500, they had sold fast. Sam wasn't going to let that get in the way. He talked to friends and acquaintances who either owned a lot or knew someone who had bought one. For Sam, the impossible was simply a starting point. His persistence paid off.

"It turned out that Cecil Horwitz had secured this beautiful piece of property at 4732 Britannia Dr," recalls Sam. "But he and his wife decided not to build and said I could have it for $5000. I could barely contain my enthusiasm and took out my chequebook. The corner lot was 90 feet wide, 130 feet deep and, as far as I was concerned, a steal. It was simply spectacular."

There was only one person who would design a home worthy of such a splendid lot. Bill Milne was delighted to let his own creativity take flight while Sam took care of the practicalities of mortgaging the $25,000 cost of construction. (Later, tour buses would drive along Britannia Dr to stop and marvel at the mountains and homes, especially Milne's imaginative design. In the late 2000s, the house would sell for $950,000 – and be torn down.)

They called it The Boat House for the bulging prow that pressed massive windows windward towards the mountains. The prow was actually the living room with floor-to-ceiling windows coming together in a V shape near the centre of the lot.

Next door to Sammy's Coffee Bar was CJCJ radio, up the stairs from Shulman's Dry Cleaners. The station manager was Ted Soskin, whom Sam met frequently to talk about Jewish music. When Ted moved directly above Sammy's Coffee Bar as the manager of CHQR, he suggested Sam bring his pristine collection to the station. Soon Sam was spinning records for "Jewish Melody

Time." From klezmer to swing, Sam played them all, and with the Calgary Jewish population topping 2100 in 1951 alone, there were certainly sponsors to tap.

"Ted and I did this for two years," recalls Sam. "He got the radio sponsors and I hosted the show from 10 to 11 on Sunday mornings. It was great fun. Ted was a true pioneer, and there was nothing he didn't know about or do in radio."

The two talked about business beyond radio. The city was starting to grow fast and Sam saw a number of friends move into construction. His building experience with both his new home and the apartment behind Switzer's Grocery taught Sam the value of location and quality construction. As he drove past a house for sale in the city's Mission district, he noticed it faced the Elbow River.

"The address was 135 26TH Ave SW and it was zoned for apartments," says Sam. "I thought the price was reasonable $25,000 – and all I needed was a partner. So, I called Ted and we talked about the plan. Within a few days, he had handed me a cheque for $12,500. Now we both owned the lot."

Sam brought Bill Milne to the site and asked him to design the apartments. With Bill onboard, Sam searched for a mortgage lender. Bob Dredge, manager of North American Life, had financed a number of Calgary housing projects but Sam's worried him.

"He didn't like the fact that I was new at this and insisted on seeing the plans before we even talked mortgage," says Sam. "Plus, I had another problem." When Ted Soskin saw the interminable hoops that Sam was trying to squeeze through, he became worried and wanted his money back. Who could blame him?

"Sam, I don't know anything about the apartment business," Ted told Sam. "You know only a little bit. I'm a radio announcer... Why don't you find a partner that can help you and teach you, because I'm useless to you. So, why don't you give me my money back and you do what you want?"

Sam was shocked but totally understood. He gave Ted a cheque and the two men shook hands.

"Of course I was shattered, but it was the best thing for both of us," says Sam. "Ted was right. If I was going to make it in this business, I had to talk and work directly with people in it. I set up Switzer's Construction and subcontracted all the trades and supplies. I was truly learning from the ground up."

The project was called River Plaza. Milne quickly finished the design and Sam immediately dropped it off with Dredge. Within the week, the mortgage was approved. Elated, Sam started construction – and was immediately sued. The American renting next door was sick from the drilling and incessant noise that woke him every morning.

Sam was terrified a court order could stop construction. He had every cent tied up in the building, and he couldn't afford even a day off the site. He phoned his lawyer, Abe Barron, and his friend, Bill Milne.

"I'd never been sued and could barely think," recalls Sam. "But Bill set me straight. He completely calmed me down and said that I've got to expect the unexpected. In business, you can follow all the steps, jump over all the hurdles and then, plop, you've tripped into a puddle of mud."

It was then that Sam fully started to appreciate his new "learning experiences."

"Whether they're mistakes, misguided decisions with the best of intentions, bad luck or unexpected consequences, they're all learning experiences. The important thing is to embrace them and understand what has happened so that it doesn't happen again. Realize, too, that while it may not happen again, something else will. That's life.

"Bill also told me to take advantage of the situation to meet new people. They give you a different perspective, expand your universe and allow you to see a new realm of possibilities."

Bill's optimism gave Sam the boost he needed. When Abe Barron stood before the court to argue the case, Sam stared in awe. The man was the best in the business, and Sam instantly saw why. It was the respect Barron held for the court and those that presided over her. That's why he was so well prepared.

"He was so compelling, and you waited intently for his next word or move. He never once looked at the plaintiff while he argued my case. All the while, he quietly strode about the room, until he stopped, stood at the front and pointed to the man. 'You Americans think you can come to Canada where it is a growing country and stop progress,' says Sam, recalling the words as clearly as he did the day they were said. 'If you're going to live in this country, you'd better not try to stop progress. You'd better encourage progress.' Abe Barron's words penetrated through every bone in my body, so I can only imagine how the plaintiff felt – and everyone else, too.

"And that was it," adds Sam. "We won."

The River Plaza project was the turning point in Sam's novice career. It energized him every bit as much as building the Boat House and the apartment behind the grocery. Yet this was more. It was the beginning of a building career if he really wanted it. But he had to be prepared to recognize the right opportunity, take a chance, risk everything, rely on advice from close friends, trust his instincts and work until he ached. That last part he knew too well.

Now he was learning the lessons of the builder – the hard way and the only way. Sam was in his element buying land, borrowing money, building apartments, selling them, then starting all over again. He'd leverage one part of the operation to start – or finish – another part. His most important rule would guide him through industry booms and busts: location.

"Location is the key that unlocks success," says Sam. "If you don't have that, then don't bother to start."

Always good at math, Sam picked up the investing essentials for any builder, beginning with the number of suites needed to make a building profitable.

"If you can't own eight suites or more, then don't touch it," he says. "That's how many were in the apartments we built in North Hill. I paid $4000 for a lot, $25,000 to construct an apartment, then let it go, finished, for $34,000. I sold them as fast as we built them, making a profit of $5000 each. Of course, that went right into the next project, with barely a nod to the builder. On paper I'd look like a millionaire one day and a pauper the next. And that's exactly where I had started. Maybe that's why I wasn't so scared."

Then Leduc changed the face of Alberta. What had been an agricultural economy moved quickly into energy. The villages and towns that were lifelines to the farmers fell to the allure of the lights and jobs of the cities, starting with Edmonton and Calgary. When Imperial Oil spudded Leduc No. 1 in February, 1947, Alberta's population was 803,000. It would double to 1,600,000 by 1971, with Edmonton escalating from 113,000 to 449,000 and Calgary crackling from 100,000 to 403,000. During that quarter century, investors pumped nearly $12 billion into energy exploration and development.

"We were all caught up in the excitement of the city and its quick growth, with the influx of industry and people," continues Sam. "The place was on the move and we were part of that, making it happen. People needed places to live that were decent and affordable. The most efficient apartment designs featured twelve to sixteen suites. Always, they had to be in the right location. In the Beltline, we constructed sixteen-suiters that were the first four-storey walk-ups built in concrete to ensure soundproofing. For me, it was important to build quickly but intelligently, and not skimp on construction quality."

Sam brought the same basic principles to all his building projects. While his overhead was low, his abilities and expectations were not. As the builder and contractor, he got to know the best trades people in their fields. He had his list of sub-contractors so if one wasn't available for a project, he wasn't left adrift. He knew what he needed to get any job done, starting with being there firsthand to ensure he had hired the right trades.

"Hands-on is very important," says Sam. "You literally have to be able to touch it. At this point we were buying, building and selling so fast. The business was booming but hands-on was the only way to maintain quality. People would move into the top floors while we were busy plastering and painting on the bottom floors, hopping out of everyone's way.

69

"Remember the Richard Farina book, *Been Down So Long It Looks Like Up To Me*? Well, there were so many days I'd be down plastering, it really did look like up to me. Sometimes I was so tired, I felt plastered, too – and I barely drink!"

Switzer's Construction broke ground all around the city. From Mission to the Beltline District to North Hill and back, Sam was buying, financing, building, renting, and selling. He quickly acquired another rule: "When buying or selling, always leave a little on the table so everyone is satisfied."

His overhead was minimal because Sam owned no massive industrial building to house construction equipment. What he needed, he either rented or bought and then sold, depending on condition and availability. Sam learned quickly to maintain proper records.

"I kept exactly what I needed," recalls Sam. "You don't want anything to come back and bite you. My accountant, Al Menzies, was a stickler for detail. He went on to a distinguished career in his field."

Sam was on the road to becoming Calgary's largest land-lord, building over 40 apartment blocks. He would indeed reach that milestone, but it wasn't his goal. For him, life was more than making money and constructing buildings. He considered it a responsibility to create livable spaces for people to build their homes and lives in Calgary.

"I decided to start the Calgary Apartment Rental Association, and by 1959 it was registered under the Alberta Government's Societies Act as a non-profit group," says Sam. "The purpose was to protect both the owner and the renter. The industry was grow-ing and ground rules had to be established. We needed a sense of fairness so the owner's investment could be protected along with the rights of the renter.

"In a boom time especially, the tenant can really be taken advantage of. That isn't right. Similarly, if it is impossible to evict a tenant who is destroying the suite, then who would want to invest in the building? The Association worked for both. The guidelines protect a tenant from eviction and the landlord from non-payment of rent and damages. This was all about rights, fairness and respect for both parties."

Even as Sam was building affordable apartments, he yearned to repeat the feat he had accomplished after Edward Bronfman came to town. This time, though, he would build not a luxury suite but a luxury apartment building. As with everything that Sam tackled in his career, location was crucial. He looked at River Plaza and decided the two lots beside it would include the new and identical River Manor at the far end. Sandwiched in the middle of the two smaller buildings would be the first high-rise luxury complex in Calgary, River Towers, complete with a roof-top swimming pool and an underground parking garage linking the three buildings. As usual, Bill Milne was the maestro behind the concept.

"It was 1958 and I had just borrowed a million dollars to build it. The day I signed those mortgage papers, I wondered what kind of crazy kid-game I was playing," recalls Sam. "What would happen if the energy industry suddenly collapsed? The market for luxury suites would march out of town so fast. I decided to go ahead anyway because if everything fell flat, I'd have a lot of company to play penny poker with."

River Towers soon completed the troika that graced the former single-family lots overlooking the Elbow River. With its wood-burning fireplaces and vast scenic windows, the luxury tower became the jewel that glistened the brightest in Sam and Bill's ring of apartments around the city. Sam had guessed right. The suites were quickly scooped up by some of the most prominent executives in business and the energy industry. From Shell Oil to Husky Oil to Calgary Power and beyond, company presidents and senior managers quietly preferred both the amenities and location. River Towers had it all. So much so that, for the very first time, Sam decided to lease himself a small office in the city's very first luxury high-rise.

Sam's mid-twentieth century dreams have proved decidedly twenty-first century as developers try to out-dazzle each other 50 years later with elegant townhouse living on the Elbow River. Yet

Sam's initial River concept brought the dream of riverside living to all. Regardless of income, a tenant could overlook the river in a modest walk-up or a stylish high-rise. To Sam, the pleasures of God's riverscape should not be limited to the rich.

"Monthly rent in the River walk-up apartments ranged from $90 to $145 for the top floor," notes Sam. "The River Towers ranged from $550 to $750 per month for the penthouse. Today, these new river townhomes are costing owners millions to buy. What a time."

By 1962, Sam had also taken Switzer's Jewellery into a profitable and comfortable position. But he was both busy with his construction business and a bit bored with the store.

"It was never really my initiative, but my father-in-law's, although I certainly paid him back in full and I did make it work," says Sam. "But I started to feel stifled. I had some other ideas, but no time to try them out."

Sam's brother-in-law, Morris Mendelman, wanted something different, too, and decided Switzer's Jewellery would be perfect. The two shook hands and Sam gave Morris the keys to the business, with all the stock, for $12,000. The brothers-in-law were delighted with the deal as it gave each a new incentive.

Sam's challenge took him to a White Rose service station that he knew well, on Macleod Trail and 33ʳᴰ Ave. Counting the traffic coming in and out convinced Sam the station would be an easy money generator. He eagerly bought the franchise but soon realized his folly after he found his hourly wage barely touched 25 cents. Again. Within six months, Sam had passed the franchise on while looking for something to soothe both his ego and his pocket book.

He settled for a sixteen-unit Denny's Motel just down the road on Macleod and 40ᵀᴴ Ave. While the motel business was barely sustainable, Sam got another offer. The Canadian Acceptance Corporation liked the location of his motel mainly because it happened to be on the Auto Mile strip. They just didn't like his motel itself, and suggested he switch to a car business. All he had to do was demolish the motel and put up an auto mart.

Sam already knew how to develop and then completely change a business, but he wasn't about to go from renting rooms to selling cars overnight. The CAC was ready to finance Sam as soon as he built the sales office. Sam had done his share of car deals and thought this might be another good business for him. He found a partner who had actual car sales experience, Eddie Brodsky, and offered him fifty percent of the company. Sam also hired two experienced car salesmen, Ron Martin and Bernie Brosgarth.

The busy auto strip already had a car rental business across the street. In 1962, Morris Belzberg had opened the first Budget Rent A Car license in Canada. By 1965, Morris had moved to Chicago, and in 1971 he was named Budget's chief executive officer. He was elected chairman of the board in 1987.

"We seemed to have the perfect spot for the auto mart," recalls Sam. "If you're renting a car, you might think of buying one down the road. Well, I wasn't down the road but right across the street. Yet I had a little problem. I was completely out of cash because everything was tied up in my construction projects. I couldn't even afford a neon sign to attract customers. In those days, the sign cost as much as a small store. So, I asked my buddy, Bill Milne, if he had any ideas. If anyone thought outside the box, Bill sure did. In fact, he put the box right up in the air. 'Let's set an office on stilts so people will stop and see,' Bill said to me."

At this stage in both their careers, Bill's box in the air created a lot more buzz than any neon sign, and cost Sam little more than the idea and the wood. When you looked at Milne's work from the right angle, it looked like a golden eagle about to take flight. Bill Milne's creative genius allowed the mind to soar, whether it was the Boat House leaving its berth, the eagle peering from its perch, or later, the Calgary Tower blasting into space.

As for the auto mart, Sam's concept seemed simple enough. Buy barely used cars that the large auto franchisers took on trade. In theory, each dealer needed the other as a ready buyer, for trade-ins freed the big retailers to focus on new car sales. In the end, all the theory tested was Sam's nerves and the CAC's pocketbook

– he couldn't have guessed then he'd someday tell these stories of woe as he accepted an honorary university degree.

"This one guy had a Volkswagen dealership where I bought a 1955 Volks that I quickly sold to a lady. A week later, she storms into the office and says it's a 1952 and we're a bunch of crooks. I was boiling and brought the car back to the dealership. I blasted him with, 'This is a 1952, not a 1955 Volks.' He looked right at me, actually smiled and said, 'Take a look at your bill, there's no date.' The man had lied and could not have cared who he was conning. Clearly, I wasn't the only one he was deceiving. There was no moral fibre there at all. Not too long after that he got out of the Volks dealership."

But Sam motored on.

"An older school teacher drives into the lot, opens the door and starts crying. I come out and ask her if I can help. 'Well, as a matter of fact, you can,' she says. And then she tells me her story. She's had a hard year, everything has happened to her and she really needs a holiday but can't afford one. The only thing she has of value is her car. But if she could sell it to me, she'd finally be able to take a holiday and get her life back together. Naturally, I take a quick look at the car, give her a good price and she's on her way. No wonder. When a buyer comes in, he asks to take a serious look under the hood. Turns out the transmission is full of sawdust – which is precisely what my head feels full of right now.

"Not so long after that, a friend walks in wanting a Buick," he says. "I head out and find a two-year-old model with 25,000 miles on it. (Those were the days before kms took over.) He's happy, I'm happy for him and off he drives. A week later, he barges into my office. Not only did he snap, so had the transmission. It turns out the car had 125,000 miles on it. The odometer had simply turned at 100,000 and started all over again. At that point, I truly wish I could have. Not only did I have a dead car, I had a dead friendship. The car, I could – and did – buy back. The friendship was another matter entirely. That is something you can't buy."

After six months, Sam had had his fill of scammers and swindlers, charlatans and cheats, men and women who had never met a good deed that they didn't turn into dirt – or sawdust. What was to have been a bonus career in car sales was now over. He quickly sold his half share to another eager soul ready to learn and profit. In Sam's case, the only profit was what he learned. And he had indeed acquired another valuable lesson in life: "Don't go into the used-car business."

Sam decided to stick with what he knew and did best: real estate. He would go on to construct over 60 buildings and become the largest landlord in the province – but not before he learned more valuable lessons.

CHAPTER FIVE:
THE HOTELIER

SAM'S LESSONS LEFT HIM WORKING AS HARD AS HE EVER HAD, but at least he felt on top of his fate. Friends like Bill Milne and family like nephew Charlie Mendelman were part of Sam's tight-knit team that designed and built apartments. One cool, cloudless night Sam sat down with another close colleague, his former poker pal Sam Hashman. The two Sams were both developers and spent the evening sharing stories about the business. By the time they each headed home, Sam Switzer's dream was as clear as the sky. He would build a high-rise hotel in the centre of the city.

Hashman's key to unlocking Switzer's future wasn't apparent at the beginning. Like his friend, Hashman was a builder of apartments. Until, that is, he bought a Caravan Hotel in Calgary's city centre, on 4ᵀᴴ Ave SW, and then one in downtown Edmonton. Hashman hired their mutual pal, Bill Milne, to design the Edmonton hotel, which he did with his usual ingenuity. But it wasn't Milne's creativity that made Sam catch his breath – it was Hashman's math.

"Here we were, building apartments that gave the renter a bed-room, kitchen and bathroom," says Sam of his talk with Hashman. "And our return on all that was three dollars a day. Meanwhile, the hotel gives the overnighter a bedroom and a bathroom, and the owner gets nearly nine dollars a day. Well, like they say, 'Do the math!' What were we doing?"

Sam Hashman had figured it out pretty early. After marrying his sweetheart, Dina, Hashman moved into real estate, and by 1950 was building four-plexes and then six-suiters.

"Two decades later," writes Jason Markusoff of the *Calgary Herald*, "he was one of Calgary's most prominent developers, helming a firm with $130 million in projects and a private jet that got him hopping daily from a mall in California to a skyscraper in Vancouver to a hotel in Toronto and eventually back to his wife and four daughters in Cowtown."

Hashman had created Great West International Equities, which would be taken over by real estate giant, Trizec Properties. He knew Edward Bronfman from his Calgary days, and Edward and Peter Bronfman, through Edper, would invest in Great West. For a period, Hashman became president of Trizec, while the two Bronfmans joined the board, assuming a nine percent share of the company.

For the two Sams in the early 1960s, "Do the math" meant developing hotels. Even as the days grew harder, each hoped the dollars would flow faster and stay longer.

Sam Switzer found the ideal location for his hotel little more than a block from Sam Hashman's Caravan. It started with a vacant corner lot on 4TH Ave and 1ST St SW. The owner, Bill Schwartz, accepted Switzer's $275,000 offer and Sam was on his way to owning the entire block. He scooped up a number of Chinese-owned family homes with the right price. Now all he needed was the parking lot owned by the Alberta Wheat Pool and construction could begin. Suddenly, a huge problem threatened to stop Sam's dream.

"The Wheat Pool wouldn't talk to me about money," recalls Sam. "They wanted their parking lot and to heck with the hotel. Of course, they had a point. When the freeze comes, everyone working downtown wants to drive, park, and hustle inside. As I'm scratching for solutions, I suddenly stare across the street at this large, unoccupied lot. Why, it looks like it's almost begging me for company. I find the owners, make an offer, purchase the lot and sit down with the Wheat Pool people. 'Let's swap lots,' I say. 'You get an even bigger space for your parking and I get to build my hotel. Why not?'"

Why not, indeed. The Wheat Pool accepted Sam's offer and the two did a straight swap. Sam's location was a logical choice for an upscale hotel, as it was right across the street from the legendary and luxurious Braemar Lodge. Later purchased by Calgary Motor Products, the Braemar's beautiful façade would fall to fire in March 1965 as the building was being demolished.

Sam knew only one man who could develop a visionary design for his new steel and concrete hotel. It was 1963, and Bill Milne had in mind a circular skyscraper where the elevator and services met in the middle of the hotel and the pie-shaped rooms radiated from the centre core. There would be no single rooms, as every suite would boast double and deluxe accommodation.

"There were no closet-sized singles next to noisy service areas," notes Sam. "We wanted our hotel to be a destination, not an afterthought."

Sam also wanted each floor to have 16 suites. Milne felt that was impossible, with 14 pushing the limit. Had quality and quantity come to an impasse?

"Absolutely not," insists Sam. "I looked at profitability and efficiency and ultimately proved to Bill [Milne] that 16 was doable. A hotel employee could clean that number in one day and remain on the same floor."

Sam rented a warehouse where Milne penciled in the room's perimeters. Sam studied the space, then outfitted his sample suite with bedroom, bathroom, closet and necessary fixtures, including a window onto Calgary. He fussed and fidgeted until the room fit both Milne's and his design – one creative and one financial but both innovative.

"Everyone was telling me the circular concept was crazy except the very guy who was behind it," adds Sam. "And I was a hundred percent with him. Bill was a genius and after our "suite" talk, I knew the hotel would be a success and a landmark."

Switzer Construction broke first ground with Sam at the helm of the excavation loader, and foreman Johnny Anderson delegating his seasoned team to the monumental task. In the middle of it all was Sam, so hands-on that he even tied the steel girders.

"It would be the tallest hotel in the city with its 142 rooms on 12 floors, plus the penthouse," reminds Sam. "I called it the Summit."

The Summit it was, and all Sam needed was cash flow during construction. He understood from his investing days that the public market could provide the opportunity if he had the financial fundamentals in place. Sam wanted a steady stream of cash to finance the hotel and provide a guaranteed rate of return. He reasoned that the shares would generate between six and eight percent return for investors, nearly double what the banks were delivering.

"It seemed simple," says Sam. "We'd raise the capital needed to construct the hotel. The profit on the rental from the suites would go to the shareholders after all the costs were met."

Sam had already developed the company called Amalgamated Properties Ltd. It included modern apartment buildings that he had constructed as well as a shopping centre. Why not a hotel?

"Sam had Amalgamated Properties and was planning to build the Summit Hotel," says Frank Nelles, a close friend since 1964. "Amalgamated became a public company on the Alberta Stock Exchange and sold shares. Lots of us bought shares, and that was great. It was all used to build the hotel."

Sam hired about twenty salesmen to travel around the rural towns and villages, explaining the concept and the expected rate of return. The venture proved so popular that within eight months the shares were sold out.

Although the hotel was far from complete, the salesmen had done their job and wanted to move on. But Sam didn't want them to quit. He valued their expertise and hoped to use their abilities in his next building ventures. He devised a plan to keep them busy by selling mutual funds. Sam flew to New York and visited investment counselors at Lionel D. Edie.

"Lionel D. Edie was the largest firm then, and the best as far as I was concerned," explains Sam. "That's why I went to see them. At the time they didn't have any business in Canada, so I asked them to take on my venture, as it would be their first. They had a serious look, we had another series of meetings, and they agreed to invest in this new mutual fund called Amalgamated Financial Fund."

In the middle of the Summit construction, the two Sams met to discuss a similar venture in Regina. Hashman had purchased the land for $225,000 and secured the necessary leases to construct The Regina Inn. Everything was ready to go but Hashman, whose plate was piled too high with other projects. Sam agreed to take The Regina Inn and handed Hashman a cheque.

Having talked to his banker and gained his verbal guarantee, Sam felt confident that funds were in place. Soon Switzer Construction was breaking ground in Saskatchewan. By the time they had moved from a hole to building the first floor, Sam had made another appointment with the banker.

"He wouldn't advance the funds," recalls Sam, still smarting over a broken promise. "He did offer to take it over himself and allow me 10 years to pay him back the $225,000 – with interest."

Sam got up, opened the door, walked out of the office and never looked back. But when he ran into Hashman a week later, he could barely contain his anger over the betrayal.

"Sam Hashman listened to me and then said he had just unloaded a few of his properties and was free to take this one back on. He would take no profit and I wouldn't lose my shirt. We shook hands and that was it. I had just done business again – with an honourable man and a friend."

Sam was back to managing both the Summit construction and his mutual fund company. Yet the physical and psychological pressures continued to climb. Then the Alberta Securities Commission came calling.

"Suddenly I had a new problem," explains Sam. "Remember the hotel shares that sold in just eight months? Well, the shareholder was expecting a quick return, but there wasn't one right away because the hotel wasn't finished. Obviously no rooms have been rented, and hence, no return. I've sold $1.3 million in shares to construct the hotel, but it's going to take another four months before the hotel is fully completed and at least six months before it's producing a profit.

"That does not make the farmers very happy. They have invested in good faith and, rightly, expect their return. I'm requested to appear before the Securities Commission to explain why the interest payments are deferred. I explain that it is only temporary until the hotel is operating and generating a profit. I promise to drop everything else and focus my energies solely on completing and opening the Summit."

Sam gets a reprieve and steps up his grueling pace. Yet the cost is eating into Sam's very existence. He's arriving home late every evening and missing his family. After checking in on the sleeping kids one night, he glances towards their pet gerbils racing in the cage. They're chasing one another over and over the circular ball, all for a piece of cheese. Sam feels a lump in his stomach as he sees himself trying to spin the ball faster, always finding the cheese is just too far away.

He resolves to rid himself of at least one piece of cheese and takes a long look at his separate mutual fund company. It is returning 14 percent to investors, which makes them very happy. But for Sam, the return is minimal. He decides to sell.

"The investors are doing fine and so are the portfolio managers," adds Sam. "For me, there's nothing there except the work plus the glory of owning a mutual company. That kind of glory I can do without."

Sam contacts a wildcatter and investor named Lowell Williamson to see if he's interested in buying the company. The Calgary oilman has married a certain Dorothy McGuire on Dec. 6, 1958 in New York. She had an older sibling named Christine and a younger one called Phyllis. Together, they were known as the McGuire Sisters and became the most popular singing trio in North America. They will appear soon enough in Sam's life, to make beautiful music in his nightclub at the top of the Summit.

For now, though, the only music Sam is hearing is decidedly

off key. He explains Amalgamated Financial Fund and its portfolio of returns to Williamson, who sees the opportunity. They agree on price and then shake hands – it's a sealed deal the Calgary way. Williamson is pleased and Sam is relieved.

"It was another one of those lessons where I sure learned a lot about working hard, doing a good job, but seeing the rewards split evenly amongst everyone except me," says Sam. "I didn't have any time to feel bad, though. Every waking hour was now taken up with getting the Summit built and opened. I completely immersed myself in what the Summit would be for this city. And then I got excited all over again."

It started with Bill Milne's circular plan and continued with Arthur Fishman's impeccable taste. The interior designer was already making a name for himself.

"He was my friend, of course, and he was also the best," adds Sam. "When you hire such talent you have to step back and allow them the freedom to create."

Arthur Fishman recalls with fondness his days with the Summit and being able to design and carry out what he wanted to do.

"Sam was extremely easy to work with, and he never interfered," says Fishman. "He simply let me go with it. I don't even recall a budget. He was, and continues to be, very easy to get along with. We never had an argument – not even once."

The result was an elegant, warm interior replete with rich wood paneling, striking wall tapestries, stained glass windows, exotic carpets, and numerous objets d'art. The theme was classic Italian, and a note of quiet sophistication resonated throughout the public rooms. It started with the intricately carved reception desk in the lobby, developed by the Swiss master craftsman Otto Steiner.

"Otto was an artist," says Sam. "Above the desk we had a Medici crest that was over 400 years old. It was hand carved and of course Arthur found it when he was in New York."

Arthur Fishman knew where to look for striking and unique pieces. Often he found just what he needed in Calgary with companies like Superior Wood Products, owned by Steiner.

"The Summit was something for Calgary at the time," adds Fishman. "That's Sam. He had the brains to build buildings on the river and a circular hotel downtown. He saw things for the future that most people didn't."

Sam brought the soul of the everyman to the Summit. The hotel was chic and distinct, starting with its second-floor swimming pool for the tired traveler. Yet it was also accessible in price, offering more than competitive rates.

"At the end of the day, you want your rooms filled, so you better offer the best price," says Sam "With the good downtown hotels posting $8.50 to $9.50, our rate had to be $7.50. An occupied room is better than an empty one."

The Summit was the place to go for weddings, birthdays, bar mitzvahs and other family celebrations. It also catered to the business class needing meeting rooms or something much larger, including banquet and convention areas.

Yet the hotel was soon known for much more than its unique circular design and exceptional amenities. The penthouse became a sophisticated nightclub featuring first-class dining, dancing and entertainment. It was called the Top O' the Summit with a view that made snow-capped mountains seem just a window-touch away. Music legends like Rosemary Clooney, Danny Kaye, The Mills Brothers and The Ink Spots braved the vagaries of the Calgary climate to bring their acts to the appreciative audiences.

Cab Calloway was another matter entirely when he showed up during a normal January blizzard.

"The Hi-De-Ho Man hated Sam's band, so Switzer scuttled out to round up new players," wrote Tom Keyser. "Calloway tolerated the replacements for the 10 p.m. show, but packed his bags before the 1 a.m. nightcap. 'You can take your weather and shove it. I'm leaving,' he told Sam, hailing a taxi.'"

Sam laughs as he recalls Calloway's disappearing act.

"The musicians I found were first rate. They were members of the Calgary Philharmonic and the audience loved them," adds Sam. "After all that drama, we just sat down and enjoyed a great show."

Sam's most popular act in the cold Calgary winter wasn't comedian George Gobel or even the McGuire sisters. It was fan dancer Sally Rand, who got her start as an exotic burlesque dancer and never really left the stage. "I haven't been out of work since the day I took my pants off," she once said, and the male audiences loved her for it.

By strategically positioning her pink six foot ostrich fans over and behind her seemingly bare silhouette, Rand managed to out-dance any police officer sitting in the show waiting for violations in that far more prudish era.

"By the time she came to Calgary, she still considered herself in her prime – and she must have been at least 65," recalls Sam smiling. "Her props were these huge pink fans, and she always had music blaring her on. She wore a tight skin-tone body suit, so she was never nude, but the audience didn't know."

Sam was in his element on the Summit stage. Whether he was with a legendary showman like George Gobel or finding a band that lost its way in the snow, Sam relied on his one-liners to get through the night. It was like spinning records on Jewish Melody Time, but this time he could see and hear his audience.

"George Gobel was known as the short man who told tall tales," adds Sam. "He was only five feet five inches and he used to say: 'Did you ever feel as if the whole world was a tuxedo, and you were a pair of brown shoes?' There were some nights when I completely related to that, especially when the customers were waiting for the featured act and it hadn't yet arrived."

Sam delighted in introducing some of the old stars of the screen and stage. But sometimes it wasn't the name acts that got people jumping for more.

"There was this coal miner from Blairmore who was a Tom Jones type. His voice was like velvet," recalls Sam. "We had him here for a year and then he moved on – I don't know where. But what a voice!

"Then there was Subway Elvis. He played the subways in Toronto and did cabarets in basements. He had just the look of

Elvis, and would dance while the women swooned. We hired him and women lined up around the block, screaming just to see and hear him. He was quite the act."

That he was, until arrested and wrongfully convicted of robbing a bank. Michael McTaggart – as he was really called – went to jail before being exonerated.

"Every now and then I'd hear that Subway Elvis was back at it in Toronto, but I never did see him again," adds Sam. "He sure was something."

Just like Sam. The man was not only ahead of his time in building the Summit and bringing the stars, but he was also the first in Alberta to hire female bartenders. Ever since 1928, women had been barred from entering taverns and other such establishments for even a drink with a male companion. It took nearly 40 years – until 1967 – to strike down this draconian Alberta act and allow "mixed" drinking. By 1969, four years after the Summit's opening, Sam had renovated the hotel and built both a parking lot and a 375-seat saloon where women would feel as comfortable as men. It was named Ye Old Mill Tavern and Sam was adamant that women also be hired as bartenders and beer servers. He didn't imagine he'd have to make three trips to Edmonton to convince lawmakers and others that women should be allowed to serve spirits and beer.

"It just seemed so logical. I felt that women would be a calming influence in the tavern," says Sam, recalling his visit before the Alberta Liquor Board. "Men on their own wouldn't be so keen to swear, fight and behave badly with women in the room watching, hearing and also serving them."

Sam won his battle, and by the time the new decade of the 1970s arrived, women were allowed to be cocktail waitresses and bartenders. It's amazing to realize that until then, women in Alberta could cook, clean and serve, but only in establishments that didn't offer alcohol. As David Parker notes, it was quite the victory.

"The Summit Hotel … was the talk of the town, not only for its design and its popular Top O' the Summit … but because Switzer had the nerve to hire the first female bartender in the province."

Sam's elder daughter, Darlene Switzer-Foster, has worked closely with her dad in real estate and other ventures. She points out that Sam has always supported women and their right to equality.

"He's listened to women all his life," she explains. "Remember, Dad grew up with four sisters and a very strong mother. Ever since he was born, he saw and knew that women could work. Dad respects women and has always been an advocate for our equality. Not only has he not been threatened by women on the job, he has always encouraged them."

Sam simply didn't let convention restrict his innovation and imagination. Of course women should be allowed to take on traditionally male roles. It was the same attitude Sam had consistently used throughout his life. If it's about talent, hire the best. And if you look locally, that's just where you might find it.

That's why Sam championed local musicians in his many acts at the Summit, something that pianist and singer Joyce Kelly fondly remembers.

"The Summit was a leader in music and Sam opened the door to a lot of musicians in the area," she says. "He was an original and wasn't afraid to try new acts."

Kelly's husband, Gordon Shoults, reminisces about playing saxophone, clarinet and upright bass at the Summit. "Sam was very conscientious in his business and an incredibly hard worker. At the same time, he was very supportive of all of us musicians as we tried to make a living doing what we loved."

Sam was clearly doing what he loved, too, but he was at it night and day. He wasn't seeing as much of his family as he wished, unless the kids were working at the hotel. In the end, that's exactly what happened.

"All of us had jobs at the Summit," recalls Darlene of the myriad of duties that lay before them. "Switchboard operator, reception clerk, bellboy, parking attendant, we did it all."

Her brother Lorne, now a business professor at Concordia University in Montreal, remembers going to synagogue to pray and afterwards to the Summit to work. Initially, his duties were similar to Darlene's, yet there were a number of jobs where only pure heft would help.

"These were the harder and heavier kinds of work where we were carrying and moving boxes, furniture and all that," he says. "Plus the time that I broke my foot, which didn't please my mother at all."

What didn't please Lorne was precisely what would bother any teenager who eagerly wished for the weekend and found it slowly passing him by. The kids found themselves working hard, just as their father had, although not, in his case, at the tender age of five.

"I was always jealous of my friends who didn't have all these responsibilities working on the weekend," remembers Lorne. "On the other hand, though, I got a chance to see a different sort of crowd. The work was physically and mentally demanding. You needed to keep your wits about you."

Ronald Switzer remembers starting his Summit career as a 10-year-old bellboy anxiously awaiting his monthly pay in books. His love of print and pictures ultimately propelled him into his career as an award-winning photographer.

"I'd be going from 6 or 7 in the evening until 2 in the morning," he says. "But I did love the Top O' the Summit. It was exciting. People still come into my studio (Switzer Photography) and ask if I'm related. When I tell them Sam's my father, they'll eagerly say such things as: 'He sure took care of us.' I like that I was a part of that."

Ron has his own fond memories of the Summit and people like Tom Lynch, the head bellman and Bill Shamman, the general manager.

"Tom was the city's Bellman of the Year," recalls Ron. "He was 75 when he won that title – and deservedly so. Dad was known for bringing the best people to work at the Summit, including Bill Shamman who came over from the Pete Club [Calgary Petroleum Club]."

Ron also remembers some of the more notorious nights at the saloon that had been added in 1969. Ye Olde Mill Tavern was as hip and cool as The Top was urbane and sophisticated. The

Top was for dining and dancing. The Tavern was for drinking and smoking – and sometimes, just outside, there'd be a whiff of the funny weed – marijuana.

"One time," adds Sam, "the police raced into the Tavern hoping to round up some dealers. They went up and down with their sniffing dogs but found absolutely nothing."

What patrons found – whether long-haired or short – was a tavern with top talent. It was the happening spot for country and western music.

"It was the best tavern in the city and so much fun," continues Ron. "Ten to one, Ye Olde Mill Tavern was the best. Again, people come into my studio and still talk about it."

Another legend at the Summit was George Stephenson, who was hired as the Director of Sales but who could well have been taken on as the Director of Tall Tales.

"What an absolute character," says Darlene. "He was such a hoot. There were times when the Summit stage was suddenly empty and he had to fill it. Perform, play the piano, you name it."

Stephenson had worked in the oil services field and was employed to fill the banquet halls and conference room with energy entrepreneurs and chief executives. His duties quickly expanded as new challenges arose – such as jailed entertainers.

"Our band that night was rockin' and the whole place was lit up," says Sam. "Including, it seems, the band. Except that what they were lighting wasn't legal. They were arrested at the break."

Stephenson looked to Sam and wondered what to do.

"No worries," said Sam, as Stephenson suddenly found himself on the stage.

Years later, *Calgary Herald* columnist Valerie Fortney gave a glimpse of Stephenson's funny side.

"A fellow asked me the other day if I lived in Calgary my whole life," says the native of Saskatoon who moved here in 1949, "and I told him, 'Not yet.'"

After he retired from the Summit, Stephenson continued his career as an entertainer, only this time he sauntered from the stage to the track. Stephenson became the legendary announcer of the horse races at the St. Louis Hotel. When the author was there in 2001, everyone from former Calgary mayor and Alberta premier Ralph Klein to the bricklayer at the next table piled into the Louis at noon to hear George bark out the latest race. Money was placed – no more than a buck – beside the beer and wings on the crowded tables.

Yet it was all a delicious ruse. The horses raced around the track of Stephenson's eagle-eyed imagination.

"When the bugle call rings out and the race begins, the crowd noise from the track is almost deafening," wrote Rick Overwater for *The Globe and Mail*. "Sweat glistens on Stephenson's skin. 'Native dancer is coming up on the outside, oh it's close!' he yells. The excitement is indeed palpable. The septuagenarian has been making the races up in his head for 17 years now, bellowing out the results over a pre-recorded soundtrack."

If the Summit were a cast of characters, Sam Switzer was the star, pulling off feats at the Top O' the Summit even as he wished he could spend more time at home. But if he couldn't be there in person, he would be in spirit and, if allowed, in creature.

CHAPTER SIX:
THE ADVENTURER

SAM WANTED HIS FAMILY TO HAVE THE MATERIAL COMFORTS HE never had, including the big Britannia home and the kind of four-legged critters that didn't land in a stove pot – as well as a few that actually did.

"Dad always loved animals," says Ronald.

"After all," adds Darlene, "His parents had no pets. How do you feed pets when you can barely feed yourselves?"

Sam started small – gerbils and such – and graduated quickly to huge. The Weimaraner is an impressive hunting dog bred for German royalty. How fitting that Sam should have such a dog, except that it enjoyed hunting the mailman or milkman. When the aptly named "Rogue" wasn't tracking two-legged creatures, he was scrapping with the kids for the dog door.

"I only hunted once," says Sam. "We went pheasant-shooting near Brooks. It was my first time with a gun and I got the bird. When I picked her up, I felt so bad that I never used a gun again."

Sam stuffed the pheasant and placed it on a mantel in the house as a reminder of creation stopped cold.

For every daughter who ever wanted a pony, Sam played the role of father perfectly. He brought home a pony that Darlene loved unconditionally. On it, she and her brothers and sister galloped through the fields in front of their home until it was time to round up their dreams and corral them for another day.

"We kept the pony in our backyard, but he kept on jumping over the fence," says Darlene – not a serious issue in the countryside, perhaps, but a crisis in a city neighbourhood.

The horse raced through Britannia, leaping through yards and darting into the road, zigzagging between the cars. The Switzer horse was having the adventure that wild horses thrive on, but that burgeoning neighbourhoods abhor.

"Aneta and I were out for dinner and suddenly I got a frantic call," says Sam. "We rush home and the horse is still running wild. It was quite the sight. Police were racing all around, trying to lasso the poor thing. As soon as they got within roping range, the horse would gallop off again. Finally I said to them, 'Let's just calm down a little here. It's not the Stampede. If we leave him alone, he'll come home. That's where his food is. Sure enough, after a few squad cars leave, the horse settles down and heads home to feed."

The crisis over, Sam tethers the horse to a secure spot in the yard. The next day, the horse is off to the stables in Forest Lawn, signaling the end of one little girl's dream.

But that didn't stop Sam from making his backyard a farmer's reverie. Aneta never knew what might be back there after Sam came home. There could be little chicks that grew into chickens – and who doesn't like chicken? Care for some? The horse is gone, but how about a pig?

Aneta was still in the hospital after the birth of their youngest son, Mark. Her mother, Lucy Newman, was at the Switzer home, caring for the children.

"Dad slips into the home with six little piglets as a surprise for us," recalls Darlene. "Baba Newman (Aneta's mom) sees the pigs and goes absolutely batty. She's on the balcony bellowing at Dad: 'You don't bring pigs into a Jewish home.' Of course Dad thought they would be such cute pets."

That's all that remained of the pigs – the thought. Sam

grabbed the little critters and swiftly left. He would return later with no forbidden creatures in tow but plenty of travels in mind.

Sam loved to take the family on trips, whether a simple Sunday drive – if that were even possible with such a growing household – or a long weekend in the mountains or the Okanagan.

Then there were the great getaways that he and Aneta coura- geously plunged into with the six kids, the 17 foot Scamper trailer and the long white Cadillac limousine Sam had proudly purchased from the Belzbergs at their lot on Macleod Trail. They had bought the car at auction in Montreal and brought it back to Calgary.

The car had once carried a different kind of cargo, maybe a little less noisy – or not – but definitely more political. It had belonged to the controversial Quebec premier Maurice Duplessis, a man not known for any concern for the Jews. That his telephone, glass-dividing-window, and siren-equipped limo would carry the growing Switzer family, with Sam at the wheel, is karmic justice.

When Aneta first saw the 1958 black Caddy she was momen- tarily speechless – before cutting loose.

"Mother was furious," recalls Darlene. "To her it looked like a hearse, and she refused to set foot in it."

Within days, the "hearse" was transformed into a gleaming white carriage complete with three rows of seats. On any outing, the spot beside the driver was prime real estate for the good kid – or the bad. As Sam says, it's all about location, something the kids learned early and often.

"Mother always sat in the back with the youngest," continues Darlene. "The rest of us grabbed our spots, and then it started – the trip, the teasing and, of course, the fights."

Thus, as for any normal family embarking on a long road trip, the excitement of the journey loudly gives way to pent-up adrenalin locked within a packed cage of steel. The monotony of tedious grey asphalt cut to the quick by the hypnotic white line turns cruising into bruising. The driver pulls over, stops the car, turns around and glares. The kids fall momentarily silent. The trip begins yet again with another set of stops and starts until eventually everyone has changed seats except the driver – the one who truly wishes he could fly home and fish alone.

But the picnics by a mountain stream were always worth the trek, especially the campfire-roasted marshmallows, flaming hot dogs on a stick and other "exotic" foods forbidden at home. Spam topped the list and no one asked what actually went into the fat-laden brick that caused quarrels for seconds. All rules changed when you were on the road.

By 1964, Sam and Aneta had six children under the age of 10. Piled into the Cadillac were Darlene, Lorne, Susan, Ronald, John and Mark. Each trip was more frenetic than the one before, and everyone wished that he or she could be sitting alone in the towed trailer resplendent in turquoise and white glory. And yet, like thousands of Canadian families who toured in the newly evolving age of car travel, they had tremendous fun.

Sometimes the trips were short jaunts to Chestermere, Lake Minnewanka or Banff. But there was nothing simple where six kids in a car were concerned, plus a 21 foot canoe plopped on the rooftop. The turquoise and white boat boasted room for the kids, rods, tackle, bait and any fish that were unfortunate enough to have been biting in the vicinity of the lure.

"Over the years, we caught many fish that didn't make the news," notes Lorne. "But it was the one that got away that did."

They were fishing on Lake Minnewanka, just outside of Banff. All boats were on the lookout for the legendary Big Sam, an elusive lake trout that had beguiled the anglers for years. Lorne and his dad threw in their bait and bantered quietly, bringing in their lines and tossing them once again. Suddenly, Sam felt a hard strike on his line. This was no ordinary fish, and soon it began to pull the canoe. It was Big Sam in mortal combat with Little Sam and it lasted all afternoon. As the sun started to leave the western sky, the battle slowed and Big Sam prepared to meet his namesake. Little Sam stared at the massive trout and gently reeled it in. At last it was over. Without a net to scoop up the fish, Sam plunged his hands into the icy water. As Sam grabbed his gilled nemesis, Big Sam smoothly slipped his hook, and swam further away into legend. He had skipped death again.

The June 21, 1967 *Calgary Herald* headline said it all: "Calgary Angler Loses Bout with 'Big Sam.'"

"A Calgary fisherman fought a five-and-a-half-hour battle with a lake trout before losing the fish to Lake Minnewanka Monday, in what is believed to be a record for holding a fish on a line in the lake.

"Sam Switzer was fishing about half a mile from shore when he hooked the lake trout, believed to weigh more than 40 pounds. The fight lasted from 1 p.m. to 6:30 p.m., and fishermen from five other boats stayed with Mr. Switzer's party to offer suggestions. A spokesman for the fishing camp at the lake said he believes the fish is the legendary Big Sam for which a reward has been offered."

Lorne laughs as he vividly recalls the day that his dad and Big Sam dueled it out. "It actually made the news. Can you imagine such a headline today? But that's exactly what happened. Over the years, we caught many fish. One time in Mexico, my dad and I pulled in a 16 foot sailfish. That never made the news."

But there were plenty of adventures that made headlines in their own vivid news of the mind, with each trip more trying than the last. It was the longer drives that deserved headlines, especially if the target was Las Vegas. That called for more than four days on the road with kids crazed and parents perplexed as to why they had thought this was such a swell notion only weeks earlier. The drive is exacting in the best of circumstances with steep hills and hairpin turns that leave no space for speculation.

"We were outside of Lovelock, Nevada when the car started to steam up," recalls Sam. "This is just what we need, a cramped car full of tired little Switzers, plus the trailer. Mercifully, I was at the top of a hill and could coast down into town to find a service station close by."

The mechanic came out, took one look at the tired Cadillac and its sweltering crew and quickly offered his diagnosis.

"The motor is blown," declares the mechanic.

"How long will it take to fix?" asks Sam, barely keeping his anger at bay.

"Well, I have to order the motor from Los Angeles, so we're looking at quite a few days," replies the mechanic. "It's the weekend you know."

"I didn't know, because on a road trip, every day is the weekend," says Sam.

The family troops out and leave the car and trailer at the lot beside the service station. They walk around the block to the hotel, check in and meet at the restaurant next door. As they sit and order their food, the waitress wonders why all the glum faces. Sam tells her the story.

"Oh no," she exclaims. "You better be careful. That guy can be the biggest crook in Nevada. Your car is probably just overheated. I'll bet it's fine in the morning."

The waitress tells Sam where to buy the necessary part and off he goes. Early the next morning, Sam inserts the $9 thermostat into the Caddy's innards, swings behind the wheel and turns the key. The car purrs as Sam drives back to the hotel, trailer in tow. After the family checks out, they stop by the restaurant once more and warmly thank the waitress.

Then the Switzers squeeze into their freed sedan, drive past the closed service station, offer the appropriate salute and motor on to Las Vegas.

In the 1950s and 1960s, a road trip was hard to beat. The escape from predictability to fantasy-fueled endless hours of staring into the eternal landscape of dreams and illusions. Just one thing trumped the road – the water. Any water would do, but sea and sun were far preferable to asphalt and sun, and especially cement and snow.

Sam's road trips to Vegas in the Duplessis limo were about to be bested by a boat in Fort Lauderdale named "My Fair Lady." She was a 57 foot seafaring beauty boasting three staterooms, three bathrooms – or heads, as the budding sailors would quickly learn – and a separate salon. Built in the mid-1950s, the Chris-craft Constellation featured a handsome wooden hull as well as two wheelhouses – one inside and one on the bridge. Instead of a canoe, she carried a 17 foot Boston Whaler ready for fishing, water-skiing, swimming or any other water sport Sam and the kids could – and would – devise.

It was Sam and Dina Hashman who had introduced Sam and Aneta to the climatic pleasures of Miami and Fort Lauderdale.

"They were such fun to be with," says Sam of the Hashmans. "When he invited us aboard his yacht, I thought, *Someday I'll have a boat like this.*"

When he saw My Fair Lady, Sam was smitten. The tag was US$45,000, a fair price considering that in those days the Canadian dollar was worth 10 cents more the American greenback.

"I got out my chequebook and received my first boating lesson: never put your chequebook away," says Sam smiling. "But I had the boat of my dreams and figured the kids would be delighted. They were used to sleeping in small spaces on the road. The boat would be a breeze – a sea breeze – for them."

Sam's new boat presented a few immediate problems, not the least of which was where to moor her, where to sail her and, especially, who would sail her. The Bahai Mar catered to vacation boats, and Sam had his first problem solved. My Fair Lady moored there for over three years before moving on to Pier 66. Sam's second problem was directly dependent on solving the third. Friends stepped in and helped him find a captain – and then a second, a third, oh no a fourth, and finally, a fifth.

"A friend who was a captain showed me around the boat and explained the essentials to keeping her in good shape," says Sam. "Because of the Florida heat, it's important to maintain the water level in the six mega-batteries. Each one of them costs $250."

The first captain Sam hired blithely allowed the batteries to dry up and blatantly lied that he hadn't.

"Have you seen the batteries?" Sam asked the captain.

"I certainly have," the captain confidently replied.

"Maybe you better go look again," said Sam. "After that, maybe you better look for the gangplank."

The next captain seemed able and hearty, so much so that he wanted to take the Switzers for a hearty sail. Actually it was more like a ride.

"We're heading down the Intracoastal Waterway and every-one is pretty excited as it's a beautiful day and the sun just dances off the water," says Sam. "There are lovely apartments, beautiful homes, massive mansions and all manner of boats to get around. They don't call this the Venice of North America for nothing."

And "Venice" is where they want to stay, but the captain has other ideas. With no warning, he heads into the open Atlantic, away from the Intracoastal's tranquility and right into the ocean's vast wall of grey cloud. A sudden squall tosses the boat deep into a trough. The vessel rides the wave up, and as it crests, the boat nearly crashes down. The captain slows the speed to the wind and My Fair Lady rides with the waves, pitching and rolling from side to side but refusing to broach. Her seaworthiness is commendable but her comfort is non-existent.

"The weather in the Atlantic can change on a dime," says Sam's son John. "The waves are huge, at least six or seven feet with whitecaps even higher, and if you don't hit the waves just right, the boat feels like it's going to tip. All I'm thinking is, *Please get us back to Port Everglades. As soon as we get there, we'll be safe. In just a few minutes, we'll get there. I know we will.*"

The kids are praying, screaming and dropping to the floor, sick. Aneta is already lying on the floor, unable to move. Sam is frothing, but not from seasickness.

"The only thing that's keeping my sanity," says Sam, "Is imag-ining the many ways to say goodbye to the captain, if we ever manage to escape this nautical nightmare."

Without consulting Sam, the next captain rented My Fair Lady for a lovely cruise. Sam might never have known about the charter business had he not decided to escape the whirlwind of work and winter for some leisurely days of sun and sea.

"We arrived at the berth looking for My Fair Lady, but she wasn't there," says Sam. "So much for my stress-free holiday. At least she wasn't stolen or sea-jacked – just borrowed, for the last time."

Sam's next captain was more interested in a good steak and an even better bottle. The routine work of keeping My Fair Lady in pristine condition was alien to this man of the sea and spirits.

With four captains down, there was only one thing to do: find a sea dawg who would treasure My Fair Lady and treat her accordingly.

"So, Dad and my brother Lorne went to a Power Squadron course held in Calgary to learn all about boating," says son Ronald. "They offer lessons in safety, navigation and care of your boat. With his 57-foot yacht, Dad was the envy of his classmates. I was too young to enroll, but came to classes anyway. We learned all the basics and I understood tides and currents, how to read the stars and also which side the buoys are on. In the end, Lorne passed the course."

Sam didn't bother to take the exam, but that never stopped him from taking the helm.

"Those captains he hired gave him so many headaches that he figured he could do a better job without them," adds John. "Dad was never happier than when he was around his yacht. He was in heaven."

Except for the times he went aground. It seems that My Fair Lady and her skipper were known to the coastguards.

"Dad can be pretty fearless," says Ronald. "He was definitely a coast guard favourite. Switzer was a name they got to know."

Brother John agrees and offers a few more stories of the Switzers and the sea.

"Oh, he did run aground a few times," laughs John. "And it can be scary, because when you're stuck on a sandbar, it's impossible to get off on your own. The coast guard would arrive, throw us a gigantic rope and then pull the boat off the sandbar. In the process, we'd often lose a propeller and need to be towed into port."

All in a day's work for the coast guard and a day's sail for Sam.

"Well, we all know that port is left on a boat," laughs Sam. "In my case, more than a few times, it became a place from which I should never have left on a boat."

Sam sometimes worried that the boat was becoming a money pit, as it seemed to spend more time in dry-dock than in the water. Such is life with a yacht for pleasure. To own such a boat is to patch up holes in the water – the bigger the boat, the larger the hole. In the end, the sea sucks away everything that's thrown at it, leaving only flotsam of memories to float over time.

But oh, what memories!

"When we docked the boat, it was like a family circus," recalls Ronald. "You need to know all kinds of information. How fast are the currents, and is the tide coming in or going out? What is the wind speed? Even though it was a 20 ton yacht, it was still like a big sailboat in the wind, and it doesn't take much of a breeze to have it hit the dock really hard.

"Dad got pretty good at docking the boat. But one time he brought it in and instead of putting it in reverse, he put it in forward. Suddenly we're getting too friendly with a concrete dock. Thank goodness the wood in the boat gave a little when it hit.

"Usually when Dad docked, he would throw the ropes over and then jump on the dock. How many times would something fall in the water – a hook, a fishing reel – and Dad would always say, 'Oh, don't worry, we'll go down and get it.' Who got it? Why, Lorne and me. Whatever fell in, we were right in there after it. And oh my! That water was warm, and not from the heat of the ocean. To this day, I don't want to even think about what was in that water!"

At least it wasn't Sam. That time. Sam was in the wheelhouse, deftly navigating the Intracoastal Waterway as his guests Sam and Dorothy Katchen basked in the rays of the sun. They were enjoying their hosts' hospitality and Sam was in his element, full of stories of the sea. Food and drink flowed with the tide until it all slowed down as Sam prepared to dock. He hooted the horn and waited for the dockhand. When no one appeared, Sam took matters into his own hands. Confident in his captaining, Sam left the wheel, grabbed the ropes, and, with a mighty heave, hurled them over the yacht onto the dock. The sheer power propelled not only the ropes, but Sam, too. Off he flew into the churning water. Seldom had Sam's overconfidence sent him into the brink. If anyone could handle a rebuff from the laws of physics, it was Sam.

"A cartoon couldn't have caught it better for my guests," says Sam. "I was embarrassed of course, but could only wave and laugh with them. What a sight to see me sailing through the air, flapping my arms like an albatross attempting to take flight. Aneta seemed to be the only one worried I might be hurt."

Sam simply climbed out of the dank water. Soon he and the kids were off on another adventure.

"I loved sleeping on the boat," says Ronald. "It would rock you to sleep with its gentle movement."

One time Sam took the boys fishing in the Florida Everglades. They booked into the Holiday Inn and Sam bought nine foot bamboo rods for bass fishing.

"We had a great time and caught 10 huge bass," says Ronald. "But what are we going to do with them? We're staying in the hotel and can't cook them. Dad says, 'Put them in this big black plastic garbage bag. We'll worry about them when we get back.'"

For two-and-a-half smelly sweltering hours, the Switzers endured the musky heat of a cramped car and the stench of 10 flopping fish. When they arrived at the hotel, they escaped the car and were about to race to the shower.

"Not so fast," says Sam. "Have you forgotten about the fish?"

Hardly. The boys were hoping they could simply outrun the stench. But Sam had other ideas.

The hotel was proud of its lush landscaped grounds replete with a stream and a goldfish pond. For a brief moment, it could also boast bass.

"The next day, the hotel staff were actually quite happy with us," recalls Ronald. "Bass are very tasty and the staff were delighted with these big fish in the pond. They knew exactly how they got there."

The majestic bass had survived the stifling ride in the garbage bag to enjoy one last flash of freedom in a goldfish pond.

Ronald and John recalled their father's love for deep-sea fishing and the day when brother Lorne caught a sailfish. "It was pretty big – at least nine feet – and they were both excited," adds Ronald.

Sam especially enjoyed taking the children out in the Boston Whaler to swim and water-ski.

"The Whaler was known for being unsinkable, but I sure wouldn't have wanted to test that theory," says Ronald. "Ours had an old motor that smoked more than our fired captains. You had to pray it started. Dad would go through the port and into the ocean and that's when we'd start asking questions."

"Is this motor going to stall?" continues John. "If it breaks down you'd be swept back into sea, so it could get pretty scary. Then we'd go water-skiing and hope the motor could pull us."

Ronald remembers skiing about a mile off shore when Sam prepared to pull him up.

"With no warning, my ski hits something dark real hard and splits in two," says Ron. "I'm suddenly in the water with what I'm sure is a shark. I didn't take the time for a real serious look. Believe me, I almost flew into that boat."

No wonder why the kids would ask each other, "Do you really want to go back into the water?"

"Oh, I was scared sometimes on the boat," says John. "When it moved, anything could happen – and did. It was a beautiful boat but between the danger and the work, I think I was happiest when the boat was moored."

Boats can be a pain in the pocketbook as well as a pain in the posterior. They're a lot of work, especially when they're big and built of beautiful mahogany.

"Dad was frugal with his money, and bang for the dollar it was a very nice boat," notes Ronald. "But every time the boat went out, whether it was twenty minutes or twenty hours, we all knew what waited when we returned. We always had to swab the deck, because the salt eats away at everything."

But it could never eat away the wonder and sheer joy of the boy who had nothing but thought he had everything.

No wonder he goes in with such huge confidence, says John. "I think he feels he's invincible."

Sadly, Sam's marriage to Aneta was not invincible, but not for want of trying. The two had taken romantic cruises and European holidays to forget all the work and remember the thrill of first love. Aneta was as much a driving force in his desire to succeed as he was, and Sam didn't want to disappoint her or himself.

"My parents took pride in their family," says Lorne. "But as the family grew, the business grew and Dad was at work these long hours."

The bond that had deepened with the birth of their children had begun to break. Sam's relentless drive ultimately bore a hole in their marriage as he succumbed to longer stretches away from home.

"Maybe if her mother hadn't come to Calgary, we could have gone back to what we had," says Sam wistfully. "Her mother never stopped believing Aneta could have married a lot better, and never stopped letting me know it. That cut."

Sam's kids remember a happy home and then one as charged as an electrical storm.

"Mom and Dad were both big personalities," says daughter Darlene. "Sometimes it seemed that they were getting along best if they were yelling at each other."

The reality was that Sam and Aneta loved each other, but couldn't live with each other.

"Dad was always very respectful of Mom and she of him," adds Darlene. "They always worry about the other. In the end, it was not a match made in heaven, but she was part of his inner voice to succeed."

From the Switzer Grocery to the Summit Hotel, the two had grown a huge family and a massive business concern. Now, they had grown irretrievably apart. After six children and 22 years of marriage, Sam and Aneta separated in 1974. They divorced a year later, with Aneta winning the largest Alberta settlement ever granted at the time.

While Aneta sued for the civil decree, it was up to Sam to arrange a Jewish bill of divorce, called a 'get' in Hebrew.

"I traveled to Montreal and talked with three rabbis about the reasons for the divorce," says Sam. "They granted the get, and both Aneta and I were able to move on with our lives.

CHAPTER SEVEN:
THE INVESTOR

The siren song of the Summit beckoned Sam incessantly, and the call consumed his life. The tall letter "S" that spun atop the Summit signified more than the name of the hotel. Sam was not going to let his life spin out of control. As the initial of Sam's first and last names, it was the symbol of all that Sam had accomplished and all that he could lose. When his marriage irretrievably tore apart, the large "S" seemed to shout: "split." Although three of his children were away at university, Sam scurried to spend time with the kids still at home with Aneta.

In the end, so much of what he owned and what he did was embodied in the Summit: managing, promoting, working, being there. Sam had poured every bit of himself into the Summit and was indeed the cement that held the hotel and all its investors fast. Safeguarding the Summit was what he had to do to protect his investors, his friends and most of all his children. The Summit must do well. It was the premier property within Amalgamated Properties Ltd., and the two were co-dependent:

"Calgary's new Summit Hotel ... owned by 1800 Albertans," declared the headline from the article: "What makes a great hotel?" The 14-part series on the Summit appeared in the *Calgary*

Herald just as the hotel made its grand entrance onto the Calgary hospitality scene.

"To date the 'Amalgamated Family' has grown to include over 1800 Alberta investors," stated the fifth piece in the series. "Coming from all walks of life throughout the province, they hold shares in the company in amounts from $100 up, thus permitting many small investors to enjoy the advantage of group ownership previously available only to investors with large amounts of money.

"In less than five years, participants in the 'APL Plan' have seen the holdings grow to include 16 modern apartment buildings, a shopping centre and a new Calgary hotel. Investment in these properties has enabled the company to pay 18 consecutive dividends."

The Summit Hotel had opened in the summer of 1965, and its unique mortgage-free ownership caught the attention of investors and headline-writers alike. The hotel was indeed unique in its structure, both architectural and financial. All of that had sprung from the free-flowing mind of Sam Switzer. His passion for the future of his city and province, coupled with his belief in the wisdom and design of his close friend Bill Milne, propelled Sam to expand his ideas on investing.

"The concept of Amalgamated [Properties Ltd.] was not based on a desire to speculate," the article continued. "Rather, it was the goal of company president Sam Switzer to provide the means for small investors in Alberta to participate in the ownership of large revenue-producing real estate such as office or apartment buildings, shopping centres, hotels, industrial or other real estate investments of established merit. Mr. Switzer himself knew that this was possible, for he, by investing in Calgary's future, had become an authority on apartment construction and management."

As president of the Calgary Apartment Rental Association, Sam was convinced that many Calgarians would follow the paths taken by renters in the large central Canadian cities.

"Metropolitan cities like Toronto and Montreal have long been predominantly apartment cities, and the trend of the last two years is finally catching on here," Sam explained to the *Calgary Herald*'s Ted Hewitt in early January 1964.

Comparing the three apartment permits recorded for 1950 to the 123 registered for 1962, Sam pointed out that Calgary was "long overdue" for apartment growth, especially in the Beltline, Lower Mount Royal and Mission areas just south of the downtown core. In addition, noted Hewitt, Sam "predicted greater emphasis on high-rise units."

"In comparing ratios of apartments to private housing in Calgary with other metropolitan areas, [Sam] said this city is just beginning to catch up with the trend in Canada," reports Hewitt. "At present, [Sam] said, about 25 percent of Calgarians live in apartments. This compares with ratios of three apartment dwellers to one private housing dweller in Montreal and a ratio of about two to one in Toronto."

Sam fully believed apartment living would dramatically increase in Calgary, and he remained in the vanguard of that demographic trend. Amalgamated Properties includes apartment buildings he had constructed. In the end, Sam reasoned that if apartment buildings could be part of the Amalgamated Properties portfolio, why not include the construction of a hotel?

Frank Nelles was working in Winnipeg as the regional manager for RCA in their commercial division when the company asked him to consider Calgary. It was 1964, and Nelles would never look back. He met Sam and discussed Amalgamated Properties and Sam's plans for the Summit.

"Sam is one of the greatest guys," says Nelles. "He's also an entrepreneur from the word go. I was excited about his concept for Amalgamated and told him I would certainly buy shares."

Nelles had secured the RCA contract for video, sound systems and room television sets for the new hotel. When he was asked to sit on Amalgamated's board, Nelles was thrilled.

"Amalgamated Properties Ltd. was a great company and loyal to its investors. I was proud to sit on the board," adds Nelles. "After two years I was elected president."

Along with Sam and Nelles, the board consisted of such

respected Calgarians as Dr. Carl Safron (appointed Chief Super-intendent of the Calgary Board of Education), Lionel Alberstat (later appointed a Justice of Alberta Court of Queen's Bench), veterinarian Dr. Bernie Tonken and farmer Soren Jensen.

Amalgamated Properties continued as a public company with annual meetings and quarterly dividends. Everything unfolded as expected – until one meeting, when it didn't.

"Ouster is sought," shouted the *Regina Leader-Post* headline of October 4TH, 1969. The *Canadian Press* story stated that, "a group of directors and shareholders had started a proxy campaign to oust Sam Switzer as president of Amalgamated Properties Ltd."

Sam was shocked, but he was not about to succumb to such a brazen attack. The charge was a common one in a hostile takeover: shareholder value was not being realized, the critics shouted, when what they really wanted was to capture the equity of a successful company. Sam was adamant that Amalgamated was especially transparent in its financial operations and was reaching its goals, given the economic times.

"Everything must be, and was, by the book," says Sam. "This was a public company. Transparency and record keeping were crucial. Spending was approved at our annual meetings. We were certainly performing well compared to our peers."

It was a standard takeover attempt, and Sam, with most of the board, was under attack. But not for long, once many of the shareholders realized that Sam's management team, with him at the helm, was best for the times. The takeover bid was thwarted.

"When it happened, it was devastating given how hard everyone worked and how committed the board was to the company and its shareholders," adds Nelles. "Thankfully, that takeover process failed. And it never happened again."

Amalgamated owned 70 percent of the Summit, which was valued at $3.5 million in 1969, as well as the 16 apartment buildings.

"I had so much tied up with Amalgamated, and the takeover attempt really woke me up," says Sam. "A hostile takeover is a very scary thing. I was extremely vulnerable and I never wanted to be in that position again."

Less than a year later, the Leier family from Saskatchewan came to see Sam. They Leiers owned the Marlboro Hotel in Prince Albert as well as the King George and Cavalier Hotels in Saskatoon. Brothers Don, Joe and Jim and sister Pat Sikler were the children of another proud prairie pioneer, James (Jack) Peter Leier. Born in Odessa, Russia, Leier was brought by his parents at age one on their grueling trek to a homestead in Salt Lake, Saskatchewan. Now his children were creating a Canadian wing of the Sheraton Hotel chain, with their three hotels as initial partners.

"Don and Joe wanted the Summit to be part of the Sheraton family," recalls Sam. "They were very experienced hoteliers and very convincing. At that point, the Sheraton had little exposure in Canada. I thought that we could grow the chain and gain a lot of advantages for the Summit, and, of course, for Amalgamated Properties. There was a big opportunity here if we all worked together."

The first person Sam wanted to work with was another old friend, Art Smith, who had handled all the publicity for the original opening of the Summit. Smith, who has, sadly, passed on, was one of the great Calgarians who would and did do anything for his city, province and country. Having earned a Distinguished Flying Cross in the Second World War, Smith had faced death every day he flew into the flak-packed skies of those dark years. After the war, Smith continued serving – as an Alberta MLA, MP, and UN delegate. Smith's early work with Sam was just the beginning of a brilliant business career that he topped off with community giving. Appalled by the growing number of homeless in the city, Smith formed the Calgary Homeless Foundation that remains a powerful force today – but still necessary, unfortunately.

"Sam was a great boss," Smith told Tyler Trafford. "He has superb integrity. He's a character. I still look back on those days as the happiest of my life. Sam and I grew together. I had a small company, Smith and Associates. To me, any deal was a big deal. I proposed to Sam that I could handle the opening of the hotel for the princely amount of $200 per month. Everybody was optimistic. But Sam was the most optimistic. I'll never forget that."

This time, though, Sam was a little overwhelmed. After the Leier brothers left, his euphoria over the Sheraton franchise began to cool. So many things had to be in place.

"It's the second largest hotel chain in the world," Sam told *Calgary Herald* writer Patrick Tivy. "It was a big plus when they asked us to join."

Even his buddy Art Smith had trepidations over whether they could pull it off; and these two were usually overflowing with optimism when talks of expansion occurred.

"I wasn't convinced that the Sheraton would happen," Smith added. "When it did, it was quite a coup for Sam."

Frank Nelles noted the positive impact on Amalgamated Properties' bottom line.

"The Sheraton business arrangement was a very good move from a marketing point of view, and at APL we were most pleased with the arrangement. It definitely increased business."

The Sheraton was an American company with plenty of global plans. The launch of its automatic electronic reservations system in 1958 – the "Reservatron" – was a first for the hotel industry. The chain followed that up in 1970 with another first, the toll-free 1-800 number. The company that Ernest Henderson and Robert Moore started in Springfield, Massachusetts in 1937 launched its 100TH Sheraton franchise in 1964, the Sheraton Boston.

"When the Leiers saw the success of the Sheraton Summit, they wondered whether I'd talk with hoteliers I knew in Edmonton and Vancouver," continues Sam. "Wolfe Margolus was a good friend and soon his Caravan Hotel became the Sheraton Caravan."

Sam flew to Vancouver to visit Ben and Morris Wosk, owners of The Landmark and Plaza 500 hotels as well as Wosk Furniture. He discussed the advantages of the Sheraton franchise and convinced them to come on board. Sam was also instrumental in seeing a number of Canadian hotels join Sheraton's network from Montreal, Toronto, Sudbury and Winnipeg as well as new American franchises from Seattle, Spokane and Detroit.

In 1973, Sam won the Sheraton Inns Award of Excellence. The plaque stated: "In recognition of his valuable services and contributions to the regional and national council concept as Canadian Regional Council Chairman."

In May that year, Sam was re-elected as chairman of the Canadian Regional Council for a second term, making him chairman of the Canadian Council of Sheraton Inns.

"I was traveling across the country promoting Sheraton ventures and meeting with the hotel managers about standards and procedures, plus problems, and just getting to know everybody," says Sam. "It was exciting. I enjoyed flying to the Sheraton headquarters in Boston and talking with the Leiers. We looked at where we were going, at other expansions and at all kinds of industry issues. The Sheraton was global and growing, and it was great to be in the middle of it all."

Being in the middle meant the Summit had to meet the Sheraton's high standards. Sam insisted on first-class dining at the Top O' the Summit and lured Gabriele Battistessa away from The Calgary Inn (later the Westin Hotel), to become head chef. Battistessa credits Sam for the lessons learned on the way to buying his own restaurant, the popular and enduring Buon Giorno on 17TH Ave SW, along Calgary's Red Mile.

"The Top was the place to go in Calgary and it was truly the top with food and fun," says Battistessa. "People felt they were in an exclusive night club with fine dining as well as dancing. Calgarians loved it and it was packed."

Battistessa also noticed that Sam liked to hire the best, listened to what they had to say, gave them the latitude to do their jobs, and paid them well.

"I learned about business from Sam," he explains. "Sam attracted the talent and also earned the loyalty of his staff. He believed in people and always gave them a chance. He felt that if you asked people to achieve and do well, they would."

"He respected what you knew and I always appreciated the fact that he listened to me and gave me the control I needed in the restaurant," says Battistessa. "And I also learned to smile at the customers and the staff. Sam always did, no matter what was going on – and there could be a lot going on."

A number of years later when Battistessa began Buon Giorno, Sam's mentorship had grown further into friendship.

"When I opened my restaurant, Sam would buy gift certificates for all his staff. He spent a lot of money in my restaurant and became a very good customer. He did a lot of promotion for me and never asked for a thing. I was overwhelmed with his kindness.

"Sam's been very generous to me. He's simply a great gentleman and I'm proud to have learned so much from him."

It's obvious to anyone who has seen Gabriele and his brother Giorgio at Buon Giorno that they've both picked up the best of Sam Switzer's hospitality tips. They're always smiling, always hands-on and always at the restaurant. No one works harder than the two brothers.

"Sam sponsored me when I immigrated to Canada," says Giorgio. "He's a wonderful man."

With those kinds of accolades, it's no wonder the Summit thrived as a Sheraton franchise.

Sam continued to hire talent as he came across it. When he called Betty Casat as a reference for a prospective nanny he needed, she was quick to offer her frank assessment. Casat was the business manager for the YWCA, and Sam thought he just might be able to deal with two employment challenges at the same time. Impressed with her kind but no-nonsense manner, Sam thought Casat might be perfect as the hotel's front office manager.

There was just one problem. Casat had been at the YWCA for five years and felt fulfilled and happy. Her accounting abilities and people skills blended beautifully at the Y to make a difference in people's lives.

Casat's compassion was born from her Saskatchewan childhood where love, hard work and giving were as ingrained as her rural roots. Losing her father, a farmer, at the age of four could have pushed Casat onto a path of singular self-absorption. But her mother, a teacher, pulled her family closer together, even as Betty stayed with her grandmother until she could reach the stirrups of her horse and ride to school.

For Betty, the Y was the perfect fit. It took Sam quite a few discussions to convince Casat that her current calling was simply a stepping stone to her next post. When Casat saw that there didn't seem to be a massive leap from a career in helping to one in hospitality, she relented.

Betty's business savvy paired with her basic benevolence proved perfect for the Summit as she moved into the job of banquet and catering director in 1973.

Gabriele Battistessa recalls working with Casat at the Summit. "Betty was very professional and very nice with staff."

As Sam's life unraveled at home, he hardly left the hotel. He had revealed to only a few friends his growing unhappiness and by mid-1974, he sat down with Betty Casat for some simple advice. She was a single mother who had raised three children into happy and giving adults. Most of all she was content with who she was and what she had.

"Betty was just about the most genuine person you could find," says Rabbi Howard Voss-Altman. "I felt that when you were in her presence all was good. She was practical, wise, unpretentious and filled with gratitude. Betty was a terrific woman. She was raised on the plains of Saskatchewan and her perspective on life was unwavering whether you were worth 20 cents or $20 million. Her attitude was: 'We're plain folk; we do good work; we give back to the community.' Betty was so down to earth. She listened. Few have it, but Betty had that great gift for truly listening."

Sam simply wanted to confide in someone who understood the challenges of the hotel business but was also so caring, kind and non-judgmental. Betty and Sam became good friends, but Betty was also quick to establish boundaries.

"I kept asking Betty out for dinner and she kept refusing," remembers Sam. "It took quite some time before she would see me beyond the daily work and Summit meetings. But I persisted. When she said, 'No, thank you, Sam.' I finally asked what she was doing."

"I'm going horseback riding," replied Betty.

"Great. Why don't I come with you?" answered Sam.

"Oh, isn't this what I need – my boss wanting to ride horses with me," Betty later told Sam. "I didn't even know if you could ride."

At the same time, Sam was asking himself, "What am I doing? I've owned a horse but I've never actually ridden one. I'm going to make a complete fool of myself. Ah well, that's nothing new."

It took Sam only one ride on a horse to realize he was in love.

"With the horse," he laughs. "Because it was the horse that brought Betty and me together. Betty used to go to school on horseback in Frontier, Saskatchewan. Every Sunday, she'd go back to her roots and ride. If I wanted to get to really know Betty, I had to get to really know horses first.

"The thrill of riding in the country was liberating," continues Sam. "But Betty was very proper. Slowly we allowed our friendship to grow. I felt blessed in her presence whether we were riding far into the foothills or walking along a river path."

Horses had liberated Sam once before. He remembered the little boy sitting beside his father in synagogue, starring at the massive steeds on the second floor as they waited to walk down the ramp to the Union Milk wagons. It was their magnificence that had allowed his imagination to take flight all those years ago. Now he realized that the magic of the horse never really left him. He fully understood what the exhilaration of the ride was all about, the freedom to shed the complexities of time and space to race with the wind.

"When you get close to a horse, it's a deep and profound connection. The horse will carry you places that you would never go if you stayed on the beaten paths. A horse allows you to feel a world that God originally intended and that we have too often allowed to slip away."

As Sam's bond with horses grew, so too did his bond with the woman who would become his close friend, mentor and the love of his life.

For now, though, Sam was content to find a few hours at first light to saddle up the horses and break free of responsibility. By the time the sun had settled high on the horizon, Sam had soothed his soul and was ready to meet the rest of the day.

Before the 1975 Grey Cup came to Calgary on November 23RD, Sam Switzer had a plan to punch up the image of the Sheraton Summit. At first, he felt he needed horses and cattle to celebrate the city's heritage and attract hotel visitors.

"The Summit had the large driveway in front plus the parking lot on the side. I thought there was ample room to build a corral for the animals," recalls Sam. "But a parking lot isn't a pasture and a hotel certainly isn't a farm. However, the cows and horses don't know that. They do their business whenever and wherever they please."

The stench certainly was not the drawing card that Sam envisaged for his hotel. He needed a new idea fast. Betty Casat talked to Ralph White, a longtime Summit customer who lived in Bragg Creek.

"Why not a mule?" suggested White. "They only do their business after they've fed. You can train them when and where to go. No manure or other mess to clean up."

Why not a mule indeed? By the time Betty told friends and other customers that Sam needed a mule, the Calgary Stockyard came calling.

"As soon as I saw her, I knew I'd be out $200," says Sam. "She was a dark bay beauty and the friendliest mule I'd ever met. She was also the only mule I'd ever met.

"Now I owned a mule. This was going to be so easy. Just find somebody to train the mule to pull a cart. Then build or buy a cart with a comfortable seat. Attach the reins from the cart to the mule. Hop on the seat and hold the reins. Gently guide the mule around the Summit driveway or parking lot or recesses of my mind, whichever seemed even remotely accessible at the time."

Ralph White answered Sam's plea with the perfect person to train a mule. Elmer was his name, and he lived in a stark log cabin on the Elkana Guest Ranch outside Bragg Creek.

"Maybe I should have talked with him about my mother-in-law," joked Sam.

Then he got serious, and soon the mule and Sam were on their way to talk to the trainer. "Who am I training?" asked Elmer, and Sam quickly took his cue to leave.

Then he called another friend, Calgary Stampede president Stew Barker, and asked a simple favour. "Do you know where I can find a cart for my mule?"

"Of course I do," said Stew.

Soon Sam was leafing through Stew's carriage catalogue to find an idyllic mule cart complete with bicycle wheels and a seat for Sam.

"Now all I need to do is contact a man in Spokane who can fly it to Calgary," he said.

"What are you smoking?" said the man from Spokane. "This cart can't fly."

"I know the cart can't fly," replied Sam. "What I'd like to do is buy the cart and have it shipped by air."

When the cart touched down, Sam quickly took it to the Elkana Ranch, where Elmer would train the mule to walk and trot and pull its load.

"When Elmer was finished training the mule, he set his sights on training me," says Sam, recalling his suspicions. "I'm used to pulling a heavy load, but this was ridiculous. Hooking up a pony harness to an unhappy mule attached to an unsteady cart with a bumbling rookie on top trying to drive the clumsy contraption was madness. I felt like a last-minute entry to the Marx Brother's Day at the Races. I may just as well have been heading for a three-ring circus as a hotel."

Besides, where would Sam house his mule and cart? The Summit was a sumptuous hotel, not a 12-storey outbuilding. Sam turned to another old friend, master cabinetmaker Kai Smed, who smiled at his plight and told him to relax.

"I thought he was making fun of me and my mule," says Sam. "But no, Kai was making a corral for us. Well, actually it was just for the mule, but it was built of beautiful walnut and there were times I felt I belonged there more than the mule. But the mule and I soon got into a routine. Every day after she fed, I'd take her to the banks of the Bow River to drink."

The Summit sponsored a month-long contest to name the mule, and received hundreds of suggestions – some refined, several ridiculous and a few downright rude. Yet one name stuck, and it wasn't Sam.

"We called her Sally, and with all the publicity she became quite the hit," recalls Sam. "Then the Grey Cup Committee called and wanted to know if the player of the year, Willie Burton, could ride in Sally's wagon for the Grey Cup parade."

The 63RD Grey Cup was played at McMahon Stadium on November 23RD, 1975. There were 32,454 boisterous fans and one mule named Sally. The Edmonton Eskimos defeated the Montreal Alouettes 9 to 8 but one of the most talked-about stars of the game was the one who really knew how to kick butt: Sally.

"Now I had a famous mule, so there's no way I could suddenly say goodbye to her," says Sam. "Besides, Sally and I became buddies. But she didn't belong in the lobby of the Summit. I needed to find her a good pasture."

On one of his jaunts to Bragg Creek, Sam had come across Don Saunders, a respected horse trader. Sam called to see if Saunders would board Sally until a more permanent solution presented itself. Saunders agreed and took Sally for a monthly fee that would barely cover her feed: $10. Relieved that his star had a home in the country, Sam said goodbye to Sally and headed back to the city.

Barely a month later, Sam received a furious phone call. It was Saunders, and he was hopping. So were his horses, and that was the problem. Sally was a breakout artist, and every time she smashed a fence, Saunders' horses fled their paddock.

"Poor Saunders and poor Sally," says Sam. "It was a blow for both of them. And I'm not feeling so good myself. In any event, Sally's out of a home and we're both into a new dilemma."

Which is how Sam purchased a ranch. Of course, the property didn't start out as a ranch, but simply 320 acres of pristine wilderness. Sally needed a permanent pasture and the half section just two miles south of Bragg Creek seemed perfect.

"Betty and I toured the property and we fell in love with it," recalls Sam. "There was no house or any building on it, except for this ramshackle of a cabin that looked like it could well have been the original quarters. I offered the asking price and expected an acceptance."

The property was owned by Bill Richards, the CEO of Dome Petroleum, who considered the offer and then decided to take the land off the market. Bolstered by the beauty of the property, Sam persevered and in the end Richards agreed to an all-cash deal. Now Sally had a place to roam, once her corral was built, and Sam had some peace of mind – at least until his next adventure. Sally only increased her fan base when she again starred in the Sheraton lobby during the 1976 Calgary Stampede. The *Calgary Herald*'s Johnny Hopkins was captivated by Sally, calling her out in his column of July 17, 1976.

"A lot of entertainers probably would have been happy to have received the attention the Sheraton's mule did," Hopkins wrote. "The beast (steed?) is called Sally and has been in the lobby of the hotel during Stampede. Owner Sam Switzer is very pleased because she is the only 'employee' who hasn't asked for a raise. She'll be used in a lot of the Sheraton promotions from here on in. Says Switzer: 'She's really popular and I couldn't begin to guess how many times she has had her picture taken the last few days.' Switzer also admits that not one person has asked him for his picture."

Sam's faith in Sally did not go unnoticed by the Sheraton brass. Her popularity with the public during Grey Cup and the Calgary Stampede won him a Sheraton Hotels' award for the best advertising campaign of the year.

"You had to love the industry, because it consumed you," says Sam, and then he remembers the very words he told the *Calgary Herald*'s Patrick Tivy over 35 years ago. "I got romanced by the hotel business."

Sam was delighted that the Summit was a respected member of the Sheraton franchise. The hotel was also a critical component of Amalgamated Properties, and the public company continued to produce dividends even when the new Four Seasons appeared on the competitive scene in 1976. It was a challenging time, as the *Calgary Herald* reported on May 30, 1977, after APL's annual general meeting.

"Revenue from the hotel operation increased less than the rate of inflation in the 1976 fiscal year to $3.3 million from $3.2 million. APL chairman Frank Nelles said the slow revenue growth was due to increased competition in the Calgary hotel market with the full impact of the Four Seasons hotel showing up for the first time. Equally, apartment revenues were stable during the fiscal year because of rent controls, he said."

The meeting offered an update on the first stage of Summit renovations and plans for the next stage, where the cavernous tavern would be converted into a smart dining room plus a cocktail lounge with a dancing floor. But it was the first phase that had created quite the stir on the Calgary entertainment scene.

"I loved the Top O' the Summit and everyone enjoyed the entertainment," says Sam. "But the reality was that it was losing a lot of money – close to $60,000 a year. The last straw was when I got a fascinating phone call from the hotel in the middle of the night."

It all began when a loyal hotel guest had returned from the Top restaurant to his room. As he opened his floor-to-ceiling windows, he was shocked at the spectacle unfolding right before his eyes. Boxes of food were being lowered on a rope from above his window to a car in the parking lot. The guest immediately phoned the hotel operator – duly noting that this was quite the customer service.

Sam had an inkling about the constant thefts, and when the call came, he raced to the hotel. From his front-row seat, he gaped at this unannounced pre-dawn performance. Sam rushed upstairs to the restaurant and confronted the thief.

"I knew something funny was happening," he said. "When I saw the boxes of food, I was furious. They were filled with the best steaks, lamb, butter and cheese. Anything that was expensive was in the box. I asked him, 'Why?' I was beyond shocked. We paid good wages and benefits. When I confronted him, naturally I wanted to fire him on the spot."

The chef convinced Sam that the recalcitrant was gifted at what he did and deserved another chance.

"I wouldn't call theft a gift," countered Sam. But in the end, he relented and allowed the contrite thief to remain at the Summit. Overjoyed, the thief promised to mend his ways, and a disillusioned Sam walked away.

By the end of February 1977, the celebrated Top O' the Summit was no more. It was the end of an era of entertainment extravaganza that had transported Calgarians to Las Vegas and beyond. On the eve of the Top's closing, both *Calgary Herald* columnist Johnny Hopkins and feature writer Patrick Tivy took an introspective look at the Top.

"Switzer, who at one time owned enough apartment blocks to be called, quite properly, the city's biggest landlord, pretty well pioneered the dining-entertainment concept in the city," wrote Hopkins. "He stood alone, so to speak, here when Edmonton had a dozen or so such operations going.

"The Sheraton was just about completed, and it was the tallest building in the city, which is more than ample evidence that a lot can happen in 10 years," Hopkins continued. "Although the hotel is no longer a landmark, it will remain as something resembling a tribute to Switzer's courage. He knew nothing about the food business, but he elected to press bravely ahead without the funding that existed, say for such projects as The Calgary Tower and The Calgary Inn."

Sam recalls Hopkins' words with affection although he still begs to differ on the "food business" point.

"Johnny was very kind when we closed the Top, but I did, indeed, have food business experience," says Sam. "I had the Yavvis coffee shop, of course. What I didn't have, until the Summit, was the very distinct experience of fine dining. And dancing. And all that amazing entertainment. The Top O' the Summit was surely something!"

ABOVE: Sam at the Wailing Wall, Jerusalem, 2010

TOP LEFT: Wolf Baer Scwajcer and wife, late 1800s.

TOP RIGHT: Myer Switzer's Polish passport.

LEFT: Myer and Chaiya Switzer at their 50th anniversary.

FACING PAGE TOP: The Polish Jewish Family Loan Association in 1936.

FACING PAGE BOTTOM: Sam's sister Becky's wedding to Morris Mendelman, 1931. From left to right: Sam's sister Jessie; Sam; Sam's sister Lily; Frank Skolve; Morris Mendelman; Becky; Ralph Switzer; Minnie Gorasht; Dave Switzer; Sam's sister Diane; Bertha (Switzer) Gold; Lily (Fishman) Manischewitz.

NON-NEGOTIABLE NON-TRANSFERABLE

No. _____ $ _____

Founders
and
Charter
Members
of

Founded
October 11th
1931

Calgary, Alberta

The Polish-Jewish Family Loan Association

This is to Certify that _____ Isshel Switzer _____ of the City of Calgary,

in the Province of Alberta, has made contributions to the Society for the year ending December 31st,
A.D. 19__, to the total amount of $ _____ Three Dollars and Too

Dated at the City of Calgary, in the Province of Alberta, this __ day of _____ A.D., 19__

PRESIDENT   SECRETARY

TOP LEFT: Sam and Aneta's wedding, August 1952. TOP RIGHT: Sam, Aneta and first-born, Darlene, 1953.

BOTTOM: Sam at the wheel of My Fair Lady.

TOP LEFT: Sam and Aneta in Cuba, 1959.

TOP RIGHT: Sam and Aneta in Berlin, early 1960s.

BOTTOM: Darlene, Aneta, Lorne and Sam in Acapulco, 1966.

CALGARY'S NEWEST DOWNTOWN EATING PLACE

Welcomes You

SAMMY'S COFFEE BAR

SAMMY'S COFFEE BAR — is located just West of the First Street West Subway at 208A - 9th AVE. W. Next Door to the Chesterfield Shop, Calgary's most modern Furniture Store.

We challenge you to find a coffee shop in Calgary that offers you ● **A more Friendly Atmosphere** ● **Quicker Service** ● **More Delicious Food** ● **Than at Sammy's.**

SAMMY'S was the first Coffee Shop in ALBERTA, with TELEVISION, and Sammy invites you in to watch your favorite programs as we are open 7 days a week.

SAMMY SWITZER
Owner

ALBERTA TURNER
Manageress

A very unique item at SAMMY'S is the Caricature-sketches on the east wall, of your favorite Calgary Radio Personalities and Announcers, which are personally autographed, and make for interesting reading. They are hand drawn by Calgary's Own Artist, John Bowen.

Each Day SAMMY'S have a Business Men's or Ladies' Special, besides what is on the menu. You have Four Specials to choose from which includes soup, dessert, coffee or tea at no extra charge.

ROBERT JACKSON
Head Chef

IRENE FULBROOK
Manageress

ABOVE: Sammy's Coffee Bar, 1955.

FACING PAGE TOP: A 1962 Greyhound bus tour flyer features two architectural highlights of Calgary: the historic Lougheed House and the futuristic Switzer house, 1962.

FACING PAGE BOTTOM: Architect Bill Milne also designed Sam's futuristic Auto Mart, 1960.

TOP: Sam at the River Towers roof pool, 1959; note the Elbow River in the background.

BOTTOM: Groundbreaking for the Summit Hotel. From left to right: Bill Milne, Sam, Mayor Grant MacEwan, Dave Halpern, CIBC bank manager Jack Williamson.

TOP: The Summit dominates Calgary's skyline!

BOTTOM LEFT: The Summit's Library lounge.

BOTTOM RIGHT: Top O' the Summit with, left to right: Danny Kaye, Sam, Aneta, Dave Halpern, Tibele Halpern.

**THE MANY FACES OF SAM,
1931 TO 2011.**

Sam's sisters:

TOP LEFT: Lily Fishman, Becky Mendelman, Diane (Dinah) Shore.

TOP RIGHT: Becky, Lily and her daughter Jessie Silver, Marsha Stein.

MIDDLE RIGHT: Becky, Diane, Sam and Lily.

BOTTOM LEFT: Lily, Diane, Becky.

BOTTOM RIGHT: Becky, niece Jessie, Lily.

TOP: Sam and his family at the entrance to the House of Jacob-Mikveh Israel, 1990.

BOTTOM: Sam and his family at the Switzer Family reunion, 2010.

ABOVE: Sam at Dragon Mall, the project for which he
received the White Hatter Award in 1995.
Photo: Calgary Herald

TOP LEFT: A postcard view of the Marina Motor Inn in Fort Lauderdale, Florida.

TOP RIGHT: Sam with his White Hatter Award.

BOTTOM: The Elbow River Casino; from left to right are: Carolyn Reu, Sam, Anne Christopoulos.

TOP LEFT: Sam and Betty on their wedding day, December 18, 1981.

TOP RIGHT: Betty and Sam at their ranch.

BOTTOM: Betty and Sam at his 71st birthday.

TOP LEFT: Betty's daugher Laurie Paradis, Sam, Betty. TOP RIGHT: Ron Casat.

BOTTOM: Betty's daughters Merrena Thompson and Laurie Paradis.

TOP: With granddaughters Valentina and Juliana.   BOTTOM: With grandsons Joshua and Noah, son Ronald, and grandson-in-law Brad Markus.

TOP LEFT: Rong Wang, Sam at a Chinese New Year ceremony.

TOP RIGHT: Sam, Peter Kearns at Suncreek.

BOTTOM: Grandson Robert Foster, Sam.

TOP: Magen David Adom ambulance dedication in Tel Aviv; from left to right: unidentified medical technician, Bill Foster, Darlene, Sam.

BOTTOM LEFT: Sam, Mark, Martin and Betty at Mark and Martin's wedding.

BOTTOM RIGHT: Sam and family at grandson Eliyahu's wedding.

TOP LEFT: Sam with daughter Susan.

TOP RIGHT: Helmi, Sam, Darlene at the opening of the Little Synagogue.

BOTTOM: John, Christine, Erica, Juliana, Valentina.

TOP: Sam driving wagon on trail ride.

BOTTOM LEFT: Sam driving carriage with Betty.

BOTTOM RIGHT: Sam the elephant whisperer and Betty, in Thailand.

TOP: Suncreek ranch in winter.

BOTTOM LEFT: Sam and Betty on the trail ride.

BOTTOM RIGHT: Sam fishing at his Loon Lake.

TOP: Sam and family enjoying the
2009 Calgary Stampede parade.

BOTTOM: Sam and Lorne with First Nations dancers.

TOP: Sam on his Fat Jones stagecoach in the 1991 Calgary Stampede parade.

BOTTOM LEFT: The Elbow River Casino chuckwagon.

BOTTOM RIGHT: Sam at the Stampede grounds.

TOP: Original Switzer's Grocery (early 1950s). BOTTOM: Switzer's Grocery, Haskayne Block, Heritage Park (2012).

OFFICIAL DEDICATION

Dean Bicknell, Calgary Herald

Sam Switzer, right, carries the Torah during the official opening and dedication procession for the Montefiore Institute, the "Little Synagogue on the Prairie," at Heritage Park on Sunday. Originally built in 1916 to serve a colony of Jewish pioneer farmers, the synagogue was abandoned in the 1920s, then was a private home in Hanna. A $1-million campaign has restored it and placed it at Heritage Park.

TOP: Little Synagogue Society and dignitaries.

BOTTOM LEFT: Little Synagogue on the Prairie dedication; left to right: Aron Eicher, Ralph Gurevitch, Sam. Photo: Calgary Herald

BOTTOM RIGHT: Official photo taken of Sam for the Jewish National Fund.

TOP: Sam, Betty, Colleen Klein, Premier Ralph Klein.

BOTTOM LEFT: Calgary Mayor Naheed Nenshi, Sam (2011).

BOTTOM RIGHT: Mary Kwong, former Lieutenant Governor Norman Kwong, Sam (2009).

FACING PAGE TOP: Alberta Transportation Minister Ric McIver, Sam, former Alberta Deputy Premier Ron Stevens.

FACING PAGE BOTTOM: Sam, Calgary Herald Publisher Guy Huntingford; entrepreneur and philanthropist Allan Markin (2012). Photo: Calgary Herald.

TOP: YWCA Gala with (left to right): Sam, Don Hewitt, Carolyn Reu, former Governor General the Right Honourable Michaëlle Jean, Anne Christopoulos, Dave Christopoulos, Rong Wang (2011).

MIDDLE: Sam and family at the JNF Water Recycling Reservoir, Sederot, Israel (2012).

BOTTOM: Sam and Prime Minister Stephen Harper at the 2012 Calgary Stampede.

TOP: Sam and family at the JNF Negev Gala, 2012.

BOTTOM LEFT: Sam receives an honorary Calgary Flames jersey.

BOTTOM RIGHT: Left to right: Frank Wilson, President, JNF Canada; Sam; Joshua Switzer; Dahlia Stenzler and Efi Stenzler, World President JNF; Helmi Switzer.

ABOVE: Sam receives his Honorary Bachelor of
Administration Entrepreneurship degree,
Mount Royal University, 2011.

As Hopkins chronicled the evolving nightlife of the Summit, he grew close to the impresario behind it all. He admired Sam's gusto, and the two even vacationed together in Florida. He knew what Sam had put into the Top O' the Summit, and that's likely why he wrote about it so poignantly.

"The city isn't going to wither and die because the Top of the Sheraton is closed. But neither is the city going to be quite the same without it."

Calgary Herald librarian Norma Marr remembers fondly the first and only time she got to experience the Top. For a kid growing up in Calgary, the Summit represented the fantasy of dreams in the clouds.

"I went to the Stampede parade with my friend and her mom, who was a waitress at the Summit," she recalls. "That morning she took us to her workplace as a treat. Not only was it the tallest building, it had the best view. We thought we had died and gone to heaven because that's how high it seemed to reach. I still feel to this day that I'd hit the big time."

That's precisely what Sam wanted Calgarians to feel, whether young or old. He had worked hard to create the mystique of the Summit, a place where legends came alive for Calgarians as they entertained and pushed back the long prairie winters.

Always hands-on, Sam was intent that the Sheraton Summit be a premier performer itself. The management had to be as good as the talent.

"Sam had to fire three managers before hiring himself to run the hotel," wrote Patrick Tivy, who noted that Sam not only took Sheraton management classes, but enrolled in correspondence courses, too.

"The hotel industry has got to be one of the toughest industries in the world," Sam told Tivy. "For instance, you buy your raw meat and you've got to store it, keep it cold, cut it, cook it and serve it. You've got to price it right."

And that was just meat. Everything comes to the manager's door, and if the standard isn't set to excel, the service suffers accordingly.

119

"You've got to sell service," continued Sam. "You've got a chance to use your personality."

That meant, of course, that you have to use it well. The hospitality industry isn't so large and intimidating that people don't talk. There are no secrets when it comes to management style. Hotels and those who run them are known for whom they attract and how well the employees are treated. Sam realized intuitively that respect, through actions and pay, would reflect a standard of business that drew any in the industry willing to work hard and bring their best game. To achieve that, Sam had to be on top of the buzz.

"The hotel developed quite a reputation," wrote Tivy. Yet he pointed to one problem that Sam was determined to stamp out fast. "The tavern on the ground floor developed another sort of reputation – that of a drug centre. Mr. Switzer met the challenge of the drug pushers by installing a closed circuit TV surveillance system with the controls right on his desk. He's also trying to discourage drug users by changing the atmosphere of the tavern."

Sam explained to Tivy that they would be renovating the tavern, "going after the older crowd – the 21s to 30 and up – that was what you might call pushed out by the 18-year-olds."

Sam detailed the renovation plans at Amalgamated Properties' annual meeting in May 1977. The first phase saw the conversion of the former Top O' the Summit into 31 luxury suites at a cost of $1 million. The second phase would be completed in the late fall and would transform the tavern; the 375 seats would be replaced by a discotheque called Daddy's Money, and there would also be a Dr. Munchies snack bar.

Johnny Hopkins lauded the changes when everything re-opened in early January 1978. "In doing away with the tavern, a great many problems have been eliminated," he wrote. "There are dress restrictions; not too rigid, but jeans and cords aren't permitted."

At the same time, Amalgamated's accountant and Sam's former brother-in-law, David Halpern, told Hopkins: "I think we have proved there is definitely a place for this sort of spot in Calgary." The Top O' the Summit was gone, but Sam Switzer wasn't about to let Calgary's dining-and-dancing scene escape his grasp.

He was convinced his new formula for casual dining and a disco-theque would be embraced not only by the Summit's former night clubbers but by Calgarians wanting an evening on the town.

CHAPTER EIGHT:
THE SEAFARER

WHENEVER THE FURIES FROM WORK AND LIFE STOLE SAM'S peace of mind, he headed to Florida. He could relax on My Fair Lady whether she was in harbour or under sail. It was Sam's place of peace, where even gale-force winds couldn't break the calm of his idyll. Family, friends and colleagues alike were quick to succumb to the warmth of both the climate and their host in Fort Lauderdale.

"Sam was able to be a different man in Florida," says Laurie Casat, Betty's daughter. "His personality totally changed. Sam would still be running at 100 miles an hour but he took time for fun and to show his guests the best of times."

Sam hadn't intended to fly his two main managers to Florida after the hospitality conference in New York. The plan was that food and beverages director Bob Perkins, and banquet and catering director Betty Casat, would attend the pertinent industry seminars and then head back to Calgary. Sam had booked the conference and confirmed three rooms with the organizers. But when they checked in, they were told there were no rooms, even though he'd been assured there was ample accommodation. For an hotelier to be denied rooms that he had confirmed for an industry conference seemed as absurd as a pilot expected to fly his passengers without a plane.

"What's more, the whole city seemed booked," says Sam. "Every convention on the continent must have been happening that weekend, or so I was led to believe."

There was no time to argue for phantom rooms and Sam was beginning to feel like Alice confronting the Mad Hatter.

They searched the directory for three- and four-star hotels. Every phone call brought a rebuff, sometimes friendly, but often not.

"Reminds me of how not to do business," grumbled Sam.

Then they turned to the two-star premises. Finally, Sam found them a place for the night.

"Well, it wasn't actually two-star," adds Sam. "But it was better than one-star. I think. I didn't want to test that one."

And a test it was. When the three finally arrived to check into their rooms, the clerk looked up at them askance.

"What do you mean rooms?" he asked. "I have a room. One. Not two. And definitely not three."

"But there are three of us, and that's what I was promised," argued Sam.

"Take it or leave it," replied the clerk.

With the area dubious at best in daylight, they were not about to venture anywhere else in the midnight darkness of lower Manhattan. Sam already felt like he had fallen down the rabbit hole.

"Maybe it will be a large room," offered an optimistic Sam; then he saw what resembled a former storage shed for cleaning supplies.

Squeezed into the room between a set of drawers and night table were two shabby single beds.

"We need three," said Betty.

The clerk who had trudged up the stairs behind them shrugged.

"I'll put a cot in there," he said.

"Where in there?" they answered. "There's no room. And

none of us is sleeping in the bathtub."

"You couldn't," replied the clerk. "There isn't one. But if we move the dresser and the bedside table out of the room, we can do it."

After a day of plane switching, seminar attending, room hunting and suitcase schlepping, they'd graduated into furniture moving.

"Is it me or is this dresser not heavy?" asked Sam.

"It's you," said Betty.

"And it's constructed of cardboard," added Bob Perkins.

"Thankfully the cot isn't," said Betty. "I'll take it."

Bob and Sam flopped on the singles and shut their eyes, worried only about whether the city that never sleeps would allow them six hours of peace. And bed bugs be damned. Betty was a farm girl who could make light of anything, except maybe those little red welts growing alarmingly on her arm.

The next day Sam booked flights to Fort Lauderdale and My Fair Lady.

"It was the least I could do, given the weather – the wind was howling and the rain was rushing after it. I'd gotten them into this jam. I still feel we were lucky to escape that – I hate to call it a hotel – flophouse feels about the right word. We'll forget about the bed bugs.

"When we landed in Florida, the weather was spectacular. Our little adventure in Wonderland was over. For now."

Betty was beguiled by the Florida climate that draped on her like a soft cashmere shawl. After a lifetime of harsh prairie winters, she understood the lure of Fort Lauderdale. It was a place where a visitor could take the tranquil moments and mould them into reflection and relaxation. Cloaked in a sense of renewal, the vacationer could return to Calgary invigorated and ready to forge ahead at full speed.

"Betty and I had worked together and become close friends," says Sam. "That was it. When we all flew to Fort Lauderdale after our New York experience, the three of us could relax and laugh at our adventure. The next time, I invited Betty to Florida alone.

That was when and where we saw that we would have a future together."

It was the winter of 1977, and Sam suggested he and Betty sail to Nassau on My Fair Lady. The trip would take two days on the open Atlantic, where a squall could come on board with the crack of a cloud.

"We headed out for an afternoon cruise to collect our captain and check that everything was in order," says Sam. "Then I heard a ping in the motor and I knew this wasn't a good thing. I called the experts, Suncoast Diesel marine, but they needed it for the day to determine what was wrong. Betty and I were staying on the boat, which was now in the shipyard. So much for a sunny winter cruise to the Bahamas."

My Fair Lady rested in the shipyard for 10 days as the shop foreman searched for the ping maker. From changing a ball bearing to stripping the transmission, the cost grew to $8000.

"I didn't need that nonsense," says Sam. "For those kinds of dollars I could journey around the world, come back and do it all over again."

The simple reality was that My Fair Lady, for all of its streamlined dream making, was an elegant hobby too expensive to sustain. Indeed, the tied-up funds could find a more practical and ultimately more lucrative Florida investment.

"I spent my last day at the shipyards, said goodbye to my yacht-weary cash, sailed back to Pier 66 and called a boat broker I knew," recalls Sam. "Three days later, he had a buyer."

All the new owner needed, besides the bill of sale, was an assurance My Fair Lady lived up to her claims of comfort and seaworthiness.

"Take her for a two-day ocean cruise and see for yourself," said Sam. "I'll be here when you return and I'll say my goodbye to her then."

Betty flew back to Calgary while Sam stayed in Fort Lauderdale and walked along the docks, preparing to leave his oasis of calm and contemplation. He sauntered across the street for a slow coffee at the Marina Motor Inn, where the unobstructed views of sleeping sailboats became imprinted in his memory.

"Why was I memorizing the waterways of my past?" asked Sam. "I'm here staring at the sailboats and this is happening right now. Just because I'm selling my yacht doesn't mean I'm selling my love for this place. I'm not searching for memory makers."

What Sam was searching for, he wasn't quite sure, until he finished his coffee and gently inhaled the 360-degree view of the marina. Then he knew.

"Are there any marinas for sale in the area?" Sam asked the folks at L.C. Judd and Company's real estate branch, just down the road.

He was jolted by the reply and energized by the prospect. The three-storey Marina Motor Inn on three acres of waterfront was both bankrupt and for sale. For a mere $1.8 million, the 142-room Marina could be his, including the restaurant, patio and bar. Sam fantasized over the motel's floating docks, the 42-berth marina and the traffic they could attract.

"I talked to a realtor there, Douglas Christy, who was a retired naval officer," recalls Sam. "I said, 'You've got a deal, providing it is as it says.' We drew up a contract, and I handed him a cheque for $100,000 with the remainder due in 60 days when we closed."

The very next day, Sam's yacht broker rang to say his buyer was delighted with My Fair Lady. As that deal closed and the marina door opened, Sam quickly called Betty.

"We've just sold the boat and got all our money back," exclaimed Sam.

"Wonderful," said Betty. "When are you heading back?"

"In a few days," replied Sam. " I just need to make sure that the motel deal goes through."

"The *what* goes through?" asked a shocked Betty.

"Remember that little motel with the marina, across from Pier 66 where we docked, My Fair Lady?" continued Sam. "Well, we bought it."

Sam was back at it. Whether in Calgary or Fort Lauderdale or points in between, if Sam sniffed a failsafe play, he wanted in.

Yet all Sam remembered was "the silence on the phone." He was quick to describe the Marina Motor Inn and her myriad advantages.

"As you know, it's all about location, and this one doesn't get much better," declared Sam. "It's the first marina that boats meet as they sail from the ocean into the Intracoastal Waterway. The depth of the water at the marina is 24 feet. There are so many possibilities to expand the small sailboat trade that the marina currently caters to."

The Marina was built by Leo Goodwin Sr. who had formed GEICO (Government Employees Insurance Co.) in 1933 and taken it public in 1948.

"Leo Goodwin Sr. amassed a considerable fortune, but unlike his son and grandson, he was not ostentatious," wrote Larry Keller of the *Sun-Sentinel* in 1989.

He moved his family to Fort Lauderdale, where he managed the hotel and his many other investments until his death in 1971 at the age of 84.

"He was a self-made man," Helen Furia, his secretary the last nine years of his life told the *Sun-Sentinel*. "He was just a wonderful man, humble and sincere."

The man's millions were left to his son, grandson and many institutions that Goodwin Sr. had supported philanthropically.

"Leo Goodwin III's driving mishaps were the subject of sensational headlines in the 1970s," continued the 1989 article. "He got dozens of traffic violations, and in one 1975 crash a Fort Lauderdale teenager died and another was crippled. A drug overdose ended his life abruptly in 1977. His death at age 25 triggered a legal battle for his grandfather's fortune and his own that only now is nearing an end."

Only seven months after his son's demise, Leo Goodwin Jr. died of cancer at the age of 63. He had been the executor of his father's holdings. As his son hadn't written a will, any heirs would automatically benefit. If there were no heirs, everything would revert back to the father.

But there was a daughter, Elizabeth Anne Goodwin, born out

of wedlock. Goodwin Jr. would learn of his granddaughter only after his son's death and seven years after her birth.

"By that time, Leo Goodwin Jr. – the man who once was worth $100 million – was strapped for cash. One year earlier, he had filed for Chapter 11 bankruptcy protection, reporting assets of $48 million and debts of $110 million. As the stock market plummeted in the 1970s, so did Leo Goodwin Jr.'s assets – much of which were in GEICO stock. From a 1972 high of $60 a share, the price dropped to less than $4 a share in January 1976, when the Securities and Exchange Commission halted sale of the stock for a few days."

Those days are far behind the multi-billion dollar performance of GEICO. In 1996, Warren Buffet bought the outstanding stock of the auto insurance company and has watched it thrive as a wholly owned subsidiary of Berkshire Hathaway Inc.

The death of Leo Goldwin Jr. provoked a glut of lawsuits and countersuits. It would take Elizabeth Ann Goodwin 12 years to finally claim her rightful inheritance.

Into this maelstrom marched Sam with his offer to purchase the Marina Motor Inn. Sam was certainly not averse to doing business over properties in bankruptcy, receivership or other legal entanglements. Like other smart entrepreneurs, however, he much preferred a clean-cut deal with a handshake and paper to follow.

"He is both a dreamer and a doer," the *Sun-Sentinel* wrote of Sam in March 1978. "A person with great patience and determination. Once he decides he wants something, he usually gets it! In this case, he had a master negotiator in his corner – Douglas G. Christy, one of L.C. Judd Company's realtors."

Sam's foresight in bringing the Summit Hotel into the Sheraton franchise impressed the *Sun-Sentinel*, as did his rise to chairman of the Canadian Council of Sheraton Inns.

"If I hadn't been the kind of buyer I am and Christy hadn't been the negotiator he is, the deal would never have gone through," Sam told the *Sun-Sentinel*. "I never quibbled about price – and he never stopped applying the pressure."

Sam's purchase of the Marina was quietly noticed back in

Calgary, where he was quick to reassure Sheraton colleagues and Amalgamated investors.

"This will be an important year for me," Sam told the *Prairie Hotelman*. "But we've accomplished so much with our reorganization of the Sheraton Calgary that I'll be able to divide my time between the two properties without difficulty."

Yet it was Sam's description of his new property that convinced any cynics that Sam had done it again. Even as property prices were rising in Calgary, Sam was shying away from paying top dollar in his hometown. Florida offered a warm alternative – where the price and location merged into a deal.

"This is the hotel you always notice as you bring your yacht into port," he explained to *Prairie Hotelman* magazine. "It is ideally located right at the lift bridge on the causeway. It's as easy to reach by road as it is by water, and it is just a few minutes from downtown, from the Sunshine State Parkway and from the International Airport."

Sam had flown back to Calgary to convince Betty of the merit of the Marina deal and to acquire the remainder of the cash needed for the close. Excited by his new venture, Sam also met with his brother-in-law and associate David Halpern. In the end, however, the two felt it was best to go their separate ways. They dissolved their partnership and equitably divided or sold their mutual investments.

"While I was caught a little off guard, I was happy that we were able to wind everything up fairly quickly," adds Sam. "At this point, I was more than a little concerned about securing the critical loan. I met with folks I knew at the Canadian Imperial Bank of Commerce. This is where friends and a respected track record take over. I was told that because of my reputation and collateral, the million-dollar request was considered risk free. The CIBC agreed to the loan and I flew back to Florida elated and determined to finish the deal."

He discussed the matter with Betty, whose business acumen he'd long relied on, and decided the Marina was a wonderful opportunity to enhance the company's investment and enjoy the balmy beauty of his own little corner of the sunshine state. What he didn't fully appreciate was the state of decay the owners had allowed the once pristine property to fall into.

Sam was no stranger to hotel renovations, and with Betty now beside him, headed into four grueling years of scrubbing and scouring, then painting, rebuilding, and more of the same.

The cleanup didn't just happen to the building, but to the books as well.

"They were a mess," recalls Sam. "We found all sorts or irregularities. One day the bookkeeper showed up with a big bag of coins and wanted to know what to do with it – after he kept his 25 percent. 'Say that again,' replied Betty, as wide-eyed as I'd ever seen her."

"Well," said the bookkeeper, "This is the money from the pop and candy machines. I take my cut and the owners get theirs."

"Not anymore," replied Betty. "This goes on the books and into the bank. That's the way we do business."

Not too much shocked Sam. But if profits were going into pockets, anything was possible. The amounts may have been small – or not, who knew – yet the culture of grab and go needed to stop. Within a year, the staff had completely turned over.

Sam and Betty continued to clean and revamp, turning the rundown restaurant and patio into a convivial spot for dining, drinking and relaxing.

There was really only one place where no one could relax. Yet Sam and Betty didn't fully realize how a person could take his life into his hands – or feet – by walking on the Marina's floating dock.

"True, it was a little dilapidated, or maybe a lot dilapidated," says Sam. "But we didn't think it could have lethal implications until one day Betty and I were walking on the pier to meet a friend. Suddenly, my foot crunched through the decayed plywood. I knew I had put on a little weight in Florida, but this was ridiculous. Thankfully, the rest of me didn't follow. I looked like a pylon deflecting people from joining me in the brink. All I needed was an orange wetsuit. I may have fallen, but I definitely wasn't finished. I couldn't say the same for the rotting dock."

That was it. Sam sprang into action. Within weeks, he had his plan, blueprints, city permit and work crew in tow. The floating docks disappeared by intent, not accident. Standing docks with concrete footings would rise in their place alongside a permanent seawall.

"We had just pulled the decaying dock down when the Army Corps of Engineers came to call," said Sam. "They wanted to see our permit, which I quickly presented."

"That's from the city, not us," they replied.

"This time, I'm shocked," said Sam. "I've been building for years and I know how important permits are. That's why I make sure I've got every piece of paper in hand."

"Well, you don't have one piece of paper," they continued. "You don't have ours."

"Why do I need yours?" asked Sam, gingerly.

"This is the Intracoastal Waterway that leads into the ocean, amongst other things," they replied. "It's our jurisdiction and you need our permit."

"I wish someone had told me that," offered Sam.

"They are now," replied the Army Corp. engineer.

"But I've hired contractors, a work crew and bought all the materials," answered the dejected Sam.

"Well, I guess you better get to work and get that permit," replied the Army Corp. engineer.

It took Sam three months of wrangling and wrestling with bureaucrats, but he finally finished his quest as the sought-after permit sat sweetly in his hand.

It was all worth the effort. What had catered, belatedly, to 42 sailboats would now serve 62 yachts each ranging in length from 40 to 70 feet. The daily price of 75 cents per foot would more than double as new amenities arrived, including electrical hook-ups and potable water.

With their Sheraton hotel experience, Sam and Betty knew the advantages of joining a franchise. They liked Best Western because the motels were individually owned, yet there was a set of standards, and members renewed annually. With the expanded

157 rooms, the motel soon became the Best Western Marina Inn and Yacht Harbour.

Over the next few years, Sam would increase the size of moorage that the Marina accommodated, moving into larger slips that anchored yachts from 150 feet to even 320 feet in length. Sam's foresight in constructing a permanent pier would ultimately attract one of the most famous floating fantasies in the world.

In early December 1988, a 282 foot castle of the sea was set to dock at the Marina Inn and Yacht Harbour. Donald Trump had wanted to moor the Trump Princess at Pier 66, where Sam had spent many years floating in the sun on My Fair Lady. But the channel was far too shallow for the massive boat, and Sam's Marina boasted the only dock deep enough for the Trump Princess. Yet Sam had serious doubts, the most critical being whether the huge yacht would breach his sea wall.

In the end, an assured Sam relented, and the *Sun-Sentinel* sent its gossip columnist, Martha Gross, to record the spectacle and interview Sam.

"That yacht will dwarf everything around here," Sam told Gross. "The fuel tanks hold 136,000 gallons. Imagine paying $150,000 for a fill-up! And it carries a crew of 35. Not just boat hands, but engineers and specialists from all over the world. It's a regular United Nations."

"The yacht also stocks enough grub for 100 people for three months," continued Sam. "And its cruising range is 8000 miles – one-third of the way around the planet. "It draws 15 feet, so it was here or Port Everglades. And we have 25 feet here. I'm glad it worked out."

Worked out? The Marina had garnered the kind of publicity that other hotels along the waterway wept for. There was the Trump Princess, nestled in her slip, at Sam's Marina.

Sam and Betty's deep commitment to Fort Lauderdale and the Intracoastal Waterway at their front door led them, in 2001, to donate $250,000 to the renewal of the area under the 17TH St causeway bridge. It was to have been a throwaway area – a parking lot. Instead it became a beautiful recreational area with a gazebo and a spot for fishing. On April 13ᵀᴴ, 2002, the city honoured the couple, naming the new park after them.

"The east side under deck area will be dedicated to Betty and Sam Switzer for their generous donation that provided funding for bulkheads, parking, landscaping and park-like amenities."

Duly noted in the Fort Lauderdale community newsletter, the Betty and Sam Switzer Plaza ensured there would be no wasteland on their watch.

When Sam wasn't working his nights and days away in Fort Lauderdale, he was doing the very same thing in Calgary. He needed to keep the Sheraton Summit thriving even as he moved the Marina into that phase called profitability. Sam and Betty buzzed back and forth between the two cities so often that they wondered whether they should simply buy an airline. That they didn't do, although they would soon buy the perfect Cessna for a number of their trips.

While the Summit Hotel and a number of other buildings still made up Amalgamated Properties Ltd., Sam continued to be a little wary of market fluctuations and having so much of his worth tied up in the public company. He never wanted to be subject to any kind of hostile takeover again and worried that the rapid escalation of property prices could trigger just that.

"Sam decided to take the company private," said Frank Nelles, the former chairman of the APL board. "He paid out all the shareholders and everyone did very well. They had earned between two and three times their original investment. It was a good venture."

While Sam would always be concerned about the value of his properties, he would no longer have to worry about quarterly fluctuations in the marketplace. He could concentrate on his holdings, and in particular, his two hotels. Their performance depended completely on his management and, in the case of the Marina Inn and Yacht Harbour, improvements that would increase profitability.

A year after Sam bought the Marina, Albert Reichmann called. He wanted to chat with Sam, who quickly flew to Toronto. They met at the Olympia and York offices in First Canadian Place, a fitting spot for the builders of Canada's tallest skyscraper. Albert was partners with his brothers, Paul and Ralph, in Olympia and York, a property development company that would first go global and then go broke. O&Y would better its peers and then collapse dramatically into bankruptcy in the spring of 1992. A year later the assets would scatter, but not irretrievably, as the next generation took what remained and began anew to build and thrive.

In 1979, Calgary had a number of important properties that the brothers had either bought or were interested in. Now they had set their sights on the Sheraton Summit. After the meeting, Sam was invited for dinner in Albert's home. What impressed Sam was the simplicity of Albert's life. As an Orthodox Jew, he lived without pretension and certainly without any servers to wait on him.

"We next met in Calgary, where I drove him from the airport to the Westin Hotel and then back again," recalls Sam. "Everything was very cordial, and the following week, I accepted their offer of $17.5 million with conditions."

Real estate was bubbling in Calgary, with properties in the core selling from $350 to $400 and more a foot.

"Things were moving fast and doubling in value," says Sam. "You could smell the boom."

But the Reichmanns seemed in a bind, recalls Sam. "The deal just dragged on. They had begun building Esso Plaza across the street from me and didn't seem so keen on closing our contract. Then we ended up in court."

It certainly didn't help that property prices continued jumping even as the deal didn't. The dispute appeared caught in the barbed wire of court solicitations, preventing each side from moving beyond the stuck deal. Yet the boom in property prices was going to bust. Prime Minister Pierre Elliot Trudeau's National Energy Program was about to land a left hook to the Alberta economy. It would flatten the province and bring Calgary development to a gut-wrenching halt.

That Sam's court dispute with the Reichmanns would occur over the climactic rise and fall of Calgary property prices seemed cosmic mockery at first. By early 1982, when Calgary businesses had fallen eerily silent, the NEP had done its work. Bankruptcies rose dramatically as the NEP took between $50 billion and $100 billion from the provincial coffers. Many Albertans smouldered in the ashes of bankruptcy and even homelessness.

Sam was caught in the middle of the court case and could neither buy nor sell. In the end, that worked to his favour as he wasn't caught in either the euphoria of the boom or despair of the bust.

"I had so much tied up in both Fort Lauderdale with the Marina and in Calgary with the Summit," says Sam. "Plus I was working from dawn to dusk hammering, painting, tearing down or putting up. There were days when I looked at the sky, I wasn't so sure the sun was about to rise or set. Yes, I'd played this part before, and the only person applauding me was Betty. You know what? That was more than enough. In the end, I was lucky."

How could Sam feel lucky?

"Because I was working my butt off in Florida, I didn't have a chance whatsoever to even think about buying more property in Calgary. I was focused on seeing the Marina become a moneymaker and the Summit even more successful. Of course, I had friends who were completely caught up in the buzz of the boom and they couldn't stop buying. But it was still all paper – even if the paper amount was $200 million and more."

With the NEP hit and the crumbling economy, a recession took hold. The former multimillionaires scrambled for cover.

"No one escaped," said Sam. "I felt so bad for my friends who were ecstatic only months before. They lost it all. It reminded me of the stock-market bubble and bust in the late 1940s. I was just plain lucky to be working away from it all most of the time. Even the court case was a blessing, but it sure didn't seem like that at the time."

But the real blessing was Betty.

"Betty was the compass," says Carolyn Reu, Sam's long-time business manager. "After they married, Sam would say of Betty: 'She is the perfect wife.' And now he says: 'She was the perfect wife.' They balanced each other."

Betty knew who she was and never put on airs. She steadied Sam's ebullience with her serenity.

"She was kind, considerate and caring." says John Ashleigh, proprietor of Avenue Hair Salon. "She gave great advice – whether on personal matters, business, leisure or travel. Betty knew I loved to see new places and she offered all kinds of tips for my trips. She was so down to earth, and whenever she walked into the salon, I knew I was going to have a great day. Her warmth and compassion were contagious, and everyone held her in such high regard. She said you always must give back and she continually did. Betty had a great sense of community and family. When she talked about the family or Sam, her eyes simply glowed. She absolutely adored him."

For Betty, simplicity was a reward for success. She never strove for wealth and opulence. What was important was giving, never taking. In that, she and Sam were similar. Neither had searched for a lavish lifestyle. Together they thrived, first as business colleagues, then as friends, and, more completely, as husband and wife.

"Betty could read people," adds Sam. "She was my best friend, my confidante and my business barometer. And I was the luckiest man on this earth when she agreed to marry me. I honestly felt like a big kid who had conquered the world. I ask myself to this day: what did Betty see in me? In her, I saw an angel."

Sam and Betty would marry in their favourite place in Canada, their acreage in Bragg Creek, where she introduced him to the magic of listening to the land and the creatures that wait in the bush. Sam learned to recognize the shrill of the hawks, the squawks of the raven and the screech of the eagle. He had never known the life of the cowboy, except for the thrill of the rodeo at the Calgary Stampede and, of course, the paperback cowboys he devoured in his youth. It was only at the tender age of 50 that Sam's boot hit the stirrups for his first horse ride. Within five years, he would become a cowboy.

For now, though, with Betty beside him, Sam truly had the sober second look at prospective offers and opportunities. She was the cool head for any deal that looked too good to be true. "There is no such thing,' she often said. And Sam trusted her implicitly. As for the court case that looked like it would live forever in limbo, all Betty said was, "Wait. It will resolve."

And it did. The case dwindled away with the economy as the Reichmanns and Sam parted ways for good. The Sheraton arrangement that Sam had been so proud of was also on the wane. Sheraton head office wanted Sam to agree to a 15-year contract that included his investing millions of dollars into a substantial renovation as well as expanding the number of rooms.

"Betty and I seriously considered the redevelopment, but it would have been a costly gamble in a difficult economy," says Sam. "We decided to give it a pass and return to being an independent hotel. Since we could no longer use the Summit name, we chose the Calgary Centre Inn. We also chose to think hard about the future of the hotel."

In the end, Sam decided to let his landmark hotel go, but only with the right proposal. Princeton Developments of Edmonton liked the downtown location of the property and pitched $325 per foot. Sam accepted the offer on condition that they lease it back to him until the 1988 Calgary Olympics were over.

The *Calgary Herald*'s Patrick Tivy lamented the Summit's closing while hoping it would "still escape the wrecking ball."

"Final checkout is 1 p.m. Saturday [April 30TH, 1989]. It's the end of an era in more ways than one. Twenty years ago the Summit [only tourists called it the Sheraton] was one of the tallest buildings in downtown Calgary. It stood all by itself on the edge of what was still a quiet residential district in Chinatown.

"Despite the changes of identity and paintjob, the brain behind the Summit has always been Sam Switzer. He dreamed it up and he built it. He hired the best acts he could find to fill the rooftop dining room, Top O' the Summit."

Citing the Summit's "unique example of futuristic architecture," Tivy called it "a genuine Calgary architectural landmark if ever there was one."

Sam was used to seeing architectural wonders smashed to dust. It had happened to the sandstone marvels of his youth as schools and buildings were blasted from memory. The innovative circular Summit hardly fit the concept of a heritage building for the few who even thought beyond Kremlin-style cement boxes. Bill Milne's ingenious conception and Sam Switzer's inventive construction defined the boundless creativity of Calgary after the mid-twentieth century. That the Summit fell to the allure of a parking lot is a travesty. Heritage and vision do not deserve to be buried in the dust of ignorance or greed.

"They paved paradise and put up a parking lot," Joni Mitchell sang. The lyrics for "Big Yellow Taxi" resonated just a little too cruelly for Calgarians who remember the Summit. The parking lot that replaced the Summit still sits there, looking forlorn, knowing its eternal job is to cover the grave of a grand idea.

Sam and Betty needed to move beyond the Summit. They were turning their talent and energy to two more hotels they had quietly acquired: The Inn O' Wizard in Orlando and the Elbow River Inn in Calgary. Both ventures were full of promise and anxiety, yet the risks would ultimately fill the coffers of Calgary's charities and more.

CHAPTER NINE:
THE SUN SEEKER

Sam had eyed holiday hotels before, and he yearned to add Banff and Las Vegas to his hospitality basket. Yet each would elude him. The panoramic charms of Banff had beguiled Sam since his first car trip from the mountains, on battered rims.

"I always wanted a hotel in Banff, and one time the King Edward was for sale," recalls Sam. " I owned the Summit and traveled with my good friend Ralph Kalef to have a look. It was up for $250,000 – imagine that. A pittance, today."

Sam was keen, but Kalef brought him back to reality. Ralph reminded him of the immense toil just to bring the place to where they wanted it, and to then market and manage the daily operation.

"We were so busy with the Summit and everything else, plus I would have had to rush to Banff every day overseeing renovations and general upkeep," says Sam. "I know I needed to be two people, but only if I could have cloned myself! All these years later, it still aches in my memory as if I'd rebuffed my best friend. Banff always seemed like a buddy to me."

Then there was the allure of Las Vegas. It was a place to fly away and forget a few dollars – and only a few dollars – Sam says.

"My limit was low – $200 tops – that's a lot for me," he adds. "Otherwise you could get caught up in the grit of gambling rather than the glitz," he adds. "In just a few hours from Calgary, you have left another blast of winter for the bliss of desert warmth. See a few shows, play a game or two and then head home. It was great for relieving stress and simply relaxing. In today's terms, consider it a spa for a guy on the go."

Sam understood the lure of Las Vegas and the simplicity of its formula for making money. He talked to his brother-in-law Harry Shore, who knew a few people in Vegas through his work with the Royal American Shows. It brought Sam back to the Calgary Stampede of his youth when his whole family worked the Switzer food concession where sister Dinah later met and then married Harry.

Through Harry, Sam was introduced to Johnny George, the games manager at the Dunes Hotel. The two hit it off and discussed buying a hotel. As only an American could oversee the gambling, George and Sam would partner a bid, with Sam owning the hotel and George operating the casino.

Backing off from the King Edward bid still rankled Sam. This time he thought he'd go with his instinct, plus he liked and trusted George. The first hotel that came their way was the Hacienda. A publicly owned company controlled the hotel, with the majority interest owned by a recent widow. She wanted to sell.

"We met three times and we had an agreement," recalls Sam. "When I flew down to close the deal, the lawyer she had hired told me that everything was off. Later I found out that he bought the place. That land was to become very valuable."

A few months later, the Aladdin Hotel and Casino came up for consideration. Again, the hotel was controlled by a publicly owned company.

"I liked it and made an offer. The owner accepted everything," says Sam. "Two months later, I headed down to close and went through the very same drama. Yes, the lawyer bought it. I felt like the fool in someone's silly farce. I can picture them talking now: 'Let's bring in the Canadian to set the price and then get on with our business.' What a waste of my time."

When the third hotel presented itself, Sam did not.

"They were eager to sell, but I was fed up," says Sam. "I told them, 'Forget it. I'm through with Vegas property.' I love Las Vegas and will always visit. But buy? That yearning is gone. I'll never offer again. As for my pal Johnny, he went to work for Caesar's Palace."

Sam turned his sights again to Florida. He already owned the Marina Inn and Yacht Harbour, but saw another opportunity only 340 km north on the Florida Turnpike. Orlando had been a tourist destination before Walt Disney opened its world resort in 1971. Then it boomed, until too many hoteliers overbuilt and went bust.

"In some ways Orlando was like another Banff – a beautiful tourist spot – but they overdeveloped when Disney announced they were coming," says Sam. "Builders were everywhere, and not too far behind them were bankruptcy lawyers. Sadly for those people, it was the right time to buy."

Sam offered on a 200-room hotel in bankruptcy and was accepted – verbally. That wasn't good enough for the simmering market. When a better bid came, Sam lost out.

"I did not want a repeat of Las Vegas," says Sam. " When the 240-room Red Carpet Inn on International Dr presented itself, so did I."

The location was perfect, as Sam always insisted, straight on the strip to Disney World. When Sam bid $2.7 million, the sellers shot back with $3.2 million.

"It was a reasonable counter," continues Sam. "This time, though, I was ready for no Las Vegas silliness. They signed the conditional deal first, before I dropped a deposit for the new price."

The Red Carpet Inn had modestly priced rooms and a restaurant to match. By the time Sam finished tweaking the hotel and dining room, his investment smelled of success. Or, more precisely, of bacon, eggs and pancakes. The diners loved the aroma in the attached restaurant called Granny's Kitchen. Granny may or may not have existed, but the myth hardly mattered when the food was so plentiful. Always hands-on, Sam and Betty carried and served the plated food to satisfied diners.

"We were serving over 900 full breakfasts in the morning," says Sam. "We used a cooking shovel to turn the scrambled eggs over on one stove and the pancakes on the other. The quantity was high, but so was the quality. The food tasted great."

The fast food chain across the street was no doubt furious that Granny's Kitchen was out-serving them by the shovelful.

"We were jammed, and customers were lined up past the door," says Sam. "First thing in the morning, the parents, each with their three or four kids in tow, were hungry for food and fun. As soon as they'd packed breakfast in, they packed themselves in the shuttle bus. Then off to Disney World."

Sam was often off with them if he had any spare time at the hotel. When Betty flew into Orlando, the two would quickly finish their chores and then choose to be kids again.

"It was only 20 minutes away, and we loved it," says Sam. "You got to be a kid with all that joy and wonder. The rides and the candy floss were a bonus."

The hotel was as deserted during the day as Disney World was packed. By the time the families returned in the early evening, they were exhausted and famished. But Sam was ready for them.

"Granny's had pizza waiting, and the crowd poured right back in for dinner. Remember Yavvis coffee shop? I was following the same formula. Give them comfort food, just like Grandma used to cook — someone's grandma, anyway — and you've got repeat customers. Granny's was a goldmine!"

As soon as Sam bought the hotel, he turned to his trusted friend Dr. Bernie Tonken, who was managing the Sheraton Summit in Calgary. Tonken immediately talked with Carolyn Reu, who had worked for Sam and Betty since the fall of 1977. Now they needed her administrative expertise as well as street smarts to tackle the new venture in Orlando. Carolyn arrived to oversee the actual purchase and remained to instill the standards she practiced at the Summit.

"Obviously, we wanted to make the hotel profitable," says Reu. "It was very different from the Sheraton Summit, where 100 occupied rooms meant no more than 130 guests. The Orlando hotel was completely oriented to families. In every room there were parents plus children. While the environment between the two hotels couldn't have been more diverse, management principles remained the same. There was a set of standards that worked."

The Sheraton Summit offered more sophisticated amenities and dining options. The Red Carpet Inn – renamed Inn O' Wizard – catered to families en route to Disney World. Sam and Betty had a comfort level with Carolyn Reu at the helm. All three were well versed with the Switzer family blueprint of hands-on hard work.

"Our customers were happy, and somewhere in between the slog and sweat, we were having a blast," adds Sam.

But the trip between their home in Fort Lauderdale and the hotel in Orlando most definitely wasn't. Sam certainly didn't want to sell their pleasant home, especially since he had purchased it as a surprise for Betty.

"It was so amazing when I bought the house, although Betty was a little stunned at first," says Sam, smiling. "I was just out walking one day and saw the For Sale sign. It was right on the Intracoastal Waterway, and you could fish from the front lawn."

Betty was accustomed to surprises, especially when Sam was in Florida and she was home in Calgary.

"One time, Betty wondered whether I might be heading up to Cape Canaveral to join the astronauts," adds Sam. "Betty relented as soon as she saw the house. It was so full of joy with family and friends. We lived there for over 20 years."

One of Sam's buddies was Ralph Klein, who, before his days as Alberta's premier, had been a Calgary reporter quick to break stories on the downtown scene. While Klein was on the hunt, he and Sam got to know each other well, trading tips and quips. Later, Ralph and Colleen would join Sam and Betty in Fort Lauderdale for a holiday getaway.

"We had great times together. Ralph and Sam had been close friends for so long," says Colleen Klein. "Sam was always a fantastic businessman, but with such a gentle soul. He and Betty were wonderful, giving people. They had big hearts and always gave so much to the community. They were true friends who never asked anything of us but our friendship."

It was the camaraderie of their Calgary friends, away from the wild and woolly prairie winters, that made Fort Lauderdale the perfect vacation home.

The kids loved the house for different reasons – it was a warm place where crazy play and exotic fish took hold more often than sheer work.

"It backed onto the entrance waters to the everglades and was the best house for fish," says son Ronald. "You didn't really have to cast your line far at all, as Dad's back yard had the most amazing types of fish. That's because when the tides came in, the water was six to eight feet deep. When the tides were out, it was comparatively shallow – no more than four feet."

Much of their food came directly from the sea. Besides fish, they dined on crab, Sam's favourite, as well as other shellfish.

"We'd join the crab traps together and throw them in the water. Then we'd wait and fish," continues Ronald. "When we had what we needed, we'd scale and clean the fish and cook them up. After hauling in the crab traps, we'd boil them and have a feast. Dad was in seventh heaven."

Benign marine critters were fine for fishers. But the ocean offered all kinds of more ominous creatures, including jellyfish, snakes, squid, stingray and sharks.

"Our joined crab traps were always fastened to the outdoor steel table on the dock," adds Ronald. "We'd pull up the traps, empty the crabs and then lower the little cages all over again. One time, as we looked out at the sea, we saw a huge six foot stingray zoom close to the dock. It saw the trap full of crabs and smelled dinner."

The stingray locked onto the imprisoned cargo, trying to pull and grab the crabs. Clearly frustrated that his banquet was beginning to fight, the stingray tackled the traps full throttle. As the creature clashed with the traps, it heaved the heavy steel table over the dock. Everyone watched it crash into the sea. The stingray thrashed against the traps and the table, paused for a moment and then started pulling.

"The whole place was in chaos," continues Ronald, and then quips: "I guess the stingray needed a table for his dinner."

Yet the Switzers weren't going to surrender their table without a struggle.

"Everybody was going nuts," says Ronald. "The stingray had this amazing strength. It wouldn't let the table go. Neither would we. It was a crazy kind of stalemate. We were exhausted – including the stingray, I guess. Because, just as suddenly, it swam away and vanished into the sea."

The clash of creatures stopped. Perhaps the stingray figured this was too much fight for food – even for such a delicacy. Fish were so much easier, and they weren't attached to a massive steel defender.

"We even managed to get the table back onto the dock," recalls Ronald. "At that point, we were so full of adrenaline that everybody was excited but nobody was scared. We stared at the water and the dock in disbelief. The mêlée seemed to go on forever, but in reality it all happened very fast."

Ronald, his wife Helmi, and their entire family were visiting Sam and Betty. That day everyone was on the dock and fully engaged in the chaos with the stingray. But the deadly creatures of the sea never stopped any Switzers from fishing. They had their priorities, and fishing was non-negotiable, even with stingrays and sharks on the prowl.

"Tiger sharks were regular visitors, and they're the worst," notes Ronald. "One time, a maintenance man was in the water, patching and painting the sea wall on dad's property. The wall took a lot of pounding and needed to be kept up. Suddenly we saw this shark fin swimming near and then it started weaving closer to the wall."

Sam was concerned that any screaming would startle the shark and send it straight to the painter. He couldn't motion the man, whose back was turned towards his work on the wall. Sam stood frozen, hoping the harsh smell of the paint would somehow mask the allure of human blood.

"Then the guy glimpsed the shark, freaked out and pretty well flew out of the water," says Ronald.

Fighting stingrays and sharks was one thing. But nearly dying when his friend's boat hit the rocks was something else entirely.

Sam's accountant, Ken Shafer, had invited him to go fishing on a quiet Friday evening outside Fort Lauderdale.

"We headed down the long rock-lined canal through the channel and into the open ocean," recalls Sam. "We were at least 25 to 35 km offshore, where the fish were biting likes wasps at a barbeque. They were everywhere."

The two were so excited, they simply ignored the sun settling into the ocean for the night. Finally, they were fished out.

"And terribly tired," adds Sam. "So we headed back, in the dark, at wide-open throttle. At which point, Ken missed the harbour entrance and smashed full speed into the rocks. I didn't even hear the crack because I was suddenly under the submerged craft. It was dark as midnight, but I saw this long spiral tunnel. I remember feeling incredibly calm and thinking, *heaven, here I come.* I felt a shove – the side of the vessel being pushed? Who knows – and I found myself swimming under the boat and surfacing on the other side. As I broke past the water and gasped that first breath of life, I felt free and without pain. Then I climbed onto the rocks and tried to see any sign of Ken.

"Suddenly I heard him yelling at me. I turned and he had his hands on the port side of the submerged boat, trying to pull the unwieldy thing onto this little island we've landed on. I grabbed onto the boat and attempted to rein it in. Abruptly, it slid starboard and squished me into the rocks, knocking me out."

Thankfully for Sam and Ken, the Sea Rescue Patrol kept their boats and services at that very island. They saw the two in trouble and sped to the scene.

"The next thing I remember is waking in the hospital with four broken ribs," says Sam. "Ken was just fine. It was luck of the draw which side the boat chose to keel over. As for the fish, they, like me, lived to tell the tale."

Sam's five-day stay in hospital was something he wanted to

keep from Betty. While recovering, Sam certainly didn't want to relate – or relive – the foolhardy fishing expedition that landed him on the rocks in the middle of the night.

"Betty would only worry and rush down here," rationalized Sam. "I didn't want her to see me like that, and I certainly didn't want to scare her. Besides, the Summit was taking up her time."

Sam asked the Marina Inn's manager, Shirley Kilpatrick, to assure Betty that Sam was swamped with the hotel renovation.

"I told Shirley that Betty didn't need to be bothered with this little incident," adds Sam. "Betty was so upset when she found out what happened. What if I had been severely injured? Of course, I should have told her. That was a dark night lit with lessons. You owe it to the person you love to tell them what's going on. Period. I never tried to be Mr. Strong and Silent again. Who did I think I was – Humphrey Bogart?!"

Sam and Betty were spending so much time in the U.S. renovating and reviving their first Florida hotel in Fort Lauderdale that their accountant was concerned their tax rate would jump.

"If we worked more than half a year in the U.S., their Internal Revenue Service would be at our door, cap in hand – well, more like a suitcase in hand," jokes Sam. "Our accountant suggested: 'Why not spend your weekends and holidays in Nassau?' Why not indeed? It was the capital of the Bahamas and member of the British Commonwealth. We flew to Nassau, reserved at the Quality Inn Hotel on Paradise Island, and settled in for a weekend of relaxation."

As they walked on the beach, Sam and Betty noticed a stunning condominium complex under development. One unit sported a 'For Sale' sign, and the two were intrigued. They contacted the developer, Franz Patella, who was delighted to escort them around the different homes. They were hooked.

"We committed to one that had a wondrous view of the boats and freighters on the ocean," says Sam. "It was a 1400 square foot two-bedroom villa still under construction, but available for $140,000. We stepped in to check it out and nearly tripped over this man on the floor. Talk about sleeping on the job."

"I wasn't sleeping," the worker insisted. "I was testing the carpet with my head and hand."

"Test yourself up," replied a curt, if somewhat bemused Patella.

Then Sam and Betty saw the unit they loved. It truly was a little bit of paradise on the namesake island.

"And it was already done," adds Sam. "We could move in – that night if we wanted. Plus, the price was the same. We shook hands right there and Franz became a fast friend."

With their work doubled by the two hotels in Florida, plus the trips to Nassau to escape the six-month tax border, Sam and Betty were burning the candle at both ends. Flying back and forth from Nassau to either Fort Lauderdale or Orlando was tedious enough. Having to continually hop between the two cities themselves was far too time consuming. With only one flight daily between Orlando and Fort Lauderdale, Sam and Betty were increasingly frustrated as they rushed to catch the plane.

"I had a customer at the Marina Inn who used to be a pilot," Sam says. "He knew planes and told me I shouldn't be at the mercy of commercial airline schedules. 'Buy a plane,' he said. 'That way, you set the schedule.' We went to the airport and headed over to a hangar where people kept small planes."

Once Sam had a sense of the size and type of plane he needed, he searched through the aircraft sales magazine. The Cessna 210 seemed perfect.

"It was tops," says Sam. "The Cessna was a safe, reliable seven-seater with a single propeller and high performance. They were asking $45,000 and I bought it out of Chicago. My friend flew it back and we were both pleased with the way it handled and felt."

Now Sam owned a plane. The trip between the two tourist spots was only 180 km by air and took him just over an hour to complete. If conditions were normal, that is.

"I enjoyed sitting next to the pilot," recalls Sam. "As we were flying from Fort Lauderdale to Orlando, the pilot suddenly looked at me and announced: 'We've got to find a place to land. We're running out of gas.'"

"Do we have a leak?" I asked, stunned.

"No," replied the pilot. "We're just out of gas."

"He didn't look scared, but Betty and I sure were," continues Sam. "The pilot got on the radio asking for the closest airport to gas up. They answered that we're half an hour from finding something. I felt like we were just sitting in the air, waiting to drop. The pilot kept calling every few minutes to see if anything was coming up. Betty and I felt like everything was coming up. I wanted to grab onto the butterflies in my stomach and fly them out of the claustrophobic cabin. By the number of fast flutters pushing against my heart, the flight seemed to last forever. We tried to keep calm by counting the seconds to nowhere. I still can't believe we landed without incident. Actually, that's not quite true. There was an incident. The first rule of flying – after you check all the gauges and controls – is to fill up. Not only was I full up, I had had it. The pilot was without a job the next day."

That may have been the first close call Sam and Betty survived with their Cessna. They got used to the others. Like the time they were flying to Nassau from Fort Lauderdale.

"As we were coming into the airport, the landing wheels wouldn't unlock," says Sam. "They refused to come down."

The pilot radioed the airport controller who told him to look in the glove compartment. There was a manual that explained how to release the wheels by hand. The pilot commanded Sam to grab the control, which Sam grasped with the clutch of a magnet to steel.

"I was glued to the control, and the next thing I saw was the pilot on the floor trying to crank the wheel down by hand," says the still astonished Sam. "Meanwhile, Betty and I were praying while my hands remained frozen to the wheel-yoke. It took the pilot more than fifteen minutes to finally crank the wheels down. I imagined us circling the skies forever, like the Flying Dutchman. Finally, the pilot succeeded and brought the plane in for an exceptionally smooth landing. Of course, I would remember any landing as smooth after that ordeal. My handprints never left that wheel. Thankfully, we did."

The kids – adults of course – still laugh when they recall the Cessna stories.

"That airplane," exclaims Sam's son John. "I remember the time that the pilot lost all our luggage in the middle of the runway at Orlando. He hadn't fastened the storage door correctly – obviously! The pilot had to slow our take-off speed and then stop so we could pick up all the luggage. Of course, we're sitting in the plane and praying that we don't take off, don't crash, and don't get smashed by another plane just landing. The air traffic controller had to radio a couple of jets to change their landing patterns, while a few others had to stay put rather than take off. We taxied back to the gate, got out of the Cessna, searched for our luggage and handed it to the pilot, who stored it back on the plane. Then we boarded once more and taxied again for take off. You can only imagine how comfortable we were taking off with this pilot again!"

"Then there was the time we were flying to Nassau and nearly missed the runway," continues John. "I know my Dad loved his little Cessna, but the rest of us weren't so enamored. I still think it was too expensive – and dangerous to boot. But that's just me, and as you can see, I survived the Cessna."

As Sam and Betty enjoyed their gateway to paradise, they still had a number of operations to manage, especially their two Florida hotels. That dropped to one soon after an English gentleman came calling.

"He was quite forthright and asked if I wanted to sell the Inn O' Wizard," recalls Sam. "After all the work we'd put in, I wanted to enjoy the place and a few profits, of course. Naturally, I said no, and expected him to leave."

But the man was undeterred. "Everything has a price," he replied.

Then he told Sam he was merely the middleman for a group of global investors who were serious buyers and hoped to receive a proposal.

"He was staying with us in the hotel, so I agreed to meet him in the morning for breakfast," adds Sam. "I called Betty, who was at the Summit in Calgary, and asked her advice."

By the time the two finished on the phone, they had figured

all the equity – sweat, time and material – that they'd invested in the Inn.

"We placed the price at $7.5 million," continued Sam. "We asked for a non-refundable deposit of $200,000 and waited for the cool Englishman to counter. He didn't flinch. He didn't blink. Most of all, he didn't say 'No.' In fact, he said, 'Fine.' That was it."

Sam gave the agent the name and number of his lawyer, Bob Miltenberg, who quickly called from Fort Lauderdale the following day.

"The cheque – for $200,000 – is here, and it's good," the eager Miltenberg told Sam.

"That's all I needed to know," says Sam. "The deal was done. I soon learned that my secret buyers were investors from Japan who had already acquired four other hotels in the Orlando area."

For Sam and Betty, the Orlando sale meant more time in Paradise to relax, boat, walk, swim, fish and eat. But mainly to escape the stress of the continent.

"Most of us who flew into Nassau were a little worried about our planes," says Sam. "It wasn't the airport, which has a great landing field for private planes. The control tower was tall and they put you on the airwave so you knew where you were flying every 15 minutes."

"No, it was the drug lords, who favoured this type of plane. We were concerned about hijacking," continues Sam. "The Cessna had high wings so you could easily see below. It was so simple to spot. I had special clamps to lock in the wheels so they couldn't move. That made theft a little harder for any hijacker."

The first time Sam and Betty took a taxi to the Nassau airport for their return flight to Fort Lauderdale, they counted all their Bahamian coins and gave them to the driver.

"We couldn't use their currency in Florida, of course, so we left the driver with everything, which included a good tip," says Sam. "It also included the $15 for our exit permit to leave Nassau. I rushed to find the driver, who thankfully hadn't yet picked up a fare. I pleaded with him to lend us the money and said we'd double it back to him.

"Just go see Mr. Franz Patella and tell him what we said," I told the driver. "He'll give it to you for sure. And he did!"

Sam and Betty loved island living because the warmth of the people matched that of the climate. It was a slow-paced life full of friends and food. Whether catching fish or conch, picking fruit or cracking coconuts, they learned to leave their watches behind and find the time by the arc of the sun. They trusted the locals for where to eat and what to see, finding the food "out of this world." How could it be otherwise in Paradise?

Their good friend Franz Patella had not only developed their Paradise villa, but lived in the complex, too.

"He had a special building for filleting fish," adds Sam. "He'd take his boat 70 km or so into the ocean and he'd always come back with a boatful of all kinds of fish. Then he'd share them with us. We had great times together."

"Want to know how to make conch salad?" continues Sam. "First you buy a tenderizer hammer. Then you pound the conch. Just when you think you've got it where you want it, that's exactly when you have to really start pounding. After that, the rest is easy."

Just like life on Paradise Island. Pound away the days, months and years working and maybe you'll find paradise on an island. Whether it's in your mind or in an actual tropical hideaway, it can serve the same menu for relaxation – if you allow it.

Yet it all ended too tragically for Franz Patella. While driving to a Miami boat show, he was brutally murdered.

"He had rented a Buick and on the way to the show, got lost in Miami," said Sam, sadly. "When he stopped and asked a man for directions, the guy shot and mortally wounded him. The murderer stole his Rolex watch and dumped him out of the car."

The *Sun-Sentinel* quickly reported the brutal slaying.

"Police charged a man with first-degree murder in the slaying of a millionaire Canadian who stopped to ask directions. After, the suspect told them, 'I just shot him,' then shrugged and laughed while showing 'no remorse at all,' detectives said. Investigators said Boris McKinney, 20, forced his way into a rental car driven by Franz Patella, 64, of Outremont, Quebec, ordered him into an alleyway and shot him five times in the chest. Patella lived only long enough to tell a police officer what had happened."

Boris McKinney was convicted of murder and sentenced to death. He later appealed the conviction to the Supreme Court of Florida. Their judgement was rendered and filed on September 13TH, 1990.

"As the foregoing argument establishes, the trial court appropriately found that the murder of Franz Patella was both heinous, atrocious, and cruel and committed in a cold, calculating and premeditated manner without pretense of moral or legal justification. It properly weighed these, and an additional aggravating factor against the sole mitigating factor found and imposed the death penalty. The sentence should not be reversed simply because the defendant disagrees with the court's assessment."

On April 8TH, 2009, McKinney's death sentence was reduced to life imprisonment.

"We were devastated when Franz was murdered," says Sam. "He was such a kind, decent and honourable man."

Patella had been part of their tight-knit Paradise pack that also included Calgary's master woodworker Kai Smed. Sam and Kai purchased a 32 foot Aqua Sport that they used to island hop.

"In Nassau, not owning a boat is like not having one hand," says Sam. "We used it for shopping, fishing, snorkeling. It was like having a car."

Sam loved to snorkel, but hated scuba diving. His foray into the sport was a disaster. Not only was Sam embarrassed, he says he was "disgusted with myself. Let me tell you the story.

"Betty and I enrolled in scuba-diving lessons when we were in Fort Lauderdale. We went to Key Largo where we had our sessions in a school swimming pool. To receive the scuba certificate, however, we needed two dives in the ocean.

"A sunken ship in the Keys was the focal point for our dive," recalls Sam. "The trainer gave us our first diving lesson in the ocean."

"There are a number of important gauges," the trainer said. "As you should know by now, your air gauge is the most critical one."

"The trainer told us what to do and precisely what not to do," continues Sam. "He also emphasized the buddy system."

"The buddy is vitally important," the trainer told them. "You need to stay close enough to touch each other. Never dive alone."

"We went on the boat with six other divers," continues Sam. "There were other commercial scuba divers around us. In fact, there were a number of boats in the surrounding sea. It gave us a comfort level."

It was time to dive. Betty went into the water accompanied by one of the instructors. Two other divers followed, and then Sam and his instructor-buddy rolled in. They were down 25 feet, in sight of the sunken ship.

"What a treat to see this old wreck covered in corral and be surrounded by all these fish," said Sam. "Now I know how they feel – well, maybe not. They've got gills and don't have to worry about getting enough oxygen – which I'm really worried about."

Sam was scared. The more frightened he became, the more oxygen he consumed. Too soon, there was nothing to inhale.

"My instructor was right next to me, and I totally panicked," said Sam. "I instinctively grabbed his mouthpiece and replaced it for mine. That first breath felt like I had won the lottery. And I had. As we rushed to the surface, I handed the mouthpiece back to the trainer. We shared it back and forth until we actually surfaced."

"You're supposed to point at the instructor and motion that you're out of air," fumed the angry trainer, just glaring.

"Then you should share," Sam shot back, not in any way aware of the etiquette of diving and dying.

"They didn't actually say what to do if you run out of air," continues Sam. "I thought my reaction was reasonable, given that I was about to die!"

Sam and the trainer chose to stop arguing and start swimming. Their vessel was visible beyond the two craft nestled in the water near by.

"We swam to the first boat, but one of the people on board slammed my fingers as they touched the side and told me to get out of the way fast," said Sam.

"We have divers coming up," they yelled.

"Startled, I moved away and swam on my back," recalled Sam. "Suddenly our own boat saw that there was some commotion and motored over. It was then that we heard the boat's radio and knew what the turmoil was all about. A diver was missing. The trainer and I were the only divers from our boat that were safely out of the deep. The rest of our crew had not yet surfaced, including Betty.

"If I had panicked before – I thought I was dying – that now measured zero on the scared scale. Someone down below had disappeared and was likely dying. And that person could be Betty. My heart was in my throat."

All the boats assembled in the area around the spot where the sunken ship lay in its corral coffin. It would have company.

"Suddenly Betty and the rest of our group surfaced and I was completely ecstatic," continued Sam. "But there was someone down below who never made it back. He'd left his buddy and ventured into his unknown. I flashbacked to my own trouble only an hour before. If I hadn't been with my buddy – the instructor – that body that they eventually retrieved could have been me. I still shudder over that."

"When we were safely back on our boat, my trainer, thankfully, didn't say anything about my behavior, which was, when you think about it, cowardly to say the least," adds Sam. "After the diver from the other boat had disappeared and died, the instructors on ours didn't bother focusing on my transgression. All they said was: 'We've lost one.' None of the trainers would actually say: 'We've lost a diver.' Or, 'A diver died.' Just, 'We've lost one.' Did they think this poor guy's death was going to scare us? You bet it did. I never put on a scuba outfit again."

When the instructors handed the students their completion cards, Betty had earned her diving certificate.

"As for me, I got a great big zero," says Sam. "I told Betty the whole embarrassing yarn. She was disgusted with me. So was I, but unlike Betty, I couldn't find myself a little spot to get away from me. Thankfully, Betty quickly forgave me, and in the end, we found a whole new love from the scuba-diving escapade: snorkeling. We didn't have to dive, nobody had to worry about Sammy grabbing their mouthpiece and Betty didn't have to learn to swim. Yes, she could scuba dive in the ocean with the best of them, dog-paddling her way to the boat. But she couldn't swim any distance if her life depended on it. Thankfully, it never did."

Betty and Sam's scuba diving was done, but their snorkeling had only begun. They'd slip on their gear – mask, snorkel, flippers – and head down the beach.

"There were hundreds of these little sea critters and we could barely avoid stepping on them," recalls Sam. "And their colours! They were a treasure in Technicolor."

The entire treasure would have been a fantasy too foolish to even contemplate for the five-year-old boy delivering found ice to the ladies of the night. That such fantasy was now Sam's reality was not simply the dream of a man who got lucky. Sam relied on far more powerful forces to move his life forward: God and family.

"Dad is a spiritual man, and honesty and integrity are what Dad is all about," says Ronald. "Plus hard work. Dad was never immune to working all day and every day."

His brother John agrees and adds, "Dad always means the best and I treat him with the utmost respect. I appreciate everything he's done."

When your children express such words that's the real treasure in life

CHAPTER TEN:
THE CASINO OWNER

SAM'S FORAY INTO LAS VEGAS MAY NOT HAVE YIELDED A hacienda, but it did nothing to dull his passion for the place. In his view, there was no better food and no better entertainment anywhere. If he couldn't have his own little spot in Las Vegas, why not create a little Las Vegas in Calgary?

Sam was never a big gambler, at least at the casinos. When he took any risks in business – and there were many – he tried to appreciate the odds before any money exchanged hands. "You always want to invest with the odds in your favour."

As a casual gamer at the casinos, Sam was just as circumspect. "When you walk in the door, put in your mind the amount you're ready to lose, not win. Make that your limit," he says. "Don't let yourself lose a penny more. This is supposed to be fun. It's entertainment. The sky's the limit for winning, but losing is not fun or entertaining."

Sam has never changed his limits of $200, even after a lifetime of betting a few bucks and winning a few more.

"I hated losing, like everybody else," he continues. "I just hated even more the thought of losing more than my limit. That always stopped me cold."

What didn't stop him was the lure of a new venture.

It began in 1974 when the North West Travellers Association contacted Sam to rent space at the Summit Hotel for their casino. As a non-profit society, the NWTA had successfully held two-day casinos at the Calgary Convention Centre, but needed a new venue. Sam agreed, and they were on their way.

"Operators liked the layout of the Summit, and as more charities were given casinos, we became their destination," says Sam. "Betty was in charge of the facilities and jumped at the opportunity."

Casinos were in their infancy in Alberta in 1974, but were soon to become an important fundraising mechanism, especially for charities. As more non-profits were granted the two-day events, pressure increased on the three casino operators in the city to find appropriate venues and equipment. Gambling net profits went to the charitable group after all the operator's expenses were paid, including the cost of equipment and rent.

The non-profits had another, more serious problem. They were required to provide the float that paid for the gambling chips. Banks were reluctant to lend the $100,000 cost of the float unless the group could prove it already had that very amount to pay for any casino losses.

Sam recognized the ludicrous Catch-22. Many non-profits must fundraise for a considerable portion of their balance sheet simply to deliver the services they provided. To prove they had the very funds they were hoping to receive after a successful casino was onerous and unfair. Why hold a casino night if you already had sufficient funds to carry on your operation? Borrowing such a large amount when it was uncertain the gambling would cover the obligation was the biggest gamble at casinos every night. Many non-profits, although attracted by the fundraising potential of casinos, simply steered away when confronted with the risk.

"It was too much of a gamble for some of these charities, which stood to lose everything they'd worked for just because it was a bad weekend at the casino," says Sam. "I told them I'd provide the float of $100,000. All they had to do was pay $200 that went straight into a pooled fund. As groups contributed, the fund would grow to cover any losses that occurred."

Meanwhile, the three separate operators providing gambling services and equipment were tripping over one another. A non-profit group would contract the operator of their choice for the same venue that another operator was managing. The current operator for a two-day casino would have to completely clear the premises of his tables, chips and other facilities just as the incoming operator was preparing for the next two-day casino. Frayed nerves – and worse – took over.

In the end, an arrangement was made between Sam and one of the three partners. The latter would look after all the gambling services for the casino holder if Sam would provide the venue, including all building costs, cleanup, insurance, advertising, and armoured car service.

"The operator didn't have the cash and needed me to co-sign a $30,000 loan so he could buy the gambling equipment he needed," says Sam."

Together, they operated the charity casinos in the Summit until it closed in 1989. During that time, the rules were far more lax than they are today.

"You didn't have the security cameras that you have now," says Sam. "Today you have special count rooms made out of concrete. Plus there's security personnel you wouldn't want to tussle with."

During the Summit casino days, the count room was on the second floor, some distance away from the gaming floor in the basement. That was rectified once Sam renovated the building.

"Before that, we transported the money in laundry carts that we'd cover with a hotel bedsheet. There was a glass door to the outside. This was not a secure operation," laughs Sam. "But somehow it worked."

What didn't work was Sam's short move into a second casino venture at the Calgary Tower in April of 1991. After two years and Sam's own investment of $600,000, the casino closed its doors.

"Betty never wanted me to invest in the Tower Casino, and I should have heeded her wishes," says Sam wistfully. "Of course,

I thought the casino would attract the downtown set. They had other ideas. Plus there was too much competition for too few casino days. Then there was the parking challenge."

Those were the days when gambling permits were so tightly controlled that only eight two-day casinos were allowed weekly in Calgary. With the Tower Casino closing, Sam took his gambling equipment, hoping to use it again soon. Eventually, he sold it to Frank Sisson for his Silver Dollar Casino.

Even though the Tower Casino fell apart, Sam was far from done with casinos.

While he was still at the helm of the Summit, Sam purchased the Elbow River Inn at 1919 Macleod Trail SE, just across from his old stomping grounds at Stampede Park. It was 1980, and real estate was simmering. While Sam paid $3.4 million for the property, he was soon shocked to receive two competing offers.

"I had formed a partnership with Dr. Bernie Tonken, whose wife Lil was my sister Becky Mendelman's daughter," recalls Sam. "We had barely finished financing the purchase through the CIBC when suddenly an $8.5-million bid arrived. Before we even had time to digest that, another offer dropped on our desk. This one's for $12.5 million, complete with a $2.5-million non-refundable deposit."

Sam and Bernie accepted the second offer and waited for it to close in mid-January 1981. It was not to be.

"Our buyer died during Christmas," says Sam. "He was a Hong Kong businessman who bought the property because it was so close to the river. He considered that good luck."

At this point, no one was having any luck. The man's heirs backed out of the deal and wanted their deposit back. Sam and Bernie believed the deposit was theirs, as per their contract, and the whole imbroglio ended up in court.

While the outcome ultimately favoured Sam and Bernie, the court case kept the Elbow River Inn away from prospective buyers. Not that there were any by then. While the National Energy Program had arrived on Alberta's doorstep in October 1980, the full brunt would be realized over the next year as real estate values plummeted.

Sam and Bernie together worked tirelessly to keep their investments intact. Dr. Tonken took over managing the Summit (now the Calgary Centre Inn) and the Elbow River Inn, while Sam kept his sights on the two Florida hotels he now owned.

Once Sam sold the Inn O' Wizard hotel in Orlando, he was freer to finance a few more property acquisitions. Soon he would be a leading private stakeholder of Victoria Park property, a fitting feat for the man who grew up there amid poverty, compassion and hope.

Sam also chose to renovate the Elbow River Inn and add a casino. Before the Summit closed, he bought and leveled a crumbling six-suite apartment building next to the Inn, then constructed the 14,000 square foot Elbow River Casino in 1988.

"We constructed Calgary's first purpose-built casino," recalls Sam. "We needed all sorts of permits for the casino approval. It took at least eight months. They even wanted to know who cut your hair and nails. The rules were very strict, and you had to be squeaky clean."

The wait and the work were worth it. Sam and Betty were pleased with the result and described the virtues to an industry website.

"The Elbow River Inn and Casino is located on the bank of the beautiful Elbow River, across the street from Stampede Park, only minutes from the Calgary downtown core and major attractions. There are 60 tastefully appointed, large guest rooms … full service hotel amenities, a restaurant, and a casino to win cash, receive gifts and be a part of the excitement."

And there *was* plenty of excitement, what with the burglary.

"It happened in the middle of the night after the casino had closed," recalls Sam. "Somebody managed to break in and get through our security that we had installed to prevent just this type of crime. They stole casino chips – $35,000 worth. Suddenly I'm left without chips and the casino is set to open the next day."

It's like offering a banquet full of empty platters. To order a new set of chips costs $50,000 and takes from two to three months for delivery. Everything comes from Las Vegas.

"My headaches just intensified," says Sam. "We called around to see if anyone had an extra set of chips that we could borrow. There aren't too many people you can call at the crack of dawn for chips to start your day – table game chips, that is. Thankfully, we were able to locate an extra set."

Sam was doubly thankful, because he had insurance for theft as well as the new set of chips. He also knew how to spot the stolen chips.

"When we opened, we knew we weren't using old chips," explains Sam. "So whoever wanted to redeem old chips, we would immediately know that they had either stolen them or purchased them from the thieves. In either event, they were both thieves because you don't buy chips on the sly."

Sam and the rest of the casino staff were especially vigilant for the stolen booty because it instantly cut into casino costs.

"Any chips that were redeemed, no matter how careful we were, would cost the casino," adds Sam. "We did catch some people who tried to cash them in, especially the larger chip amounts."

Of course, it was impossible to charge anyone trying to redeem the stolen chips, as they could – and did – readily protest their innocence.

"All we could do is keep the chips and store them away," continues Sam. "We retrieved nearly everything that was stolen, but it was useless in the end. Those chips could never be used again by a casino."

Yet if crooks really wanted to pull a fast one, they could try. Only once, in Sam's memory, did someone fully succeed.

"It was a big win," remembers Sam. "The amount was $90,000. Something didn't feel right about it. We examined the cards and sure enough, they were marked. Someone had substituted the marked ones for the clean cards. We knew who won and figured out who was involved in the fraud." Yet they never got enough hard evidence to charge the crook.

Those kinds of crimes are harder to commit in the modern casino world.

"This was something that casinos had to look out for," adds

Sam. "That's why only employees handle the cards."

When there's a large legitimate win, however, everybody is ecstatic – including the owner.

"Absolutely," says Sam. "That's why everyone's here. That's what they're hoping for. When a patron wins big, the news makes the rounds in the casino world. Whether it's here at the Elbow or elsewhere in the city – or province – people think they can win, too. Patrons come to see what it's all about or whether it's their turn on the 'hot machine.' The adrenaline is flowing, and you can feel it in the air."

What you don't want to feel is fear. The bomb scare happened during rush hour Friday, February 25TH, 2005.

"Just an FYI for anyone heading to the Hitmen game," posted the Calgary puck forums web note. "A bomb went off on the Macleod Trail bridge at the Elbow River Casino."

One post pointed out that, "the side of the bridge was charred black." Another noted that, "there was NOT an explosion – just a fire."

The chaos creative a massive traffic mess that ultimately turned out to be good news for the Calgary Hitmen. The popular junior hockey team was at the Saddledome that night. While the game was delayed to accommodate the late throngs, the team ended up playing to one of the largest hockey crowds they've ever had.

It was the exact opposite at the Elbow River as Sam had to empty his casino. There would be no crowds that night.

"We had to evacuate," says Sam. "It was the middle of a hard winter and the city sent buses for our patrons and staff. Nothing was moving on the road, cars were stuck in the parking lot, and nobody could get home. It went on for hours. Thankfully, there wasn't a bomb. The fire was blamed on some poor soul living under the bridge and going through some kind of quarrel."

Soon Sam's casino would leave the banks of the Elbow River to a new home two blocks north. He had hoped to massively expand the existing casino around its riverfront location, but the plan proved unwieldy and costly.

"The casino sat on riverfront property that was far more valuable for condominiums and townhomes," says Sam. "I decided to hold that land and find a larger space for a brand new casino. We'd build it from the ground up, and it would become the most beautiful gambling and entertainment space in the city."

Commercial realtor Wing Tang sold Sam some of the development land that would become part of the new casino property.

"I've sold a number of properties on their behalf," says Wing Tang. "I was not surprised at all when Sam decided to build a brand-new casino. Casinos are not for everybody. He saw where the market was going. He made his move, which was the right one at the time."

"Sam is a visionary and very savvy to deal with," he adds. "He's someone I could trust. In all our dealings, I've never had one single problem. The closings have all been smooth with no problems. We have a very good business relationship. Sam can be a tough negotiator, but he is always fair and upfront. He's very honourable and extremely pleasant to deal with. I don't get a lot of clients like Sam. I wish everyone was like him. I'd be laughing every day."

Sam had waited long enough. "I had to make a decision on the casino," he says. "Build it or lose out. I decided to build it."

At the youthful age of 78, he was ready for a new adventure even if it would cost him more than a few days of wonder and nights of sleeplessness.

In the end he was convinced that his little Las Vegas on the prairie was just what Calgary needed. But convincing municipal bureaucrats to sign onto his dream – or at least onto a permit – was glacially slow.

"But those many months of waiting were really a bonus," explains Sam. "The city may have been silent, but the real estate market wasn't. I was able to buy more land next to what I had already acquired. By the time the permits arrived, I was ready."

So were Sam's good friends who would be instrumental in the construction of the building. They included architects Herman Bell and Roy Lee, as well as Bob Hildenbrandt, vice president of Ledcor Group construction.

There were plenty of smiles when the project broke ground in the fall of 2004. "Even though it was a cold and miserable day, Sam was still jubilant," recalls Anne Christopoulos, his company's longtime accountant. With Ledcor's fast tracking, the building was ready to receive its visitors on June 22, 2005.

This was the very time that the Elbow River was rushing her banks, flooding numerous homes and businesses. That included the old Elbow River Inn and Casino, which Sam was forced to close when water overflowed the banks of the river and the city issued an evacuation order.

Sam refused to allow the rising river to waterlog his excitement over the new casino now opening its doors. Thankfully, the premises were dry as Sam welcomed patrons to the striking brick building on the corner of Macleod Trail SW and 17TH Ave. Situated on Calgary's famous red mile, the Elbow River Casino would come to boast a New Orleans ambience.

"We didn't create that beautiful décor until a few years later," says Sam's long-time manager, Carolyn Reu. "It was bare bones until we had the cash flow to make all the improvements that patrons now enjoy."

The prudence in that decision certainly made sense once the capital costs of the building itself were realized. Sam and Betty wanted to ensure that the new casino created more than a splash on the entertainment scene for the city, but made money, too. In the end, with Betty working constantly on the interior design, they got their wish.

"I wanted our customers to experience the feel of Bourbon St and Mardi Gras," says Sam, still excited that he pulled off a feat that would challenge even the fittest of entrepreneurs half his age. "We've got great food, entertainment and, of course, gaming."

The 80,000 square foot facility features two storeys of free underground parking – always a bonus in winter – and employs 400. There are 14 poker tables, including a 24-hour poker room, as well as 30 gaming tables and 604 slot machines. The casino also offers lottery, Keno, off-track betting and VLTs.

"It really is a glitzy place with its high-end furnishings, huge colour-changing ceiling lights and a fine dining area," wrote the *Calgary Herald's* David Parker on June 23, 2005. "Customers get valet parking or a golf cart ride to the elevators from the huge two-level secure parkade that holds 313 vehicles."

Casino legend Frank Sisson lauds the way Sam has broken the mould.

"In the casino business, he's been a leader," says Sisson. "He was in it long before I was. Sam stuck it out through good and bad. He just plugged away."

Sisson did the very same thing until he got an offer he couldn't refuse for his Silver Dollar Casino.

"People don't realize how you went to the dance to get there. It's the whole deal, and Sam worked so hard," adds Sisson, who knows a thing or two about hands-on hard work himself. "The casino business is tough, and it won't get any better. But Sam is good because he's got a great location."

"The bottom line is that Sam does a marvelous job and he's got very good staff running the casino," says Sisson. "They're long term, and they know exactly what they're doing. The Elbow River Casino Poker Room is the best in Alberta."

In the fall of 2008, Mark Breslin's Yuk Yuks franchise was searching for another venue. The popular stand-up comedy clubs are known for their take-no-prisoners form of comedy, featuring "live, uncut" comedy routines.

The license holders looked at the large banquet hall in the Elbow River Casino. It held 250 people and could easily transform into a Yuk Yuks showroom. But to rent the space from Sam, the franchisees had to acquire a different set of city permits. It took a solid six months of back-and-forth with various bureaucrats for the franchisees to acquire the necessary papers.

When the licensees finally got the go-ahead from the city, Sam was delighted that Yuk Yuks would have a franchise in his building. He told the partners he'd do anything they needed to make sure the space worked for them. Having Yuk Yuks at the Elbow River brought Sam back to the days of the Summit and its star-filled entertainment. They opened the doors to Yuk Yuks in February 2009.

"It is their show all the way of course," says Sam. "But I was thrilled the Yuk Yuks partners were at Elbow River."

Rosemarie Enslin, who worked with Mark Breslin in Toronto, managed the publicity for the Yuk Yuks opening.

"I'd wanted to meet Sam ever since he built the fabulous River Towers," she says. "He was the talk of Calgary. I loved working with him. He was always in the casino, but he was very quiet and I wondered whether he was reading my emails. Well, he was reading them, all right. Sam knew everything we were up to. He had the most wonderful approach. He always said yes. I felt like, 'Oh, the answer is yes. What is the question?' I think Sam Switzer is absolutely terrific. He reminds me so much of the late, great Toronto entrepreneur, impresario and philanthropist Honest Ed Mirvish."

Then, Enslin remembers one more quality about Sam that wasn't apparent at first. "I said he was quiet. That is until you put a microphone in front of him. He just sparkles. He's a natural. At the opening, he took to the stage with no script and dazzled with his remarks. He could have headlined Yuk Yuks all by himself."

Whether Sam is on or off the stage, Sisson is equally impressed with his tenacity.

"Sam just keeps going," adds Sisson. "He maintains solid relationships. But I firmly believe that Sam will be the last of the casino independents."

Sisson's words would be prophetic. On July 1ˢᵀ 2012, Sam sold the Elbow River Casino. Again, his friend Wing Tang handled the sale.

A few years earlier, Trent Fraser, president of Fraser Strategy Inc., a Regina-based marketing group, had examined Sam's business style.

"Sam is still the leader of the organization – an organization that he has nurtured through the recruitment and retainment of dynamic personnel who become part of the Switzer Casino family," wrote Fraser in his report. " I have worked with many of the directors, managers and staff of Elbow River Casino over the past five years and to a person they work hard to ensure they will not be the one to disappoint Sam.

"I have observed Sam making his rounds at the Casino, where he calls staff by their name, with a big smile on his face. Sam is a listener. He can often be observed listening intently to a conversation or debate, only to bring conclusion to the discussion with one succinct and intellectual statement. His time and experience allow Sam to see the world clearly, and his business acumen is exceeded only by his compassion for others. This iconic father figure understands how to build a business culture poised for success – by building a family."

Sam also understands the conundrum of gambling in modern Alberta. It's critical for the survival of many non-profits, but it can deal a blow to individuals with addiction issues.

"First of all, it's much easier and safer for charities to reap the benefits of a casino rather than the chocolate-bar and bake sales," says Sam. "I was always concerned for kids' safety when they went door-to-door selling chocolate bars and stuff. But I recognize, absolutely, the challenges of someone who is addicted to gambling. We at the casino do everything we can to help."

Sam points out that the casino places its Responsible Gaming Information Centre right next to the cash cage. He also explains how the provincial coffers are quick to consume the $1.4 billion that was added to general revenue from the Alberta Lottery Fund in 2010–11.

"We've had gambling with us from the beginning of time and most are able to do it responsibly," he adds. "I truly wish I could sit down with the problem gambler and convince him or her to gamble like I do. But I know it's part of a larger problem. That said, the profits of gambling help so many more people than it hurts. I wish in my heart it could help everyone, rather than hurt the few that it does."

The majority of the population can enjoy their time at the casino with no worry that they'll become gambling addicts. Only one percent can be cast as problem gamblers, according to the Alberta Gaming and Liquor Commission. Another 2.8 percent are considered moderate risk, while 7 percent would be categorized as low risk.

"Staff representatives in the RGICs provide support and referrals to customers that may have a gambling problem as well as assist and educate casino staff with the identification and monitoring of problem gamblers," states the Commission's web site.

Sam also donates a laudable part of the profits, after expenses, to charities. From local to national and international, his charitable giving is extensive.

"In 2009, The Sam and Betty Switzer Foundation provided financial support to such worthwhile organizations as the Alberta Children's Hospital, Mount Royal University, Heritage Park, YWCA Vermilion Skills Training Centre, The Canadian Human Rights Museum and Alberta Adolescent Recovery Centre (AARC)," states his company sheet on giving.

"Throughout 2009, Elbow River Casino, as a company, supported a number of charitable endeavours – from Special Olympics to The Calgary Herald Christmas Fund. We are proud that our staff have, independent of company funding, successfully undertaken such initiatives as collecting stuffed animals for children and donations for the food bank. The company president, Sam Switzer, sets an excellent example of giving, having made significant personal donations during 2009 to such local organizations as The Mustard Seed and further afield to such organizations as World Vision."

The donated monies are over and above the Alberta Liquor and Gaming Commission-mandated portion that goes to the provincial government.

In 2010–11, nearly $300 million of the $1.4-billion Alberta revenue from charitable gaming was funneled back to provincial charities.

"Proceeds (revenues less expenses) from licensed charitable gaming events go directly to the charities that conduct the events," states the AGLC's charitable gaming review for 2010–11. "These proceeds are used to support community projects and initiatives for non-profit and volunteer organizations throughout Alberta. Charitable and religious groups conducting a casino event keep the proceeds from the table games, less a service fee for the facility operator."

The AGLC's annual review also points out that part of the take from slot machines and electronic bingo goes to charities, too. That's good to know, since the slot machines, while a lot of fun for patrons, take their good sweet time before the player whoops out with a win.

"The difference between table games and slot machines is that slots are entirely predictable," writes Michael Sokolove in the *New York Times* magazine. "They're like ATMs, but in reverse – programmed to take money from players, usually about nine cents of every dollar wagered, while producing frequent near misses, the illusion that a big jackpot was at hand if only, say, just one more overstuffed burger had landed on the pay line."

In Alberta, the amount is lower, seven and a half cents per every dollar. In addition, even though slot machines look like a gravy train for the casino, they can hurt an establishment's reputation if the player goes away mad.

"All you have is your reputation. We were voted the best of Calgary gaming in *FFWD Weekly*'s 2010 readers' poll," adds Sam. "We want people to come here for an enjoyable evening out, spend what they've already decided on and leave feeling they want to return again soon."

For Sam, when he returns to the casino, the visit can be a little bittersweet after the July 1ST sale.

"I did shed a tear when I bid farewell," adds Sam. "It was exactly seven years after we moved into this beautiful building that I sold it. It wasn't the seven-year-itch but it was probably time. Now when I visit my favourite casino, I can actually play. As you know, owners can't gamble at their own establishments."

While the casino world had consumed much of Sam's days, he still had plenty of time for his other "learning experiences." Those weren't mistakes, as Sam readily points out, but lessons to learn by.

The Sarcee Shopping Plaza seemed like a natural fit when Sam bought it in the mid-1980s. The anchor tenant couldn't have been much stronger than Safeway – until its head office shut the store.

Sam was furious, but Safeway was done with small-footprint stores. Anything less than 15,000 square feet was on its way out. A worried Sam insisted that only another grocery mart could fill the Safeway spot. While the company wasn't keen on having a competitor take over its lease, it also knew that Sam was in a tight spot. Safeway relented, and Sam was able to bring Food City on board.

All went well until it didn't. When Food City added another new store on Macleod Trail, it expanded into insolvency. The Sarcee spot was done, and Sam was out another tenant. That's when he decided to run the grocery store himself. Sam was going back to his roots. By 1994, he had sunk what he needed into inventory for the Sarcee Ag Food & Meat Market.

"I'd run Switzer's Grocery as a teenager, so why not operate a grocery store now?" he asks. "In the East Village of my youth, $40 was a big day for us. Running this mega store, by comparison, meant that I had to clear $1000 a day, just to open the next morning. I was stocking the shelves and doing whatever it took, finding good butchers and managers especially, plus all the other staff you needed just to make the mega-store function. I did this for two years, and if I broke even I was lucky. The whole experience was mindboggling."

Sam hoped to lease the store to another city chain, but no one was interested. A liquidator of bankrupt stock soon set up shop, and Sam was relieved to find someone in the huge space. For fifteen months, everything went along smoothly.

"The last three months of his lease, the young man couldn't pay his rent," recalls Sam. "I didn't want to evict him and told him I just hoped things would improve. I also knew there was still lots of value in his stock. The last week of his lease, he pulled a midnight express and emptied all the stock from the store."

Sam was left with no rent, no tenant, no stock but plenty of steam coming out his ears. He decided to cast a wide net for an appropriate tenant. Within two months, he had signed the World Health Centre to a lease that offered Sam a whole lot more than sweat equity – stability.

Within three years, the Sarcee Shopping Plaza had earned

Sam both profits and a willing buyer. During that time, Sam and his daughter Darlene, with the Marasco family, had purchased a number of government liquor stores, including the one in their own Sarcee mall.

"We were doing fine, until a new license was granted to a store directly across the street from us," says Darlene. "Thankfully we also had a store at the Brentwood Village Shopping Centre, which isn't too far from students at the University of Calgary campus. As you can well guess, that was our most successful liquor store. We also had one in Midnapore."

Their company decided to sell the three stores as a package to the Liquor Depot chain owned by Irving Kipnes of Edmonton. In 2004, Kipnes took his entire chain public as Liquor Stores Income Fund.

Sam still wasn't finished with shopping centres. In addition to Sarcee, he also owned Forest Lawn Plaza and Glendale Plaza, all bought in Calgary during the same mid-1980s period.

He thought he had the perfect location in Camrose, 200 km northeast of Calgary. There were two major tenants when he bought the mall – Safeway and McLeod Hardware – plus a number of other shops.

"Six months after I bought it, Safeway pulls out," says Sam. Then six months later, McLeod leaves. Was it something I said?"

It also put Darlene and her husband, Bill Foster, who managed the buildings with Carolyn Reu, in the car to Camrose more often than any of them wished. Each spent far too much time on the road mopping up problems that were anything but a phone call away.

"If it wasn't the new roof, then it was the new roof leaking," adds Sam. "If it wasn't the new tenant, then it was the new tenant not paying rent."

The whole experience was making Sam question his sanity and especially his faith in shopping malls.

"During these years, I often asked myself where I should focus," recalls Sam. "I thought it would be buying and managing shopping malls. But sometimes I think if I'd just left my money in the bank that I would have been more successful with far less headaches and work. Not to mention all the stress it put on my staff in Calgary."

And yet, as always with Sam, any misstep led in only one direction: forward.

If it hadn't been for the Tower Casino fiasco, Sam would never have built the Dragon City Mall. And he would not have earned something that money doesn't buy: the prestigious White Hat Award for 1994 as citizen of the year. Every year, the Calgary Convention and Visitor's Bureau presents this award to a person who has distinguished him or herself. This time it was Sam.

The celebrated award was the direct result of one of his finest and most difficult accomplishments: the construction of the mall that led to the revitalization of the entire Calgary Chinatown, making it a go-to tourist destination. The area also solidified the Chinese community's critical role in the heart of Calgary.

When Sam saw the large and nearly vacant three-storey structure on the corner of 4TH Ave and Centre St SE, he quickly recalled its glory days as a bustling building that had sold for $23 million. Now the once proud Foothills Place sat sadly still, bankrupt and for sale.

"What a perfect place for a casino," thought Sam. "There was plenty of underground parking and so we offered $4 million."

The trust company wanted the deal done quickly and everything closed within a month. Once Sam owned the building, an envoy from the Asian community called him up for a chat.

"They were explicit, and I listened hard," recalls Sam. "They definitely did not want a casino in their community. I couldn't convince them otherwise, so that was that. No casino."

Sam refused to be dejected. He went back to his newly bought building and saw something entirely different. What was to have been a casino could be the start of a community rejuvenation. His building was dilapidated and the block was rundown. It was time for a makeover.

"Why not?" he asked himself. "It would be great for the community and for Calgary. I've built from the ground up and I've renovated and rebuilt but I've never undertaken such an important step to revive such a critical part of this city's heritage. If I could build a circular hotel in the middle of the city when no such building had ever been done before, I can create a building worthy of the Chinese community in Calgary."

Sam went to Nelson Yee, a realtor familiar with the community who suggested Sam's building could be the flagship for the community revival. Why not transform his behemoth into a mall?

Betty became a huge booster of the revitalization and the two hired architect Frank Kaspar of Abugov-Kaspar.

"I liked Frank Kaspar's work and when he showed me his designs and discussed what he intended to do with the building I was impressed," recalls Sam. "Much of the second floor was replaced with an atrium and stairwell directly to the third floor."

Sam wanted to make sure his construction conformed to Chinese cultural traditions so that the mall would look favorably on its tenants. Before he began any work, Sam turned to David Lai, an acupuncturist who was well versed in the ancient art of feng shui.

"The building itself is in a very good location," Lai told the *Calgary Herald's* Mel Duvall on Dec. 15, 1994. "The lions on the Centre St bridge are a symbol of good fortune and peace, and will guard against evil entering the building. The Calgary Tower also serves as the ball for the dragon – another symbol of good fortune."

With Lai as his guide, Sam rounded the corners and curves in his building. That in itself seemed a good omen to Sam, with the memories of the circular Summit Hotel only blocks away. They also moved the official entrance and address around the corner to Centre St.

"Pointed corners are bad luck," says Sam as he recalls Lai's advice. "Then we had a problem with the golden dragon on the ceiling. It faced the wrong way. David told us to put a ball by its head. When it's playing with the ball, the dragon can look in any direction."

Lai explained to the *Calgary Herald's* Duvall that everything must be taken into account when embarking on such a venture: "The location, the date and time it is opened – all are important to ensuring good fortune."

Dragon City Mall attracted 50 Chinese stores, services and restaurants, including herbal shops, well-priced clothing and jewellery businesses. The showcase Regency Palace Seafood Restaurant dominated the third floor.

"The thing I like about the Regency Palace is that it does feel a little decadent and royal," writes blogger Katie on *Yelp*. "It has a grand atmosphere. You step onto the top floor of Dragon City Mall into the truly beautiful lobby area. It is lush, a bit like a garden, and you cross over a small bridge that spans a koi pond."

Carolyn Reu remembers vividly all the Dragon City work and how much time Sam and Betty put into the project.

"They both believed in it, but it was a challenge," she says. "It truly contributed to the vibrancy of the community and became a convivial tourist destination. You have to hand it to Sam and his vision. He won the White Hatter of the year award because the City recognized the positive changes he made downtown."

Dragon City Mall became a stunning landmark that continues to attract Calgarians and visitors alike. While Sam would never recoup the many millions he put into the redevelopment, he would place it near the top of his life's accomplishments.

"I still get goose bumps when I go inside the Dragon City Mall and look up," he says, and then laughs. "And it's not because of the money I spent. It's a wonderful space and I'm so glad I was part of it all. It's a legacy for the people in this community and it jump-started the redevelopment. I'm proud of that."

CHAPTER ELEVEN:
THE RANCHER

THE TOWERS OF CALGARY AND THE BUZZ OF BUSINESS FADE quickly as Sam drives through the backwoods to Suncreek Ranch. Situated near the hamlet of Bragg Creek, the 340 acre spread remains anonymous, and hidden to all but the most observant passersby. Sam loves the ranch with a passion the city boy might never have known without Betty opening the door to the cowboy imagination tucked away in Sam's childhood memory of Zane Grey paperbacks.

Sally the mule may have prompted the original purchase of the ranch, but the muse behind Suncreek was Betty. Her spirit guided its direction and sense of purpose. Sam's kindled enthusiasm soon jump-started everything from its mule-fostered beginnings to its sun-coated buildings and beyond.

Romantic the ranch proved to be, but it was dangerous, too, especially for an adventurous novice like Sam. He once faced down a madman with a buzzing chainsaw aimed at Sam's neck. He survived when a buckboard overturned and landed on him. Through it all, Sam enthusiastically viewed almost anything non-human as a potential ranch animal, including geese.

Early in their ranching days, Betty and Sam would drive to

Bragg Creek on weekends to visit their land – and Sally. If daring got the best of them, they'd spend the night in the primitive original cabin where spiders, mice and other settlers had superior squatters' rights. Complete with an even more rustic outhouse, the cabin – and that was stretching the word –might well have seen better days, but those days were so far gone it was impossible to say for sure. The walls did keep the larger creatures on the far side of harm's way, although Sam didn't like to test that notion.

True, it was better to be inside, but there are certain insides that look far worse than outside. So much for the romance of the wild, thought Sam, as he scoured the classified ads for a trailer.

Soon Sam bought a 12 by 62 foot mobile home from an elderly woman. "It wasn't fancy, but it had been taken care of," says Sam. "Betty was away and I wanted to surprise her, so I had it hauled to the ranch. After she returned, I said, 'Let's go see Sally.' When we got there and she saw the trailer, I looked at her and said: 'Welcome home.' And that was our home in the country for five years."

When Sam placed the trailer on his property, he also arranged for electricity and plumbing. What he neglected to do was inform the appropriate authorities. With Betty's promise that the trailer would be only temporary living quarters, the municipality relented – but only on condition that a house be built, sooner rather than later. *Much later* turned out to be closer to the truth.

Dealing with bureaucrats was a whole lot easier than dealing with water, however, despite Sam's early belief that water was all around and that all he was needed was a drill and a bucket. He was sure he'd found the perfect spot and started drilling, expecting to be sprayed with the obvious result.

"Oh, I got sprayed all right – with advice," laughs Sam. "I found out quickly that the water doesn't come to you. You must come to it."

Soon Sam learned all he needed to know about witching a well.

"I didn't believe in divining or witching to find water, but a few people asked if I'd done it," recalls Sam. "At this point, I needed water and anything that worked was fine with me. That's how I met the one-legged witcher, an ex-Mountie. He came over and made a fresh witching stick, a Y-shaped twig. As he held each side gently and walked slowly around the property, suddenly the twig pointed down firmly. That's where we drilled and found an ample well. It was just 10 feet from my original spot. When it comes to witching a well, there's no second prize, as Mr. Know-it-all Sam soon learned."

Sam was less interested in the science or myth of well-witching than the running water that was soon flowing in the mobile home.

Their good friend Genevie Dean, whose ranch was nearby, remembers "the old trailer" and the joy Sam and Betty would take in the country. Except for the weasel hiding under the bed.

"Betty phoned me in the night and said she saw this long thin white creature dart under her bed. By her description, we were sure it was a weasel. 'You don't want to go to bed with a weasel,' I said and then we both started laughing."

Of course, weasels in the house are no laughing matter. Sam and Betty had already tried to whoosh it away with a broom. Then they struggled with mothballs, but the only creatures the foul smell repulsed were Sam and Betty. After Genevie's astute advice, Betty became confident they could take care of it. The two rigged a makeshift trap, lured the weasel in, rushed the trap outside, freed the creature, dashed back into the trailer and collapsed on the bed. Just another bliss-filled night in the country.

Genevie and her husband, Don Dean, first met Betty and Sam through the Carriage Association, a group committed to preserving and promoting vintage cutters and carriages. The founding meeting of the Jubilee Driving Society was at the Summit Hotel on Valentines Day, 1977.

"I love horses and carriages, so I guess it makes sense," says Sam. "I remembered some of the lessons I took with Sally the mule and her little carriage. I had graduated from the mule to a horse – big time, in my book. But it was so much easier than Sally. I'd take a horse and sleigh over a mule and cart any day."

And then, Sam adds dryly, "Of course there are a few who think the mule and I have much more in common."

Sam and Betty hosted the Jubilee Driving Society's first cutter rally at their Bragg Creek ranch with Genevie and Don Dean enthusiastically participating. Over the next few years the couples became good friends.

One day in the summer of 1980, Sam and his son Mark dropped in to see if the Deans knew the owners of a team of driving horses that Sam wanted to buy.

"As it happened, the owners were friends of ours whom Don had been involved with in the construction business," says Genevie Dean. "Then Sam also mentioned that he was building a new house on his property. Would Don be interested in the project?"

Sam and Don Dean talked about what they'd do, and then got serious. Only a year later – light speed by Alberta building standards – they'd completed the three-storey, 6000 square foot home.

"Don thought it was the most beautiful house he had ever built," says Genevie Dean, recalling her late husband's pride in the project.

It is a gloriously comfortable country place enclosed by a wide porch filled with chairs and tables, as well as a piano for parties. The sun-filled home with its large windows is ideally centred to take full advantage of the wonderland interplay of mountains and sky.

"It is so peaceful," says Narmin Keshavjee, whose husband, Saadat, is a fellow Rotarian of Sam's at Calgary West Rotary. "You sit on this lovely porch and see the sunset offer a gentle glow to the valley below. It's all so calming and comforting."

It was the perfect place for a country wedding. On December 18TH, 1981, Sam and Betty welcomed their blended families and friends to celebrate their joining together as husband and wife. Betty had gone to classes with Sam to study his Jewish faith. She converted to Judaism, and Rabbi Lewis Ginsberg married them. The ceremony was just as they wished: small but overflowing with the warmth of their family and closest friends.

"I was the MC after the religious ceremony, and what a great day it was," remembers Frank Nelles. "The glittering pines seemed to shine with the sun. Everything was bright and everyone was cheery. It was wonderful for all their friends and family and especially for them. Sam was all aglow, and so was his new bride. Together they were overjoyed. All I could think of was how perfect it was. Just a beautiful time."

Betty saw how much Sam loved his life on the ranch, so far removed from his city roots. Farming was in her blood, and the familiarity of ranch living brought her back to Frontier, Saskatchewan. She knew both the delights and the dangers of the farm. Sam, unfortunately, seemed immune to the menace of the unknown.

"Sam would ride his horse on the road in the dark, and we'd be so worried," says Genevie. "He had no fear. My husband knew how to ride and how to drive the carriage. He was a very careful person. There were times when he was simply in awe of Sam. 'He just does it and gets away with it,' Don would say."

Today, older and somewhat wiser, Sam shivers at the thought of some of his close calls and misadventures. Once, he almost lost a team of Belgian horses.

When he began to collect carriages, he turned to a carriage restorer near Bragg Creek who transformed Sam's first carriage from its earlier life as an 1876 horse-drawn taxi in Montreal.

The man did such a good job that Sam knew the restorer could do it again.

"I had bought a buckboard that was probably from the early 1900s and looked it," said Sam. "It was pretty beat up. I had also bought a team of Belgian horses that were already trained for a carriage. Everything was hooked up and I felt pretty comfortable."

Sam drove the team attached to the battered buckboard onto the restorer's ranch. There was a Texas gate to prevent his horses from escaping the grounds. If it was good enough for his horses, it was fine for Sam's Belgians. Besides, they were connected to the buckboard. Sam climbed off the carriage, left the reins loose and headed into the restorer's house.

"We heard the rushing clippety-clop sound of hooves beating on the grass and gravel, and then the sudden bang of the buckboard," says Sam. "When we came out, they were gone. The Belgians just flew over the Texas gate, with the buckboard behind them. Well, it was so wrecked, the gate wouldn't hurt it anyway. We rushed down the road, looking for the horses, expecting to find them down on the ground with broken legs, or worse – dead. About three miles away, we saw them standing in the grass, occasionally bending down to chomp and looking very nonchalant, as if to say, 'What took you so long?'"

In 1984 Sam decided he needed a barn and asked Don Dean to again be his contractor.

"We hired Fred Coates to mill the logs from the ranch and help build the barn," says Sam. "We started with a modest structure but changed the plans to accommodate the growing size of the building and the roofline. We wanted a traditional-looking barn, and it is, just somewhat larger.

That's for sure. It's an impressive log structure measuring 75 by 90 feet. Genevie Dean remembers the barn was to be big enough not only to house Sam and Betty's Belgians, but to host parties, dances and general get-togethers, too.

"It was to be a two-storey log barn, with a drive-in loft level," says Dean. "When it was finished, Sam and Betty hosted an old-fashioned barn dance. My husband loved working with Sam because his mind was always open to Don's ideas. Once Sam agreed, he gave Don free rein to go ahead."

When Sam had confidence in a person's abilities, he allowed him or her full independence to do the job. Sam respected people's strengths and refused to micro-manage. He believed in hiring the right people and leaving them alone.

Unfortunately, the same logic does not always apply to horses, a fact Sam learned to respect but not always appreciate.

Now that Sam and the Belgians were on speaking terms again, they became his favourite team. It was a chilly winter night as Sam and Betty prepared for a party across the road. They were setting out for the Bar KC community hall and a festive Christmas event. Sam hooked up the horses to the hay wagon, he and Betty climbed aboard, and off they went.

"We had a delightful time, said goodbye to all, and climbed back on the wagon," recalls Sam. "We were just starting on the road home when the horses had another idea. They decided to take the direct route, which does not include the road. They started to race, while we're holding the reins tight. Suddenly, the wagon struck a tree and off we flew into a snow bank. It was like landing on a big cold cushion. Betty and I looked at each other, got up and brushed ourselves off. Miraculously, we were fine. So were the horses. The team galloped to the wire fence, where they abruptly stopped."

Another time, Sam's friend Kai Smed came over to the ranch to find a Christmas tree for his family. Sam, Betty and Kai got in the wagon and started searching. When Kai found what he wanted, they cut the tree, hauled it to the wagon and put it in. Betty was already in the wagon as Sam climbed on board. Before Kai could hop in, the horses took off.

"Once more, Betty and I ended up in the snow, lying there laughing," recalls Sam. "Kai came running over, a little worried that we were hurt. When he saw us laughing, he couldn't contain himself. It was all we could do to get up and start looking for the horses. They were way ahead of us – literally. There they were, standing right in front of the snow bank, waiting."

Sam didn't notice right away that when he flew into the snow, so did his prized Bulova diamond watch. He'd been awarded the watch from the Bulova company for high sales during his jewellery store days. All these years he had worn it and now it had slipped off into the deep snow if not the deep beyond.

"I wouldn't believe my it was gone," says Sam. "Six months later, when the warm spring had melted the snow, I was determined to find my watch. I scoured the area and on a sunny day, I saw this sparkle coming from the dirt. It was the Bulova – still ticking."

Just like Sam. All his horse riding and carriage driving only intensified his love for the magnificent steeds. Luckily, Betty was equally adventurous as the two built their life together in the woodlands on the edge of the Kananaskis mountains.

"We loved camping and horseback riding in the mountains," says Sam. "One of our first trips was an overnight ride to Moose

Mountain in the Kananaskis with Ralph White, who was an out-fitter as well as a good friend. I drove my old buckboard with two super horses. Everyone else was on horseback, and a little later I wished I had been, too."

Sam and Betty packed their supplies and sleeping gear and were off with the rest of the group. Everyone mounted horses while Sam climbed onto his buckboard. As they headed into the mountain forest, a group of motorcycle enthusiasts were revving their motors as they neared for the paved road and the highway. The noise spooked the horses. They kicked and bucked danger-ously in the confined space. Some of the riders quickly jumped to the ground as they tried to calm their mounts. Others didn't have that option as they met the earth the hard way.

Later, the two-horse buckboard had just started climbing toward the mountain when suddenly the wagon tipped to the side, spilling its contents, including Sam and Betty. The horses were trapped, and so was Sam.

"I was pinned under the wagon and couldn't move," recalls Sam. "The horses were all jumbled up, too. We'd just come through the motorcycle fiasco and that had left them a little jittery. Now we were all in a mess. Betty and the rest of the crew slowly righted the wagon and I managed to stand up tall with nothing broken. Then we had to unhook the horses and guide them up. Once we knew the horses were okay, we had to start all over again, hook them up to the wagon, fill it up with what we'd retrieved and finally get back on the trail."

As they rode further up the slope, darkness descended from the close sky and thick forest. The outfitter found a clearing to camp for the evening and dismounted. The group settled and fed their horses, and then cooked their food over the open campfire.

"Betty and I slept in sleeping bags in the buckboard under the stars," says Sam. "It was a cool, brisk evening, but I felt warmed by the magic of the night as I stared at the sky, waiting for a shooting star to land beside me."

Their reverie was broken by the cold air of daybreak, their breath competing with the early morning mist. The campfire took its time to flame, but everything remained frozen.

"Our eggs, bacon, bread and butter were as rigid as rocks," recalls Sam. "They sat on the frying pan like a tray of ice cubes. Thankfully the cowboy coffee was perfect – very strong."

Cowboy coffee is a mainstay on the overnight trail ride. Water is poured into a thin tin pot or can with a tiny metal handle on top. Course coffee grounds are added. A twig or stick loops through the tin handle for the cowboy barista to hold as the coffee heats over the campfire. The coffee simmers and the cowboys throw a tiny clean stick into the mixture. That separates the grounds, leaving coffee free to be poured.

"At least there was something to chew that morning," laughs Sam as he recalls his stint at making coffee. "As we got ready to break camp, our outfitter told one of the group to rope his horses to a tree, but the know-it-all didn't think that was necessary. Guess who the know-it-all was?"

A red-faced Sam followed the frustrated crew into the mountains looking for the fleeing steeds. Hours later, there they were, gently grazing on mountain grass. By the time everyone had backtracked to the campsite, there was just enough sun and good humour remaining for the ride back down the mountain. As the riders headed for home, every two- and four-legged critter was accounted for, and nothing was bruised save one slightly deflated ego.

Despite the perils of being pinned under the buckboard and the search for runaway horses, the joy of the ride within such a pristine panorama left Sam a cowboy convert. His and Betty's weekend exploit had transformed them into adventurers on horseback, participating in the many trail-riding offerings.

"It was the Western Stockgrowers 100TH Anniversary ride, and Betty signed us up as a birthday present to me," says Sam. "We had a great day, and when we camped that first night, Betty got out the tent and we set it up, finishing with the tiny flap at the entrance. Betty said, 'Let's go in,' and I stopped cold. Concerned, she stared straight at me and asked, 'What's wrong, Sam?' I said 'I don't know what to do next – in all my life, I've never slept in a tent even once.' Betty grinned, bent down to open the flap and replied with a smile, 'Well, happy birthday, Sam.'"

George Deegan was considered one of the younger gang on this centennial cattle drive. He recalled how everyone was up at 5:30 in the morning but by the early afternoon, they were bushed.

"We'd take the saddles off our horses and just relax," says Deegan, a retired CEO of United Grocers. "Nearly all of us were exhausted. Not Sam and Betty. They'd unhitch their wagon and take all that heavy tack off. Then they'd grab their saddles out of the wagon, put them on the horses and head off to the hills for a two-hour ride. We were in awe and just amazed at their energy and strength, especially since we were so tired. They were a great couple and very hospitable people."

Sam and Betty's strength and energy would be tested during their next adventure on the Boundary Commission Ride. Again, they rode a buckboard, but this time Sam and Betty were driving a celebrated Studebaker wagon, known for being hardy under the most extreme of conditions.

"I wanted a strong wagon, and this was built like a brick you-know-what house," says Sam. "We were finishing our fourth day and it had been quite the ride. I was unhooking the horses when another carriage appeared close, startling the horses. Suddenly they spooked and started to take off. I instinctively grabbed the reins but the buckboard began to roll. As Betty raced to stop the horses, the wagon went down – and so did the horses and me. This whole scene was scarily familiar."

But it was all new to this trail-riding crew as well as another group of onlookers. Plus, the Studebaker wagon was a whole lot heavier than Sam's earlier peril-packer and where it fell, it looked like it wanted to stay. The horses, too, were in danger, struggling as Betty rushed into action. She managed to stop them and calm them down, then turned quickly to Sam's plight.

"She got everyone who was looking to slowly push the way-ward wagon back up, finally freeing me from its crippling grip," recalls Sam, still amazed that he managed to escape unscathed. "The horses were down and trying to break free from the tangled reins and traces. Thankfully, Betty chose me first, over the horses. 'She must love you,' everybody said."

The traumatized horses, not to mention Sam, had had enough. Their legs, while not broken, were badly scraped and everyone needed some tender care. That was the end of the Boundary Commission Ride for Sam and Betty. A rancher near the Alberta/ Montana border had a trailer that transported Sam's wagon and his horses back to Suncreek Ranch. There was room in his cab for Sam and Betty, too, as they returned to their truck at the trail ride's start-off point.

"Betty later related what Don Wilson, the Calgary Stampede president, joked to her. 'Your horse was down but so was your man. You chose to save your man, but you know how hard it is to find a good horse!' By that time, we were all ready to laugh, knowing full well what might have been."

Betty and Sam still loved their adventures, and a favourite was the Trail Riders of the Canadian Rockies, which had been offering rides into the mountains since 1923.

"The breathtaking beauty of the Rocky Mountains awakens the adventurist in all of us," states the Trail Riders' website. "Every mountain pass leads to endless possibilities of undiscovered valleys and hidden canyons. Carpets of wild flowers and majestic lodge pole pine provide the backdrop of what many believe is the most beautiful scenery in the world. A wide open sky framed by snow-capped mountains is the view from each horse. As you focus on the scenery, your horse watches the trail. But the horse can't do all the work. As you traverse steep canyons and climb windy paths, the rider remains aware. This walk in the park is like no other you will ever experience."

This described Sam's new passion perfectly. It invigorated his life with Betty, and he was grateful that she had transported him to his new world full of awe and wonder.

"Our most memorable ride was into the headwaters of where the Bow River begins," remembers Sam. "The river sparkled with the brilliance of emeralds." The shades of green changed with the sun as the trees stared at the river and the meadows beyond.

"Our horses acted as if they had no worries at all, stepping over these massive rocks and taking us further into the back-woods," recalls Sam.

The horses seemed to pacify any nervousness that a rider might have as they trekked further into a wilderness calmed by the serenity of such scenic bounty. The mountains' majestic glory offered a protective circle for any soul seeking refuge from the concerns of the city.

Suncreek Ranch became Sam's cocoon as it reflected his love for the mountains and wilderness. Always practical, though, he wasn't satisfied with being a hobby rancher. He wanted his spread to have a purpose. Off he went to the auctioneers – again.

"I'm their best friend and always have been," he laughs. "In a way, they're like the casino and there's always the lure of a big win. But you've got to have your eye on the money and you can't be deflected. Sometimes I've stretched that little rule."

Sam decided he needed cattle on his ranch and trucked over to the Stampede Park cattle auction. By the time he'd finished buying, he had 110 animals and a manager to look after them. But Sam stayed in close touch and was soon familiar with phone calls in the dark night. There was a cow standing in the middle of the road and Sam had better get there fast or she wouldn't be standing. Other calls in the deep of the night revealed how Sam's cattle had been taken by rustlers or cougars. His herd soon dwindled to 99 head.

"It was time to get out of the cattle business," he says. "My first clue was after I bought two Charolais heifers. One was carrying a calf and the other was ready to go into heat. I'd get up at daybreak to see how this cow was doing. Over the next two months, it got to the point where I was constantly looking for signs so I could rush her over to the neighbour who had a prize bull."

The continual hunt for symptoms of bovine romance was taking too much of Sam's time. Exasperated, in no small part due to his inexperience, he decided to take the bull by the horns – hopefully not literally. Sam trucked his heifer over to his neighbour's ranch to see if he had better luck.

Instead, he made a discovery.

"I got a call from my neighbour a few days later," says Sam, smiling. "I'd been watching the wrong cow. All this time I'd had my eyes on the heifer that was already with calf."

Sam's cattle were soon on the market. Yet the lure of the gavel remained as Sam sped over to Maclean Auction, always on the hunt for the practical and the spectacular.

"It's highly respected and always a fun place," he says and then recalls, sheepishly, the flock of sheep he bought for the ranch.

"I bid $15 for two sheep," says Sam. "At least I thought it was two. When the seller came over to me, he brought out a flock. I'd bought all 12, not two for the same price. I couldn't believe my luck and hurried them home to surprise Betty. Boy, was she surprised."

Betty asked Sam if he knew how much work sheep could be. They needed an enclosed space, because cougars and coyotes could smell a buffet a mile away.

"I talked to the neighbour across the street who had a flock," says Sam. "He told me they would be dead if I didn't quickly build a pen and scrape the field free of weeds. Sheep die if they eat weeds. I thought they were going to be perfect animal lawnmowers."

The next week, the sheep were back at the auction mart. Sam retrieved his cash but soon spent it during his brief goose period.

With the sheep coins weighing heavily in his pocket, Sam walked by the stalls and stopped sharp when he saw two beautiful white geese. Beguiled, he quickly bid and won them.

"Now what am I going to do with these geese?" he asked himself. "I can't stare at them all day."

Sam went practical and put his momentary affection for the white birds to rest.

"These weren't swans – they were geese," he says. "They were raised for someone's dinner and I guess I bought them for mine."

When Sam returned to the stalls to collect the slaughtered geese, he was shocked.

"I was handed these two plucked and scrawny birds," he recalls. "If there had been any meat on them I don't know where it was hidden. They sure didn't look like the ones I'd bought."

There was nothing Sam could do. He had bid for and bought the geese and if he was handed back dead what they weren't when they were alive, so be it.

"I guess I got goosed in the pocketbook," he laughs.

Sam's love of auctions soon became apparent to his ranch manager, Peter Kearns.

"Sam was very hesitant at investing in equipment unless he could get a deal at an auction," says Kearns. "So when his old tractor finally died, Sam figured the auction was the best place to find a replacement."

Kearns wasn't so sure: "I researched around and found what was available for $5000. Then I discovered an excellent tractor with 95 horsepower and available for a deeply discounted price."

Kearns presented Sam with all his facts for the new versus the old one. Sam's trust in auctions did not trump practicality.

"When I made my case for a new and superb tractor, with warranty, Sam agreed," said Kearns. "I didn't even realize that the cab in this unit had air conditioning for summer, heating for winter and a stereo. I thought I'd died and gone to cowboy heaven."

After Peter Kearns was hired by Sam and Betty to manage the ranch, he thought he'd do the job for a year or two. That was November 2000.

"My daughter Kelly found the ad," recalls Kearns. "It read: 'Farm help required; must know how to operate a chainsaw.' The interview was basically: 'So, can you operate a chainsaw? We're trying to remove a few of these poplars around the house.' I felled them and then Betty said to Sam: 'We really have to go. We have a dinner appointment.' Sam looked at me and asked: 'When can you start and clean all this up?' I'd cleared the trees off the road so they could drive their car down the hill and into the city. I've been here ever since."

Kearns is both thankful and impressed with the trust bestowed by Sam and Betty. They knew he'd once had a farm in Ontario and that he understood his way around the needs of the ranch. He plants the hay that the ranch sells and takes care of the many carriages and wagons that Sam collects.

Kearns also cares for the two dogs and 10 horses – his and daughter Kelly's five horses, as well as Sam's five. Stormy is Sam's favourite. Riding at the age of 80, Sam presented a certain grace on Stormy as the horse gingerly walked the grounds between the pines and poplars.

"Stormy is a Tennessee Walker and has a wonderfully smooth gait," says Sam. "You could hold a glass of wine while riding Stormy and it wouldn't spill, except into your mouth. I love that horse."

Kearns knows his horses and admires Sam's courage in riding at his age, and his tenacity in trying new things.

"Sam learned by hook and by crook," says Kearns. "He has survived. Some of the risks he took were shocking, but he did it. Plus, Sam's early concept of horses was that they'd do what they're supposed to do. Often, they did just that. What Sam lacked in experience, he more than made up for in vision and gumption."

Kearns also recalls the time Sam bought a 1923 McLaughlin-Buick at the antique auction. The pride of General Motors, this Canadian car was named for Sam McLaughlin, who retired as GM Canada board chair in 1967 and passed away at the age of 100 in 1972.

As the Tin Lizzie website states (with a nod to Bill Vance): "McLaughlin put a wry twist on the American Buick slogan: 'When better cars are built, Buick will build them,' by advertising: 'Better cars are being built, and McLaughlin is building them.'"

Naturally, Sam wanted to ride his prized car in the Calgary Stampede parade, but the entry date for participants was long past. Sam was not deterred.

"He kept at it, and we ended up in the parade," says the admiring Kearns. "All the people along the route rooted for Sam and that antique car."

Except for those at the spot where it decided to stop in the middle of the parade – and not to take a salute.

"We were right in front of the Rotary Club area and the McLaughlin simply conked right out," recalls Sam. "These were my fellow Rotarians, and I was causing the stoppage. Was I embarrassed, especially when the two policemen came along to give her a good push. We finally got going, which was a good thing because there's nowhere to hide when you ride in the parade. There were no more escapades, that is until we got very close to the finish line. Right in front of the Palliser Hotel, the McLaughlin had clearly had enough. She was done. The Stampede Quads rushed over and pushed her out of the way. I quickly called my son-in-law, Bill Foster, who hurried to the spot and towed the McLaughlin back to the casino."

Sam was no stranger to the Calgary Stampede parade. He had ridden many times in his prized carriages and wagons. On July 5TH 1991, Sam climbed aboard the Elbow River Casino Express, described as "one elegant and historical vehicle," that had done yeoman duty in late 1800s America ferrying passengers and mail.

"When the horse-drawn stagecoach was showcased to thousands of spectators at Friday's Stampede parade, it wasn't the first time it had tasted adulation," wrote the *Calgary Herald*'s Michael OKN Clarkson. "The top-of-the-line coach was used for carrying passengers and mail across the United States at about the turn of the century before it was 'discovered' for Hollywood."

Sam renovated the antique coach, retaining its oak frame, steel wheels and its impressive leather support and upholstery.

"The coach, known as a Fat Jones Stagecoach after a supplier of wagons and livestock for movies, was used in many films over the years, including Little Big Man, filmed near Calgary," continued Clarkson.

Clarkson noted that Sam had wanted an original stagecoach and found exactly that from Longview stunt coordinator John Scott.

Another carriage in his collection is an historic landau that was part of the 1750 British Parliament's opening ceremonies.

"It's wonderful but temperamental," says Sam. "At that age who wouldn't be? It has even been used at the Spruce Meadows equestrian shows. I was delighted to know that Prince Phillip rode in it."

Sam would love to show it in the Stampede parade but is

wary of the landau's ability to make it to the finish line. It's one of the very few things that Sam knows he can't make happen on pure will.

"Sam has never believed there was anything he couldn't do," continues Kearns. "I have learned so much from him. Sam has given me a positive outlook on accomplishing things in life."

Sam has also given Kearns lots of great stories.

In June, a neighbour from Turner Valley rents pasture at the ranch for his 30 cows and 30 calves. Sam is delighted with the arrangement because tall grass is a fire hazard. Hay is also grown on another 25 acres so Sam once hired contract workers to cut the hay in the fall.

"It became a real headache because most workers are busy with larger fields and you want the hay off before it becomes too ripe or the snow falls," says Sam. "We bought the equipment we needed at auction – where else? – and the only problem we had was hiring people to pick, load and carry the hay to storage.

"I finally found three people to do the job," continues Sam. "Two of them were First Nations and they were very good. The third person was a real renegade and he didn't hit it off with the first two. When we stacked the wagons with hay, this guy went crazy. He grabbed the chainsaw and started chasing the other two around the ranch. I finally managed to catch up to him. As he turned to face me with the chainsaw buzzing, I asked him to put it down and said then I'd pay him for the day. He swiftly pointed the chainsaw directly at my neck and, with no swearing or yelling, abruptly turned it off and dropped it at my feet. I gave him a full day's wages and watched him leave as he pocketed his cash. When I picture it all in slow motion – this renegade with a chainsaw chasing these poor guys – I can't believe the other crazy guy rushing toward him rather than away. It's a wonder I'm here to tell the tale."

Sam needed no convincing to buy a hay picker and baler – from the auction house, of course. After the square baler strained the belts and broke, Sam bought a more efficient round baler. In any event, he has a neighbour with a machine shop that caters to old equipment – and to Sam.

Sam's close friends were party to his daring and adventures. Frank Nelles had been brought up on a farm in Manitoba and volunteered to help Sam clear a carriage trail through the thick forest.

"We had a harrowing experience with the caterpillar one fall when I was to move it to its winter storage spot," explains Nelles. "As we drove around the lake, which had a steep decline off the roadway, the cat started to slide sideways down the slope towards the lake. Sam and I thought it was funny until the cat began to approach the lake. We were out of control. About 30 feet from the water, I said: 'Sam let's jump off,' which we did, fast."

A rock that jutted out by the water's edge stopped the caterpillar cold while the motor kept running. Nelles jumped back on, gave full throttle, and sped away from the lake.

CHAPTER TWELVE:
THE GIVER

When realtor Gordon Shoults introduced Sam and Betty to the property that would become Suncreek Ranch, he had come full circle. As a musician, Shoults had played for Sam at the Top O' the Summit as had his wife, Joyce Kelly. Now they perform at the iconic Steak Pit, a western-rustic restaurant in Bragg Creek that Shoults had owned for over 50 years.

"He's been very supportive of our restaurant and he always has a smile no matter what," says Kelly. "He's honest, warm and encouraging."

The couple are big fans of Sam's approach to philanthropy. As with everything in his life, he is hands-on.

"He's directly involved and he's enjoying what he's able to do," they say. "It's the greatest feeling to be able to do what Sam is doing and to see the results."

Shoults especially enjoys Sam's "refreshing and genuine warmth," and recalls a fellow musician that Sam loved to hire, Ernst Johanssen, who performed as Jo Hansen.

Stan Cichon, a friend of Sam's for 25 years and a fellow Rotarian, remembers the late Jo Hansen well.

"He performed at the Summit and he played at Sam and Betty's wedding," says Cichon. "Sam had a soft spot for Jo. He was born in Harlem and had played piano for a number of well-known American musicians of the day, such as Helen O'Connell."

Sam and Stan became good friends because they had so much in common, even though Cichon started out as an educator and then became an entrepreneur and rancher. Both were born of Polish immigrants and found they had a lot of overlap with friends and relatives.

"I remember when Sam was named White Hatter of the Year in 1994, something he didn't expect and he received a standing ovation at our Rotary Club," continues Cichon. "That really touched him."

Sam and Betty had attended the prestigious White Hat awards for many years, but this year he was overbooked and over-busy and wondered if he could spare the time. It was a momentary thought that Betty soon squelched. Recognizing one's peers and colleagues is a time for joy, so off they went to sit with friends and applaud the winners. When the winner of the big prize was announced, Sam was shocked.

"I didn't even think I could make it up to the podium," he recalls. "It was absolutely unexpected and came right out of the mist. People know that if I'm given a mic, I can go on. This time, I could barely squeak the words out. I said, 'I love Calgary,' and got off the stage. It was the purest speech I've ever made."

They loved him for it. Cichon wasn't surprised at Sam's reaction to winning the big award.

"Sam won't blow his own horn," adds Cichon. "He's a doer and has made a tremendous impact on the community. He'll make a contribution so other people get credit, not him. He's done that with a number of people whom he believes deserve recognition, like the late Jo Hansen, and he's done it quietly."

Cichon says that he would do practically anything for Sam. He especially respects the fact that Sam has never forgotten his roots and strives to be inclusive in a world where exclusivity too often takes hold.

"Sam respects the opinion of others, is sensitive to humanitarian needs and is a true contributor to the community and to humanity," adds Cichon.

When Cichon nominated Sam to receive an honorary bachelor's degree from Mount Royal University, he had a hard time deciding what to include in just three pages.

Sam has been a lifetime supporter of the Calgary Exhibition and Stampede, where he also volunteers as a senior associate. Sam's work with the Victoria Crossing Business Revitalization Zone was personally recognized by then-mayor David Bronconnier. Sam's a dedicated long-time member of the Calgary Al Azhar Shrine and the Rotary Club of Calgary West, two service clubs that contribute considerably to city charities. He's also a member of the Masonic Lodge #9 and the Skål Club, an international travel industry social group.

"Sam was an original member of the Skål Calgary Chapter more than 50 years ago and he's still very active, attending monthly meetings and hosting our annual BBQ at the ranch in Bragg Creek," says Howard Silver, owner of the Metropolitan Conference Centre and the son of Jessie Silver, Sam's niece. "During our monthly dinners, Skål organizes a 50/50 draw to raise money for the club and its tourism scholarship fund. There is one member who almost always has better luck – you guessed it, Sam!"

For Skål's dinner before the summer break, Sam announced the sale of the Elbow River Casino on July 1, 2012. Then the 50/50 ticket was drawn.

"It was very fitting that Sam, once again, won the draw at the last Skål dinner the casino will host under his ownership," says Silver, adding: "It was always touching to watch Sam's joy, walking slowly up to the podium to collect his winnings, unable to hide his Cheshire-cat smile. We were and remain happy and amazed for him, Sam the generous man. Why shouldn't life give him a little wink once in a while with a winning raffle ticket or two?"

Sam's philanthropic giving cuts a wide swath through the city's social agencies, as well as national and global charities from the Special Olympics to World Vision and Red Cross Haitian relief.

"I like to participate in organizations that are on the front line, doing vital work," says Sam. "That's what also moved me to donate to the Calgary Herald Christmas Fund because we know exactly who the charities are and what they do."

Sam had already donated $50,000 to the 2011 Christmas Fund. Then philanthropist and entrepreneur Allan Markin offered to match donations to the Fund, as well as finance an outcome analysis audit, worth $140,000 each, for the included charities. Excited by Markin's generosity, Sam phoned the *Calgary Herald* publisher Guy Huntingford to donate another $200,000.

"When I heard what Mr. Allan Markin was prepared to do," adds Sam, "I thought, 'What an opportunity.' God bless Mr. Markin."

Publisher Huntingford was wowed by the community participation and the matching funds, noting how "life-changing this is for all the charities."

"It's incredible," he stated in a *Calgary Herald* editorial. "It could be over $5 million this year, which is truly outstanding."

Sam has also given generously to organizations within his Jewish faith and was honoured in June 2012 for his donations to the Jewish National Fund of Canada. He supports his local synagogues and has helped many of them as they build and provide for their congregants. The Conservative Beth Tzedec and the Orthodox Congregation House of Jacob-Mikveh Israel can each point to places that only became possible through Sam's faith and philanthropy. It was the Reform Temple B'nai Tikvah that became Sam and Betty's personal place of worship. Their generosity stimulated the stunning renovation of Temple B'nai Tikvah, including its sanctuary and social hall.

"Faith and philanthropy are one," says Sam. "It is called tikkun olam, and it means repairing the world. By helping others through tzedakah or charity, we are ultimately helping ourselves because we are making our world more just for all. In our faith, it's a mitzvah or commandment to make our world a better place. It's both an obligation and a joy to give back, and I'm truly privileged to receive so much warmth for doing not just my duty, but my passion."

One of the big fundraisers that make Calgary better is the annual B'nai Brith Gentlemen's Dinner. Held at the Beth Tzedec synagogue, the dinner raises substantial funds that are shared within the Jewish and larger Calgary community. The event also recognizes two community leaders: one Jewish and one not. For 2011, Calgary Mayor Naheed Nenshi became the first Muslim to be so honoured. Sam was delighted in two ways: because he supported Nenshi politically, and because his nephew, Nelson Halpern, son of David and Tibele, received the Ben Docktor Award of Excellence.

For many years Sam's friend, educator Aron Eichler, was the master of ceremonies for the B'nai Brith dinner. He shared that honour with another prominent Calgarian, Lou Pomerance, who, with his brother Phil, had owned Western Outfitters Ltd. The man who made B'nai Brith a name in Calgary was its former president, the late and legendary Jack Feingold.

"Jack was a master at raising money for B'nai Brith and that's because he had a heart of gold," says an admiring Sam.

Eichler and Pomerance are prominent community builders and volunteers. Standing at the B'nai Brith podium, each was renowned for telling jokes and stories that would have the guests spilling their drinks, if not their actual dinner. The auction was always popular, particularly because items would be bid up far above their monetary worth.

"When the auction started, Sam – who you know loves an auction, and especially one for a good cause – would increase his bid until we'd raised way more than what we expected," recalls Eichler. "He paid an astronomical amount for what was surely a Grey Cup-worthy football used by the Calgary Stampeders."

Sam and Betty were part of the fundraising efforts for the Little Synagogue on the Prairie that sits today in Calgary's Heritage Park Historical village. The project's president, Irena Karshenbaum, led an enthusiastic cross-section of Jewish community volunteers to raise over $1 million to restore one of the province's remaining prairie synagogues. The Montefiore Institute, built in 1916, served as a synagogue, school and community centre for 30 Jewish homesteading families near Sibbald in eastern Alberta.

The Board of Directors for the Little Synagogue project included Irena Karshenbaum, Trudy Cowan, Leslie Levant, Shel Bercovich, Emanuel Cohen, Daryl S. Fridhandler, Dr. Ralph Gurevitch, Betti Weiss, Shauna Switzer, and her husband, community historian Jack Switzer, who has since passed away.

The fundraising committee consisted of Bobby Libin, Martin Cohos, Daryl S. Fridhandler, Irena Karshenbaum, Leslie Levant, Larry and Sandy Martin, Betti Weiss and Sam and Betty Switzer.

The grand opening in Heritage Park was June 28TH, 2009. The Torah procession began at the Switzer Grocery and Confectionary that Sam and Betty helped fund in the Haskayne Mercantile Block, and continued to the Little Synagogue. Sam was honoured to install the Montefiore Institute's Torah with then-Lieutenant Governor Norman Kwong beside him.

"This was an amazing community effort," says Sam. "There were so many people who volunteered to make the Little Synagogue a reality. At the opening, they stopped counting at 2000, but people continued to stream in. We were all so excited and I only wish Betty could have lived to see this. But she left this earth too soon, just nine months before the opening. The Little Synagogue meant so much to her."

They had formed the Sam and Betty Switzer Foundation and it was their opportunity to give back to the community. This way they could contribute directly to projects and people in need.

"Calgary has been very good to me," says Sam. "We wanted to do as much as we could to directly change lives. But we didn't want a major portion going to administration. Any administration that is top heavy is not doing the job it was supposed to do."

Many recipients of their gifts have written directly to express their profound thanks to Sam and Betty for making a difference. The Mount Royal University bursary for single parents is a prime example.

"Your kind generosity has been instrumental in enabling me to pursue my dreams for a quality education, a meaningful career, and has allowed me to fulfill my promise to my young son of a better quality of life," writes one student "from the bottom of my heart."

Another MRU student who used her bursary towards tuition, books and childcare wrote: "Receiving this bursary means a lot to me because I was previously employed at the Elbow River Casino and had the opportunity to meet Mrs. Switzer. She was a wonderful woman with a generous heart."

Reading the letters, Sam readily appreciates the struggles of these single parents whose goal of education to better their lives and that of their children he so fully understands and embraces. After all, Betty was once a single mother herself.

This letter says it all: "Without this funding, I may not have been able to concentrate so hard on my studies and in turn to be as successful as I have been. I have gone from believing I am stupid to knowing that I can succeed. I have a little girl who believes in me, and has been one of my biggest fans through all the late nights, early mornings and triumphs. She has seen what it takes to be successful and for that I am forever grateful.

"There are still rough times, when I wonder what I'm doing as a 38-year-old single mother of a five-year-old. When I look at the other students, I wonder what I could have achieved had I been younger and on my own. But I also know that with the assistance of organizations like the Switzer Foundation, the support of my family and friends, and the love of a little girl, all things are possible and will be worth the struggle on the other end.

"Thank you, Mr. Switzer, for this contribution. I didn't have a chance to meet Mrs. Switzer, but I know in my heart that she would be so proud. Not just of me, but of everyone who has been selected to receive this bursary."

Martin Cohos recalls the Foundation's gift to the Alberta Children's Hospital that was directed towards oncology research into childhood cancer.

"It was a wonderful ceremony that I was invited to attend with other friends and family," he says. "A young child with a brain tumour told her story. It was so compelling, yet she related it in such a matter-of-fact way that we all cried as we listened to her courageous struggle and her thank you for Sam and Betty's help."

Betty's earlier work with the YWCA compelled them to contribute to the Vermillion Energy/YWCA Skills Training Centre. Single mothers learn the skills they need for better-paying careers in trades and construction.

Sam gives generously to so many community organizations that it's virtually impossible to list them all. Not only does he donate to the Mustard Seed, a well-known homeless shelter, but he has employed people from the shelter as well.

When Robbie Babins-Wagner, the CEO of the Calgary Counselling Centre opened an envelope addressed to the CCC, she had to look twice and then wipe away a tear.

"There was an incredibly generous cheque to the Calgary Counselling Centre, and I hadn't even met Mr. Switzer," she says. "It's an immense kindness that allows us to continue helping people and families to build better lives."

"If I can influence in a small way by helping others, my presence on this earth will have meant something," says Sam. "I believe every one of us can make this world better for our having been here, whether we give our time, energy or money – and preferably all three. Nothing that we give is too small and nobody is a nobody. When you realize there's a world that needs help in any way and amount possible, you're compelled to give."

It all starts with one person; and Sam looks to the inspiring story of his Auntie Meema, the late Bella Singer, who sponsored and funded family members to escape anti-Semitism in Europe by emigrating to Canada.

"She scrubbed floors, toilets and whatever toil it took to get her extended family over here," says Sam. "She was a beautiful woman. When Betty and I last visited her, she was 104 years old and she still looked immaculate."

Sam remembers Auntie Meema as a spry and happy person who never stopped working to build and give back. He places her in his pantheon of heroes with Mohandas Gandhi, Martin Luther King, Nelson Mandela and Winston Churchill.

"She personifies the power each one of us has to make a huge difference in people's lives," says Sam. "We all carry a Gandhi, a King, a Mandela or a Churchill within us. Bella Singer was responsible for over 300 of my relatives coming to Canada and beyond. Auntie Meema is the reason I'm alive and here."

Every five years since 1990, the Switzers have held a family reunion. Lots of the festivities occurred at Suncreek Ranch, where Sam and Betty staged a barbecue, crazy games like sack races and an even crazier raffle. Aron Eichler, whose late wife Ida was a Switzer, actively participated in preparing the prizes.

"There was a colour TV for first prize," he recalls. "When the winner stepped forward to pick up his prize, he started laughing and said, 'Hey, this TV is black and white and it's also broken.' I replied, 'But that's not what we raffled. You'll notice the beautiful painting all over it. Now that's what I call a coloured TV.' Then there was the golf package we offered. The Switzer recipient came to collect and said, 'Thank goodness I didn't win first prize.' Then he pulled out his golf clubs – which were all broken. 'On second thought,' he replied. What a fabulous fun time. Sam and Betty were great supporters of the reunions."

Sam describes the third prize, a chicken dinner for four that was won by his good friend the late Moe Kowall.

"Moe came up and we handed him his prize," recounts Sam. "It was a box with a live chicken, uncooked potatoes and carrots, along with your all-important greens – some ghastly looking broccoli and a wilted head of lettuce. Moe just gasped as we all laughed."

At the reunion on July 4ᵀᴴ, 2010, the consensus was that Sam's grandfather, Wolf Baer Switzer, had over 1700 descendents – not all of whom attended.

"What a party it would have been if all of them had come to the ranch with Betty there," says Sam softly.

Jenny Belzberg and her husband Hy, who is also a relative of Sam's, have been active as community volunteers throughout much of their life together. Their philanthropy has been celebrated within Calgary's many communities and across the country. Because they've been friends for years, Jenny understands how Sam feels when he gives.

"You are included and become part of what's happening within the community," says Jenny. "There is such joy to giving and getting involved. Sam's generosity has allowed him to meet so many people in the community, and I know that Sam feels he receives so much back. Everyone who gets involved and gives ends up feeling so indescribably enriched. I know that Sam is loving it."

"When I look at how my life has grown through all the people and experiences I've had through volunteering, I wonder at those who don't or won't give some time and energy," she adds. "By giving, you get to meet people you might never know otherwise, and it's heartening to be with those kinds of people. It changes your life."

Jenny Belzberg recalls Sam's father, whom she knew when she was a young woman in Calgary.

"Sam's father was a very fine man and a gentleman," she says. "Sam is his father's son. He's such a likable character and there's always a smile on his face. I believe that's because Sam's makes the most out of every day, and I like that about him. He has such positive energy.

"Plus, he always says things just the way they are. Sam is honest about his life, and that's refreshing, too. He's straightforward and people can relate to that. He's not a materialistic man. He's been through the school of hard knocks and he's making a big commitment to so many in our community and beyond. I admire him for what he's doing, and we're very lucky to have him here."

Jenny hopes that Sam's life will inspire others to give. She points to the lives that are touched by those who volunteer and give to the community. But the person whose life is touched the most is the one who gives.

Giving, sharing and volunteering give purpose to our lives and nurture vibrant and benevolent communities. These lessons are as ingrained in Sam as his ability to poke fun at himself.

"Sam disarms you with his humility," says Calgary Flames CEO, Ken King. "For Sam, it is a completely natural act to graciously and generously respond to a philanthropic request. He treats it like it's his duty."

In a sense, it is.

"If your goal is to earn money, you won't succeed in life," says Sam. "You've got to have a higher purpose. You must give back."

Sam lives by that rule every day. He thanks God for his family and friends that have allowed him to act on opportunities and achieve. Sam intrinsically believes that his success is the direct result of the people around him and his faith.

"I am where I am because of God's blessings," he says. "It's so comforting to seek God and ask for help. I feel bad for people who don't have faith or call themselves atheists. They must carry life's burdens all by themselves, and that is profoundly sad."

Each morning, Sam takes time to be alone and at one with God. As he prepares to pray, he puts on his tallit, the Jewish prayer shawl. At all of its four corners are knotted fringes, called the tzitzit, which remind the wearer of their religious obligations.

Sam then puts the tefillin or phylacteries on his arm, representing God's freeing the children of Israel from bondage in Egypt. The tefillin are tiny black boxes that contain scrolls of scripture verses from the Torah, the first five books of the Jewish bible: Genesis, Exodus, Leviticus, Numbers and Deuteronomy.

By wearing symbols of Jewish faith, Sam is ready for his morning prayers. He moves into deep meditation and remains silent.

"I am at one with God and it is deeply comforting," says Sam. "As I meditate, I feel very calm and at ease with the world as I wade into waves of reflection."

Every day, Sam asks for forgiveness for his sins and tries to improve as a human being. He has been doing this diligently for over 35 years.

"You can never stop improving," he says. "There's so much to know, and even in your mistakes you become a better person if you allow yourself to learn. All of us go through the harshness of life where the struggle seems useless. Yet after prayer and meditation, I find that my mind is suddenly clearer, and my life appears as a clean slate to start anew. I feel invigorated and ready for the day's challenge. I believe there is a God who never sleeps, and that belief allows *me* to sleep."

While Sam went to synagogue with his father, he admits to "falling off" after his dad died. He was married with children, and allowed his work to consume most of his waking hours. When his son Lorne became a student of Torah, Sam again took notice. Dr. Lorne Switzer is also a scholar in small-cap equities at Concordia University. When Lorne's son Elyahu was ordained as an ultra-Orthodox rabbi and then married, Sam searched once more and found his connection to God.

"After I married Betty, I started picking up on my prayers," he says. "Through prayers and reading, I felt the guidance of God. The more you read, the more your mind opens and the closer you get to spiritual understanding."

Sam believes everyone should search for spiritual guidance within their religion.

"Every faith strives to make a better life for its followers, and if we all heeded that deeper message, our world would find solutions to the ills that bring nations down," he says. "History proves how faith can divide us, but it also reveals how faith can bring us together. Rather than break us apart, faith can pull us together to work jointly with all."

In his book *Jerusalem, Jerusalem*, author James Carroll points out that religion "is both a source of trouble and a way of vanquishing it. Religion, one sees in Jerusalem as nowhere else, is both the knife that cuts the vein and the force that keeps the knife from cutting."

Sam brings much of his family to Israel when he goes to celebrate and worship on Pesach (Passover).

"Israel is the only democracy in the area and it has been able to thrive even as it's under attack," says Sam. "It is a modern country that strives for equality in an unsettled and harsh part of the world. We pray at the Wailing Wall in Jerusalem and ask for peace and forgiveness in this country that I love and throughout the entire area. Peace is possible; it has been and it will be again."

Sam feels at home in any synagogue in the world, and whenever he's traveling, he goes to shul on Shabbat, the Jewish Sabbath.

"I always look for a synagogue, and when I enter and participate in the service and say my prayers, I feel comforted and safe," he says.

Sam and Betty would sometimes walk into a church on Sunday and listen to the hymns.

"They are holy places, and you can feel the worshippers finding comfort in their songs and prayers, too," he adds. "True fellowship means respect for all. The strength of humanity is that we can build bridges over our differences to connect what we share."

In 2008, Sam needed every ounce of his faith and every bridge to friendship when his beloved Betty fell mortally ill .

Rabbi Howard Voss-Altman called Betty the heart of her and Sam's "large and beautiful family. She was its glue, the family's loving, wise and pragmatic centre."

Her children, Laurie, Ron and Merrena, believe their mother "really heard your heart."

As Betty's back and hip pain persisted, she and Sam consulted a specialist.

"He discovered she had cancer," says Sam quietly. "When Betty started treatments, we knew we couldn't stay on the farm if she was going to get to her appointments. We'd better search for a place in the city."

Sam's daughter Darlene, along with Betty's daughters Merrena and Laurie, kept him busy looking at condominiums. They found one they liked, put in an offer and were turned down.

"We felt bad for a day or two, but then Merrena found another one with even better layout and square footage," recalls Sam. "We offered and were accepted. Betty was elated, except for the carpeting that we could easily replace with hardwood. We asked interior designer Susan Kaspar to help us plan. Betty picked out the flooring and all the other little changes we made and set out to make the condo perfect."

Betty was making all these choices while she was in hospital receiving treatment. The hardwood floors were finished on Thursday and the furniture arrived on Friday.

"The doctor told us that Betty would be home on Saturday so we were all super-excited," remembers Sam and then he stops and closes his eyes. "She did come home, but not to us. She went home to God, whom she loved. God removed her from her pain."

"I got the call at 2:30 in the morning to tell me she had just passed away. It was the saddest moment in my life. I rushed to the hospital. When I saw Betty, I finally understood what constitutes a soul.

"There she was, my beautiful Betty, lying in bed, with her eyes closed as if she was sleeping peacefully. There was not a wrinkle on her face. She looked so comfortable, so relaxed, and yet she was not there. She was no longer alive, and I felt a shiver as I knew her soul had departed. I felt both empty and painfully relieved. Her soul, her very essence, had already traveled away."

"I didn't think I could go on, but then my family and my faith pushed me through this void, and just as I will cherish Betty forever, I will love to the end my children and their spouses who did so much for me. Both Betty's children and mine carried me through a time too dark to remember. Yet there is a warmth knowing that Betty's soul is at peace in its resting place."

Betty's daughter Laurie recalls the many lists her mother compiled to keep her beloved family busy during her illness.

"When mom was in the hospital, she would make lists for each of us of things that needed to be purchased for their new condo," says Laurie. "It seemed like each day there was a new list of things to do. I rather suspect that she was trying to keep us all busy rather than worrying about her. On Thursday, Sam and I were shopping and trying to get our lists done. But rather than searching for towels, bedding and dishes, we spent a good part of our time looking at earrings for mom. He just wanted to buy her a present to make her feel good. She passed early the next morning and our lists were not completed.

"Mom's service was on Monday. On Tuesday night, Sam suggested that we had work to do in completing mom's lists and Wednesday would be a good time for us to do this. He also suggested that my niece Allison (Merrena's daughter) join us. Again, I rather suspect that as much as Sam needed a little bit of normality in his life, he also knew how much Allison and I also needed a distraction. So, shopping we went and between laughter and tears, we completed the precious lists that had been written for us by a woman who was more concerned about us than she was about herself."

Betty had passed away on September 26TH 2008, and her funeral was filled with serene reminiscences, because Betty Switzer was a woman admired and adored.

When Rabbi Voss-Altman visited Betty in the hospital, he was profoundly moved by her humility and empathy.

"Betty was so down to earth," recalls the rabbi. "She said to me, 'Oh Rabbi, you came to see me. That is so special that you took the time out of your busy day.' It humbled me because she was so ill but wouldn't think of herself. Betty was so magnanimous. She wasn't concerned about her own situation – she saw it simply as something to get through. She was more interested in hearing how others were doing."

"The times I spent with Betty were some of the best times of my life," continues the rabbi. "It felt genuinely good to be in her company."

Sam and Betty often attended Temple B'nai Tikvah's Friday evening worship or Saturday morning family service. Sometimes their grandchildren came. Family services can be fun precisely because they're so unpredictable, with children rushing around the sanctuary and the rabbi getting interrupted.

"Oh they can be a bit free-range," he laughs. "But she and Sam wanted to be in this welcoming place, which our sanctuary always is. I saw her eyes light up at family services, because they were symbolic to Betty. There was energy and inclusiveness, especially with the warmth of the children who felt comfortable running about. It was fun."

At her funeral, the rabbi remembered Betty's benevolence, patience, tolerance, compassion and modesty.

"In so many ways, she was one of the best people I've ever had the privilege to know, because her agenda – first and foremost – was *What can I do to help?* She wasn't interested in glory or credit. She simply wanted to see a job well done."

In that, Betty more than succeeded. With Sam and their Foundation, she put her mind and money into helping others.

Colleen Klein considered her friend Betty to be "the glue that held everything together," adding that she and Ralph "were grief-stricken for Sam when Betty passed away."

Sam says quietly: "Betty made me a better person and found in me qualities that were always there, but that I had suppressed over the years of working too hard and not spending enough time with my loved ones."

Then he recalls both the poverty and yet the richness of his youth.

"The world can be so hard for many, and we can't ignore the harshness that falls on people through no fault of their own," says Sam. "I may have been born poor in a run-down part of the city but I had what so many crave and can't find or have taken from them: love. That's the gift that gave me the will to go on after Betty."

It was also the gift that had given Sam the confidence to take risks and share the results with his family. Over his life, the community would become his extended family. Sam's nephew Benny Fishman, the son of Sam's sister Lily and her husband Jack, recalls Sam's closeness to his parents and sisters.

"All his life he's worked hard, just like my mother and the whole family," says Benny. "They stuck together with each one helping the other. Now Sam's doing tremendous things for the community and he's well respected for all he's done. You have to love him for that.

"Look at everything he's accomplished. Yet he's very low key and never one to make a lot of noise. He's the kind of person who flies under the radar. There's a gentle side to Sam, and I admire his humility. He's not out to make his name. And a lot of people have been with him for a long time. That says it all right there."

Sam and Martin Cohos have been friends for 55 years. The

architect and founder of Cohos/Evamy, now part of Dialog, met Sam professionally and marvels at the "unassuming enigma" the man has become.

"He is one of the most incredible adventurers I've ever met and is the absolute opposite of arrogant," says Cohos. "He's an entrepreneur with vision, courage, daring and insight. All the businesses that he went into, he didn't have experience in them. Just one day, he decided to do it. He has spent his life at the cutting edge."

"Why did he do all the things he did?" asks Cohos. "Where do you find the courage to just continue doing it?"

Sam has always felt he could do whatever he put his mind and energy into.

"I never lacked confidence because I was brought up to get out there and work hard," says Sam. "I never think in terms of believing in myself. I always believe in the people around me. Betty was the best at helping me pick the right people. You're only as good as the people you've hired."

Sam likens his employees to a symphony orchestra: "Each bring different instruments, but we all have to be in tune. Everyone has to know their music, when to play and when to refrain. If one of the instruments is out of tune, the whole symphony suffers."

The comparison became so apt that Betty's son, musician Ron Casat, presented Sam with a conductor's wand, an actual 14 inch Mollard oak baton.

Carolyn Reu has been part of Sam's symphony for more than 30 years. She has managed to raise her family while ultimately becoming the CEO of Sam's company.

"Sam has been very accommodating to my lifestyle with my husband and children," she adds.

Many of his employees have worked with Sam for more than a decade, including his accountant of 13 years, company CFO Anne Christopoulos.

"I feel that I have had the best time of Sam's life in working with him," says Christopoulos. "On the one hand, we operate the business, and on the other hand, we give the money away to his philanthropic interests."

Sam's confidence and reliance on staff like Reu and Christopoulos, as well as his daughter Darlene Switzer-Foster, means he can spend more time on his charities. Even past his mid-80s, Sam keeps his day running on adrenaline, habit and experience. In earlier days, most of his waking hours were spent on business ventures and the ranch; today, nearly half of his time is devoted to community and philanthropy.

"The people I have in place running the operation are first rate," he says. "I could be tough if I had to be, but what I've learned throughout the years is that you get a lot more with sugar than with salt."

Every one of Sam's missteps – and there have been more than a few – he has treated as "learning experiences."

"Success starts with taking your first step," he says. "That first step may be a misstep, but it doesn't mean it's a mistake. I have imprinted in my mind the lesson that every mistake is a step forward in the path to learning. These are lessons that improve us, but we all must be prepared to swallow our pride before we can progress."

Martin Cohos recalls Sam's positive will and motivation to do the right thing but not dwell on the negative.

"His attitude is, *Let's move on. Don't worry about mistakes. Let's get on to a better chapter.* He truly typifies the Alberta spirit of can-do – the adventurer and entrepreneur. He did it himself."

Yet Sam would say he only achieved through the good people working with him.

Sam is not a materialistic man and certainly not a clotheshorse. He owns two pairs of shoes, two suits plus a sports jacket.

"Why would I wear designer clothes?" Sam asks Benny Fishman. "No one can see the label anyway."

But when he golfs with his friend Aron Eichler, he always brings two pairs of pants.

"That's in case I get a hole in one," says Sam, grinning.

Aron Eichler enjoys playing golf with Sam because they spend most of the round laughing – usually at each other's jokes.

"They're like our golf shots," says Eichler. "Either too long or too short."

Let's just say that Phil Mickelson needn't worry about Sam's golfing accomplishments.

Sam remembers the day he broke 75. "That's a lot of clubs," he says with a straight face.

"One time I asked Aron if he had a sand wedge for me," says Sam. "He took off and brought back a pastrami on rye."

"Sam and I were playing at Canyon Meadows and I swear he hit an eagle, a birdie, a mule and a barn," adds Aron Eichler.

The two men still continue to play their rounds of golf for charity.

"And believe me, when you see the way we play, it truly is charity when they let us on the course," laughs Sam.

It was George Bernard Shaw who said: "To be clever enough to get a great deal of money, one must be stupid enough to want it."

Sam believes that strongly and adds dryly: "Of course to be clever enough to get a great deal of golf, one must be stupid enough to want it."

From golf to giving, Sam's life has been laced with good humour, spirituality, humility, sadness for the less fortunate, a powerful desire to help and a faith in the fundamental decency of humankind. It all makes for a man who inspires people around him without ever trying to do so.

CONCLUSION:
SEEKING THE SUMMIT

"A LOT OF PEOPLE SAY YOU'RE SMART OR YOU'RE LUCKY WHEN success comes into your life, but that's not true," says Sam. "If money is your motive then you've already failed. You must have a higher goal."

Sam knows what gives life meaning: finding wisdom and depth. The spiritual is far more satisfying than the material. Meditation soothes the soul; avarice slices it apart.

"When greed becomes your religion, you are truly lost," says Sam. "I have seen too much of it in my life. Where does God come into play?"

Whether a person is Jewish, Christian, Muslim, Sikh, Hindu, Buddhist or a follower of any other faith, each has lessons for living in peace and harmony with others and within oneself. Sam feels God gives grounding; greed destroys it.

"How much is enough?" asks Sam. "I hear people say how happy they'd be if only they had $10,000. When they reach that, they say they really need $20,000. Then it becomes $50,000 but they're still not happy. It becomes a cycle of suffering because they're reaching for the wrong goal. They're striving for a bubble that only grows in order to burst."

What do we need? Happiness, contentment, purpose and most of all, good health are worthwhile goals.

"When you're healthy, you're wealthy," says Sam. "There are basics that we all need: adequate food, housing and clothing. At what point do we move beyond the adequate to the opulent? We become acquisitive and lose our way."

Sam firmly believes he'd still be happy if he lost everything and landed in a one-room apartment – "but only if I had my family and friends, because if you have someone to share your life, you already are enriched."

His current residence in Calgary is a quite modest condo very close to a bustling mall. It's comfortable but far from fancy. Although he could live almost anywhere he cared to, this is fine with him.

Knowledge and perseverance produce success, but only if you're willing to bury your ego and listen. Leo Oudendammer, a friend for 35 years, has worked with Sam throughout his career as an hotelier and casino owner.

"Sam never takes no for an answer," says Oudendammer. "When other people give up, that's when Sam starts. He's also a master at picking brains. Sam's not afraid to ask questions. You learn a lot that way."

True success is to have struggled and overcome darkness. To be successful is to appreciate what one has and then consider what one needs. Compile two lists, he says, and make them fit together.

For Sam, listing his blessings is easy. He begins with his father and mother, Myer and Chaiya, who gave him life and the values that he holds so dear. He names Betty, with whom he shared the happiest and most fulfilling part of his life. He is grateful and thankful to his first wife, Aneta, the mother of his six children. Four live in Calgary with their spouses: Darlene and Bill Foster and their children; Ronald and Helmi and their children and grandchildren; John and Christine and their children; and Mark and Martin Gosselin, who married at Ronald and Helmi's home. Lorne and Nadine, who live in Montreal, have both children and grandchildren. Sam's daughter Susan resides in Florida. He names also Betty's children: Ron Casat, Laurie, with husband Wes Paradis; and Merrena with her husband Dan Thompson, as well as Betty's grandchildren.

He adds Carolyn Reu, Peter Kearns and Anne Christopoulous for their business and personal friendship.

He is appreciative of his companion, Rong Wang, who has cared for him in these last few years.

"It took her four tries to get her driving license," says Sam. "Each time she failed. On her fifth try, she nailed it."

Sam recalls the day Rong Wang came home crying.

"She was very upset," he said. "She had just been stopped by the police and received a speeding ticket."

Asked if he told her not to worry, he says, "No, I told her not to speed."

Sam tries to list all the relatives who are so dear to him, starting with his sister Dinah in Toronto and his cousin Jack Singer, Auntie Meema's son. Of course there's Benny Fishman and his sister Jessie Silver; brothers Charlie and Allan Mendelman and their sister Jessie Moscovitz; but there are so many it's almost a day's work, and he has to stop.

Then there are his many friends with whom he has shared his life, some of whom have passed away, such as Morris Mendelman, Sam Hashman, Bill Milne, Moe Kowall and Don Dean.

"I am so unbelievably thankful for these dear relatives and friends that I can't even begin to list them all," he says. "Without them, I would be like those picked-over shells scattered on a rocky shore."

Frank Nelles says of Sam: "We have been down many roads together and will continue to go down more, for he is a true friend, a true philanthropist whose word is sacred and whose heart is of gold."

Genevie Dean says simply: "May God bless and keep this wonderful man."

Sam lists his businesses that have allowed his passion for giving and supporting so many charities.

Then he writes one word: God. For Sam, it all starts with faith.

"As long as I have my faith, family and friends, I am a wealthy man," Sam told his nephew and friend Benny Fishman.

Sam's list would be a book, but when he gets to the second column of what anyone needs, Sam writes just two words: Good Health.

What we learn is that success comes from within. Before we can reach outwards, we must search inside and seek what truly matters in life. If we find faith, family and friends, we have achieved the summit of life.

Seeking the summit is both simple and complex, as we see from Sam's life. The great Jewish sage Hillel said: "Love your neighbour as yourself. Everything else is commentary."

That is precisely what Sam has learned in his life. Your neighbour is your family, your friends and your community. Together with them, you can reach the summit.

"Sam wanted to make something of his life," says Rabbi Howard Voss-Altman. "He became a city founder. Betty gave Sam a sense of life beyond business. She showed him what it meant to enjoy life. She helped him take care of business so that people would benefit. Together they did good work in the community. Sam continues that philanthropy. While he always had his faith, Betty enabled Sam to see the possibilities of happiness through that faith, and through his family and friends."

Alvin Libin and Sam go back to the days of Switzer Grocery when Alvin used to bring Sam fresh bread from his father's Palace Bakery. Libin is another celebrated Calgary entrepreneur and philanthropist who, with his late wife Mona, established the Libin Cardiovascular Institute of Alberta.

"Sam is an amazing man who has done a remarkable job of supporting so many causes within the community – and beyond," says Libin enthusiastically. "He is giving back tremendously and shares so much. Simply put, Sam is just a good guy and a good citizen. I value our history together and our friendship."

Jeanette Nicholls is an educator and community volunteer who has donated literally thousands of hours in giving governance workshops to non-profit agencies within the Calgary community, including Jewish groups.

"People like Sam Switzer are one of the reasons why I and my husband, Ron, give back," continued Jeanette. "When Sam, with his late wife Betty, gave, they did it with such joy. Sam continues contributing to make our community such a wonderful place to live. His generation knew hard times and it simply energized them to make life better for everyone."

Ron Ghitter continues to be a community leader after serving in politics as a Peter Lougheed-era MLA and later, a Progressive Conservative senator. He describes Sam very succinctly as "a very philanthropic and generous individual."

Drew Staffenberg, executive director of the Calgary Jewish Federation, admires Sam for his impact on the community of humankind.

"When one searches for definitions of human kindness, generosity and compassion, you will undoubtedly find the name Sam Switzer. In my view, Sam epitomizes the concept of tikkun olam (repairing the world) and the mitzvah of tzedakah (the righteous act of charity). Through helping families and individuals with basic human needs, seniors' housing, educational scholarships, medical research and rehab, Jewish education, support for Israel and the arts, and much more I am probably not aware of, Sam has quietly touched so many of our lives, and we are all the better for it. Sam is, indeed, one of our Calgary community's unsung heroes and super-mensch.

"Having worked in the philanthropy industry for over forty years, it is awe-inspiring to observe Sam's passion for quietly fulfilling the mitzvah of tzedakah and helping make our world a better place for all. I also believe Sam's generosity and understanding that a person in not measured by how much you have or how much you earn, but how much you share and how much you give, has been an inspiration for many others to follow."

Sam's place in history is one of building community – quite literally, cement block by cement block. Then he took building to an even higher summit by giving. He became a developer of land, people, promises and purpose.

Community volunteer Sheldon Smithens is an auctioneer,

appraiser, TV co-star of *Canadian Pickers,* and family friend. He says simply: "Some people you meet along the way are larger than life. Sam Switzer immediately comes to mind."

Sam didn't let the anti-Semitism of the early days stunt his dreams; he simply ignored it and allowed people to reconsider their intolerant thoughts before putting them to words.

Sam's approach to seeking the summit took his inward search outwards to community and beyond. It's one that has made the popular Calgary Mayor Naheed Nenshi as much a fan of Sam as Sam is of Naheed.

"As a businessman and a philanthropist, Sam Switzer works hard every day to make Calgary a better place to live," says the mayor. "His contributions have made a positive impact on the lives of thousands of Calgarians."

For Sam, seeking the summit means searching for the best in people and, inevitably, finding it.

As he assesses his life at the sweet age of 86 in 2012, he chuckles at the very notion of being young again.

"Oh, no. I'm living some of my best years because I get to continue giving. I would not want to be anywhere else or be any other age except what I am now," he says, and then smiles. "Being young again would mean I would have to give up all those memories. They are who I am, and I am grateful for every one of them. Who would any of us be without memory?

"Many, many, many times I've been asked what's next in my life? and I repeat my mother's favourite saying: 'What will be will be.'

"My life has been fortunate. I feel to have been, and I am in, the garden of gratitude to the Almighty. His greatness is beyond investigation. So to Him I say: 'Thank you. Thank you. Thank you.'"

ENDNOTES

INTRODUCTION
Page 4: "I am thrilled." (An edited version appeared in the *Calgary Herald*, June 4, 2011.)

CHAPTER ONE
Page 8: "Immigrants were bombarded." (Don Braid and Sydney Sharpe, *Breakup: Why the West Feels Left Out of Canada*. Toronto: Key Porter, 1990.)

Page 9: Bella first sponsored. (http://www.jhssa.org/266.html)

Page 10: "I was in the basement." (Tyler Trafford, *That's Me*. Unpublished ms.)

Page 11: "Where grass was up to a horse's belly." (Albert Stein, "The Jewish Farm Colonies of Alberta," *Outlook*. March/April 2001. http://tinyurl.com/3vdwjru)

Page 12: "From what I learn." (Max Rubin, "Alberta's Jews: The Long Journey;" ed. Howard and Tamara Palmer, *Peoples of Alberta: Portraits of Cultural Diversity*. Saskatoon: Western Producer Prairie Books, 1985.)

Page 12: "A stalwart peasant in a sheepskin coat."
(Braid and Sharpe, op.cit.)

Page 12: "The Rumsey and Trochu colonies." (Stein, op. cit.)

Page 13: "Prices of grain and cattle." (ibid.)

Page 14: "The coming of the Switzer." (Rubin.)

Page 15: "The object of the Society." (Jack Switzer, "The Polish Jewish Family Loan Association," *Discovery*. JHSSA, Spring 1997.)

Page 15: "Are based partially." (ibid.)

Page 16: "By the start of Calgary's boom."
(http://www.evexperience.com/about/history)

Page 17: "My father worked with a horse and wagon."
(Trafford, op. cit.)

Page 18: "How lucky I was." (ibid.)

Page 19: "Jessie and I had it easy." (ibid.)

Page 21: "She was crying." (Eva Ferguson, *Calgary Herald*. May 9, 2012.)

Page 21: "I feel so much guilt." (ibid.)

Page 22: "Who is a Jew?" (Alan Mendelson, *Exiles From Nowhere: The Jews and the Canadian Elite*. Toronto: Robin Brass Studio, 2008. Quoting from Lewis B. Namier, "The Jews," *Conflict: Studies in Contemporary History*. London: Macmillan, 1942.)

Page 23: "R.B. Bennett." (Irena Karshenbaum, "Calgary family celebrates 100 years in Canada," *The CJN*. 17 June, 2010. http://tinyurl.com/cvppwju)

Page 23: "I suggested recently." (Irving Abella and Harold Troper, *None is Too Many: Canada and the Jews of Europe 1933–1948*. Toronto: Lester & Orpen Dennys, 1982. Also see, Mordecai Richler, *This Year in Jerusalem*. Toronto: Alfred A. Knopf, 1994.)

Page 24: "We can only hope." (Bernie Farber, *The Toronto Star*. May 27, 2008. http://www.thestar.com/comment/article/431217)

Page 25: "When Douglas called." (Sydney Sharpe and Don Braid, *Storming Babylon*. Toronto: Key Porter Books, 1992.)

Page 25: "In 1947, Manning lost patience." (ibid.)

Page 25: "One time in the House." (Sharpe and Braid.)

CHAPTER TWO
Page 32: "Irreparable for occupancy."
(http://www.cbe.ab.ca/schools/view.asp?id=89)

Page 37: "I had the suppliers." (Trafford, op. cit.)

Page 38: "The principal met." (ibid.)

Page 40: "The successful man."
(http://quotationsbook.com/quote/26691/)

Page 41: "Never in the field."
(http://www.youtube.com/watch?v=Y0t-RqjMH-A)

CHAPTER THREE
Page 47: "When prohibition ended."
(http://tinyurl.com/bnuujp4)

Page 54: "J.B. Barron, who became a theatrical impresario."
(See Jeremy Klaszus, "A Landmark Languishes," *Swerve,*
January 20, 2012.)

CHAPTER FOUR
Page 61: "Milne made a significant contribution."
(Government of Alberta News Release, September 8, 2008.
http://tinyurl.com/7jqafq7)

Page 65: Ted Soskin. (His grandson Brent Martin honoured
Ted Soskin with "My Grandfather's Voice," the award-winning
film Martin produced after his pioneer grandfather passed
away. http://www.behance.net/gallery/My-Grandfathers-
Voice/1954965)

Page 66: Calgary Jewish population. (*The Jewish Historical Society of Southern Alberta*. Spring 2000.)

Page 66: "Sam, I don't know." (Unpublished interview with Sam Switzer for Calgary Jewish Historical Society of Southern Alberta. With many thanks to Jack Switzer.)

Page 69: Alberta's population. (*The Jewish Historical Society of Southern Alberta*, spring 2000. James G. MacGregor, *A History of Alberta*. Edmonton: Hurtig Publishers, 1972.)

CHAPTER FIVE

Page 77: "Two decades later." (Jason Markusoff, "Hashman built many of Calgary's landmarks," *Calgary Herald*. May 31, 2011.)

Page 83: "The Hi-De-Ho Man." (Tom Keyser, "Sam's ventures show his winning touch," *Business Edge*. March 21, 2001.)

Page 85: "That he was." (http://fyimusic.ca/industry-news/talent/wrongfully-convicted-of-bank-robbery-subway-elvis-returns)

Page 85: "The Summit Hotel." (David Parker, "Gala honours noted hotelier," *Calgary Herald*. May 25, 2003.)

Page 88: "A fellow asked me." (Valerie Fortney, "Imaginary pony tradition goes back to the races," *Calgary Herald*. March 12, 2011.)

Page 89: "When the bugle calls." (Rick Overwater, "The Stampede's underbelly, *The Globe and Mail*. June 30, 2001.)

CHAPTER SIX

Page 94: "A Calgary fisherman." (*Calgary Herald*. June 21, 1967.)

CHAPTER SEVEN

Page 103: "Calgary's new Summit Hotel." (*Calgary Herald*. August 23, 1965.)

Page 104: "The concept of Amalgamated." (ibid.)

Page 104: "Metropolitan cities." (Ted Hewitt, "Big Apartment Growth Forecast for Calgary," *Calgary Herald*. January 9, 1964.)

Page 105: "In comparing ratios of apartments." (ibid.)

Page 106: "Ouster is sought." (*The Leader-Post*. October 4, 1969.)

Page 106: "Amalgamated owned." (ibid.)

Page 107: "They owned the Marlboro." ("Hotel builders pay tribute," *The Saskatoon Phoenix*. April 26, 1977.)

Page 107: "Sam was a great boss." (Trafford, op. cit.)

Page 108: "It's the second largest." (Patrick Tivy, "Profile: For Sammy Switzer," *Calgary Herald*. February 28, 1977.)

Page 108: "I wasn't convinced." (Trafford, op. cit.)

Page 108: "The Sheraton was an." (http://www.starwoodhotels.com/sheraton/about/history.html)

Page 108: "The plaque stated." (*Calgary Herald*. October 22, 1973.)

Page 116: "A lot of entertainers." (John Hopkins, *Calgary Herald*. July 17, 1976.)

Page 116: "You had to love the industry." (Tivy, op.cit)

Page 117: "Revenue from the hotel." (*Calgary Herald*. May 30, 1977.)

Page 118: "Switzer, who at one time." (John Hopkins, *Calgary Herald*. February 28, 1977.)

Page 119: "Sam had to fire." (Tivy, op. cit.)

Page 120: "In doing away with the tavern." (John Hopkins, *Calgary Herald*. January 13, 1978.)

Page 120: "I think we have proved." (ibid.)

CHAPTER EIGHT

Page 127: "Leo Goodwin Sr. amassed."
(http://tinyurl.com/bnpmblt)

Page 127: "He was a self-made man." (ibid.)

Page 132: "That yacht will dwarf." (Martha Gross, *Sun Sentinel*. December 7, 1988.)

Page 133: "The east side underdeck." (*Focus on Fort Lauderdale*. April/May, 2002.)

Page 137: "Final checkout is 1 p.m." (Patrick Tivy, *Calgary Herald*. April 26, 1989.)

CHAPTER NINE

Page 152: "Police charged a man."
(http://tinyurl.com/7et836b)

Page 153: "As the foregoing argument."
(http://www.law.fsu.edu/library/flsupct/74867/74867brief.pdf)

CHAPTER TEN

Page 160: "The Elbow River Inn and Casino."
(http://www.point-travel.com/calgary/elbow-river-inn-casino.htm#hotel-reservations)

Page 163: "Just an FYI."
(http://forum.calgarypuck.com/showthread.php?s=a1ce22c6f316afd4d3d5312f6f380ac8&t=8644&page=2)

Page 168: "Only one percent."
(http://aglc.ca/pdf/quickfacts/quickfacts_gaming.pdf)

Page 169: "In 2010-11, nearly $300 million."
(http://aglc.ca/pdf/charitable_gaming/2010_2011_charitable_gaming_report.pdf)

Page 169: "Proceeds (revenues less expenses)." (ibid.)

Page 170: "The difference between." (Michael Sokolove, "A Big Bet Gone Bad," *The New York Times Magazine*. March 18, 2012.)

Page 174: "The building itself." (Mel Duvall, *Calgary Herald*. December 15, 1994.)

Page 175: "The thing I like." (http://www.yelp.ca/biz/regency-palace-seafood-restaurant-and-lounge-calgary)

CHAPTER ELEVEN
Page 184: Cowboy coffee (http://www.youtube.com/watch?v=gOAdPkDhTSo)

Page 186: "The breathtaking beauty." (http://www.trail-rides.ca/Wild_Adventure.html)

Page 190: "McLaughlin put a wry twist." (http://www.tinlizziefl.com/Mclaughlin-Buick_1908-1942.pdf)

Page 190: "Riding at the age of 80." (http://www.youtube.com/watch?v=BjlsS0nR5ds)

Page 191: "When the horse-drawn." (Michael Clarkson, *Calgary Herald*. July 6, 1991.)

CHAPTER TWELVE
Page 197: "It's incredible." (Editorial, *Calgary Herald*. January 24, 2012.)

Page 198: "The project's president." (http://www.littlesynagogue.ca/)

Page 205: "Is both a source of trouble." (James Carroll, *Jerusalem, Jerusalem*. New York: Houghton Mifflin Harcourt Publishing, 2011.)

INDEX

SYDNEY SHARPE

Sydney Sharpe is a journalist and the award-winning author of *Staying In The Game*, the biography of Doc Seaman; the best-selling *The Gilded Ghetto: Women and Political Power in Canada* (Harper Collins); *Storming Babylon: Preston Manning and the Rise of the Reform Party*; and *Breakup: Why the West Feels Left Out of Canada* (the latter two co-written with Don Braid and published by Key Porter). *Seeking the Summit, Sam Switzer's Story of Building and Giving* is her eighth book.

Sydney also co-edited and co-wrote the best-selling Centennial book *Alberta: A State of Mind* (Key Porter), as well as an online book, *A Celebration of 70 Years of Vision and Action*, a study of how the Alberta Medical Association fostered world-leading reproductive medicine for women.

Sydney has been a senior columnist for the Calgary Herald, Calgary Bureau Chief for the Financial Post, and has worked in the press gallery in Ottawa. Throughout her career she has written for numerous magazines and newspapers and has appeared on television and radio. Peter C. Newman described her in his 1998 book, *Titans*, as "the most influential daily journalist in the city, and one of the best business reporters covering the Oil Patch."

She has been a tenured professor at Alberta's Athabasca University and MacEwan University, where she taught anthropology and sociology. She earned her B.A. from the University of Alberta and her Master's Degree in anthropology from McGill University.

She has worked and lived in the U.S., England, the Caribbean, Quebec, Ontario, Atlantic Canada, British Columbia, and the Canadian North. She is married with two adult children and lives in Calgary.

The net proceeds from the sale of *Seeking the Summit, Sam Switzer's Story of Building and Giving* will be donated to Heritage Park Historical Village of Calgary.